Harry Shapiro has worked in the drugs field for over twenty years and is the author of a number of acclaimed rock biographies and music books. The BBC named *Waiting for the Man,* his history of drugs and music, 'one of the twenty best music books of all time' while *MOJO* dubbed his best-selling biography of Jimi Hendrix as the one against which 'all other rock biographies will be judged'.

SHOOTING STARS: DRUGS, HOLLYWOOD AND THE MOVIES

HARRY SHAPIRO

For Kay.
Always there for me so long as I keep her in apples.

Library of Congress Catalog Card Number: 2003111439

A complete catalogue record for this book can
be obtained from the British Library on request

The right of Harry Shapiro to be identified as the author of this
work has been asserted by him in accordance with the Copyright,
Designs and Patents Act 1988

Copyright © 2003 by Harry Shapiro

First published in 2003 by Serpent's Tail,
4 Blackstock Mews, London N4 2BT
website: www.serpentstail.com

Set in 11pt Baskerville by Intype Libra Ltd

Printed by Mackays of Chatham, plc

10 9 8 7 6 5 4 3 2 1

Contents

Acknowledgements

Major thanks to my ever-patient publisher Pete Ayrton, editor John Williams, my agent Mic Cheetham, and film collector Bob McCrea from somewhere so small in America that the international directory enquiries had never heard of it. Special thanks to my very good friend Julian Cohen for endless encouragement and helpful suggestions. Thanks also to Professor David Courtwright, Tim Hogbin, Claudie Mernick and a few people from inside the movie business who wanted to remain anonymous.

Introduction:
Out of the blue and into the black

There are certain words that conjure up the deepest fears and anxieties, which drive people to unspeakable acts of terror and cruelty, words of ostracism, isolation and hatred. These words are more than just words. They represent groups in society, real people, flesh and blood, on to whom, at different times in history, societies offload their troubles, resentments, anger and responsibilities: leper, Jew, witch, nigger. Scapegoats first appeared in the Old Testament: a goat was chosen to appease the wilderness demon Azazel. The animal would be burdened with the sins of all and then thrown off a cliff, cleansing the people of their iniquities. The ancient Greeks went one stage further and stoned people to death to heal the community. The sacrificed ones were the *pharmakos* – from which we get the word 'pharmacy', appropriate when considering the scapegoats of more recent times: drug users.

These days 'drugs' is a word that sends a shudder through parents, professionals, politicians and the press. Drugs have taken on an almost supernatural aspect. We talk of a war against drugs, as if piles of plants, pills and powders have a life of their own dedicated to mayhem and destruction. Like leprosy, the phenomenon of drugs is framed as an epidemic, as if you can 'catch' drug abuse. In 1989 an American drugs officer warned his British counterparts that the impending wave of crack he predicted for us would bring society to its knees 'in two years'. The then Home Secretary, Douglas Hurd, raised the ante when he told the press that crack would represent the worst thing to hit these shores since the plague of the Middle Ages. Crack did come to Britain, but compared with these apocalyptic visions of chaos, the impact of crack has been more modest.

Is this rhetoric simply a matter of protecting public health? Any reasonable person would be concerned about the dangers of injecting heroin or the effects of powerful hallucinogenic drugs on an unstable mind. But with upwards of 150,000 tobacco- and alcohol-related deaths every year in the UK and hardly a word uttered, keeping the nation healthy can hardly be the source of outrage about drugs. Many of those deaths will be among older people with a long-term history of use, but what about the hundreds of fatalities a year caused by direct alcohol poisoning in the under-25s? When did a teenage alcohol death ever make the front pages where every ecstasy death is assiduously reported?

Much is made of protecting our children both as innocents abroad and as guardians of the future. But in the light of almost daily accounts of children being battered, abused, raped and murdered in so-called civilised countries, let alone the reports of child-murdering death squads, under-age prostitution and mass sweatshops from the developing world, such good intentions ring somewhat hollow.

Is it because most drug use is illegal? Maybe. But many crooks and gangsters acquire legendary, almost heroic, status among their peers, the communities they live in and in the media. Many films and TV productions present criminals in a sympathetic light – codes of honour, love of family, loyalty to friends and so on – however many faces they blow off with automatic weapons. Police talk about 'honest villains' as opposed to those who get involved in drug dealing, tagged in the media as 'merchants of doom' or 'evil drug barons'. So whatever it is about drugs, it's not just their illegality.

The fear of drugs is very convenient for governments. It can be turned against anybody who challenges the status quo or is seen as a threat to the social fabric of society; over time, students, black and ethnic minority groups and Communists are but three groups who have been targeted.

From an economic point of view, especially during periods of relative peace, the war against drugs provides large eddies of cash for countries with established arms industries who supply an array of weapons and military hardware to competing forces. And governments throughout the world play the anti-drug game for the sake of continuing Western military and economic aid.

But without the general consensus on drugs, ultimately such actions would become politically unacceptable. Something else is at work here

– something irrational and beyond explanation. No more rational perhaps than blaming a goat for a bad harvest and chucking it off a cliff.

More subtly, American popular culture has played a key role as the ambassador of American values and beliefs throughout the world. Not surprising, then, that both the music and film industries are very conservative (and increasingly owned by the same handful of multinationals). But the movie business has been especially protective of its image and much more sensitive to external criticisms of its product. Whereas popular music has thrived on the association with drugs and been at the forefront of many drug trends, the film industry tries to distance itself from any association with drugs while still trying to attract young audiences with contemporary themes. Only occasionally have individuals and individual companies within the industry broken through the self-censorship that for many years tried to deny there were such things as drug users and drug dealing. Prime examples are Otto Preminger's determination to break the Hollywood Production Code and have his film *The Man with the Golden Arm* (1956) shown without a seal of approval in A-list cinemas, the heady period which produced *Easy Rider* (1969) and *Traffic* (2000), the first major Hollywood film generally to call into question the conduct of the drugs war.

In tackling drugs as a social issue as opposed to simple Victorian morality tales of individual decline and redemption – and even simpler 'goodies v. baddies' – Hollywood has made little progress. But perhaps that is asking too much. What film can be said to have raised and sustained the level of debate on any major issue of our time? Is film just a superficial entertainment we forget once we leave the cinema? How do we judge the social impact of the cinema beyond bums on seats and the cult of celebrity? Can we justly criticise films for not being 'realistic'?

In the early days of cinema, most film-makers were not interested in accuracy; drugs were simply dramatic props. Realism was actively discouraged in early drug films, because of concerns that a movie might instruct the young in the ways of evil. For decades the aim of these films was primarily to entertain, and then to warn the impressionable away from evil influences.

Drug films are subject both to the contemporary social and political pressures of the day and the eternal commercial dictates of any product of the entertainment business. 'Most [drug] films, even those we view today as the most ridiculous, were carefully crafted in the dramatic shorthand of the day and conceived to fit a specific niche in the market-place – and were seen without irony by period audiences.'[1] But in respect of how drug issues are dealt with, have the motivations of film-makers and the expectations of audiences changed that much over the years?

It is certainly true that most drug films were the products of their time. It may be a perfectly reasonable criticism of, for example, *Reefer Madness* (1936) to say that it was not an accurate portrayal of marijuana use. But this was a government-endorsed propaganda movie against the use of the drug. It could hardly be expected to be accurate. Yet would it be true to say that the use of drugs is now depicted with more realism and accuracy because times have moved on? Changing social mores since the 1960s has seen drug use feature regularly in mainstream Hollywood movies, and some of this has been quite explicit, focusing often on scenes of injecting drug use, like *Drugstore Cowboy* (1989) and *The Basketball Diaries* (1994). However, beyond the physical presence of drug use in movies and close-up shots of ways of taking drugs, little has changed.

Desires and weaknesses that drive characters in drug movies remain similar, even though the tastes and philosophies may change. The opium dens of *Broken Blossoms* (1919) are just like those in *McCabe and Mrs Miller* (1971) and *Once upon a time in America* (1984). The agonies of heroin withdrawal follow a line from *Human Wreckage* (1923), *The Man with the Golden Arm* (1956), *French Connection 2* (1975) and *Requiem for a Dream* (2001).

Reefer Madness is now an amusing film, showing nice educated young people driven to hell by drugs. We laugh because it is ridiculous, but the message of *Less than Zero* (1987) is not dissimilar. Exploitation movies are pretty much the same everywhere, and this has been the standard format for drugs movies the world over, whether mainstream Hollywood (vice must be punished) or independent (we'll shock the straights and show them what really happens). In both cases, drugs are fun and then they are not.

Drug use is usually portrayed as a product of individual pathology and often a pretty stereotypical view of that pathology. Where is the historical drama based on the Opium Wars? Many movies have used the 'drug cop gone bad' scenario, but no film-maker (to my knowledge) has considered the wider implications of this. What about an eco-drama on the biological war against drugs in developing countries? Or the iniquities of the drug laws? And there must be a plethora of good plot lines about American drugs policy abroad as a cover to interfere with the economic and political infrastructures of other countries. *Traffic* (2000) broke the mould by turning some of the stones on drug policy (although nowhere near as effectively as the Channel 4 series on which it was based). But an industry source told me that once *Blow* (2001) bombed at the box office, it was all the excuse anybody needed for sidelining drug film proposals.

Does any of this matter? What difference does it make if the media take a sensational view on drug issues? The biggest problem is that the mythologies which have grown up around the subject serve only to isolate and marginalise those with serious drug problems and the friends and families desperate to try to help their loved ones but shamed into silence.

Given the controversies that have raged about the drug content of movies, from the earliest exploitation films of the 1920s through to *Trainspotting* (1995), you would think that the literature of both drugs and films would be rich with extended discourse: What are the key themes and messages? How have drug themes been tackled? What do these treatments tell us about societal attitudes to drugs? How have these attitudes changed over the years? What is the symbolic nature of drug themes? What impact has drug use had on the film industry itself?

In fact, based on searches of key libraries – the British Library, the Library of Congress, the British Film Institute, the 80,000 items in the database of drug literature held by the UK drug charity DrugScope and general searches of the Internet – only two previous books have appeared on this subject, both very different in intent and structure from what follows, along with a mere handful of academic articles and some from popular journals.

Equally revealing are film study books that on first blush should at least have touched on this subject but patently fail even to mention it. Many of the early films on drugs played on the general fascination with the Orient – the mysterious and dangerous, yet exotic and alluring, world of the opium den where young white women were supposed to be lured to a fate worse than death. The advertising for a modern-day fragrance, Opium, plays on that same enticing image strong enough to be regarded as the basis for a glossy campaign. Yet in a 300-page book devoted to that same love affair with the mystic East among film-makers and audiences, there is just one passing mention of opium (the Opium Wars).[2]

The creation of 'drug fiend' mythology (drug users sent mad by the need for drugs who then kill to support their habit) was driven primarily by the demographic shift in drug user profile from mainly white middle-aged, middle-class women in the nineteenth century to young male, working-class users (both white and black) in the twentieth. This had a significant impact on the history of drug policy and public perceptions of the issue. Yet books on images of the working class in the movies fail to register this phenomenon at all.[3]

This is not to suggest a conspiracy of silence, but simply that many film researchers and historians appear to be uncomfortable with the subject of drugs, as if acknowledgement of its presence in film sullies the art. If so, they would be in exalted company. So keen were the great movie moguls and directors for their product to be regarded as art, to avoid government interference (and as many of them were immigrants) for themselves to be accepted into the upper echelons of society, that they set up their own censorship code to weed out the most undesirable aspects of film. The story of drug films is very closely tied in to the history of censorship. For many years drug films were not simply censored; the mere mention of drugs, however portrayed, was banned outright.

This delicacy over drugs was, of course, not replicated behind the scenes where movie stars, producers and directors have injected, sniffed, snorted and smoked the entire smorgasbord of intoxicating substances often to legendary excess. Hollywood's public relations machine has over the years desperately tried to keep that aspect of the business under wraps and certainly has resisted its depictions in the films themselves.

A 1984 film, *Mike's Murder*, was all but buried allegedly because of its uncomfortable portrayal of drug use among Hollywood's rich and famous. Images of rampant Hollywood drug use have only recently appeared and then at the sleazy end of the boulevard – life in the porn film business as shown in *Boogie Nights* (1997).

Some general points about this book. What counts as a 'drug movie'? There are thousands of crime films where the action is played out against the backdrop of illegal drug dealing and many others where a character casually smokes a joint. In general, though, I limit my selection of films to two general categories. First, where the presence of a drug theme or themes is a primary motivating force driving the film. Secondly, where the film has seemingly tapped in to the drug sensibilities of the target audience – *2001* (1968) would be one example. Some films combine alcohol and drugs, like *Clean and Sober* (1997), but alcohol is not dealt with in detail: to do so would have doubled the size of the book.

The focus is inevitably on America in general and Hollywood in particular, both because it has long been synonymous with the business of film-making and the art of excess. Drug themes appear to be replicated the world over, so in the main there are no fresh perspectives originating from the cinemas of other nations. That said, some major additions to the canon of drug films have come from outside the USA, notably *Christiane F* (1981) and *Trainspotting* (1995).

In Malcolm Bradbury's novel *Doctor Criminale* (1992) the narrator describes himself as a liberal humanist – a chaotic mixture of tolerance, permissiveness, pragmatism, moral uncertainty, global anxiety and deconstructive scepticism. Which about sums up my views on drugs.

I

Marks of a beast: the making of a drug fiend

Before there were drug fiends and dope fiends, smack heads, scag heads and junkies, there were people who got into difficulties with drugs. Most of them were middle-class, middle-aged women. Take Ella O'Neill, for example, who became the central character in Eugene O'Neill's autobiographical family tale, *Long Day's Journey into Night*.

According to O'Neill's biographer Steven Black, Ella 'almost at once' became addicted to morphine prescribed for pain relief following the difficult birth of Eugene himself. But her 'instant' addiction was an accident waiting to happen. She had never come to terms with the early death of her father through TB, while her eldest son Edmund had died of childhood measles. She was often lonely and depressed – following her actor-husband around and living out of suitcases with little or no company. Ella's modern-day equivalent would be one of the millions of women on repeat prescriptions of tranquillisers and anti-depressants. An official of the Iowa Board of Health wrote in 1885 that most addicts were to be found 'among the educated and most honoured and useful members of society, and as to sex, we may count out the prostitutes so much given to this vice, and still find females far ahead as far as numbers are concerned'.

Insofar as their morphine prescriptions were obtained legally from a doctor, such women presented no threat to the social order. Men drank in bars, pubs and clubs; women took opiates at home. In fact, morphine addiction could be reasonably well hidden from the public gaze. Ella's friends (who were used to her dreamy, distant demeanour) were often unaware of any drug problem. A major study of America's opiate problem published in 1928 reported that for many years husbands, wives and other members of the family lived in complete ignorance of addiction within their midst. In 1914 Ella O'Neill returned home after another stay in a sanatorium – only this time she did remain free from addiction until her death in 1922 from a brain tumour, even though

she underwent a mastectomy where morphine would have been prescribed for post-operative pain. A hundred years earlier, in 1822, when
Thomas De Quincey published his pioneering autobiography of addiction, *Confessions of an English Opium Eater*, opium was the miracle
panacea. By Ella's death, opium and its derivatives morphine and
heroin (together with cocaine) were the drugs from hell and all users
were the devil's disciples – drug fiends.

What follows is a brief sketch of drug use primarily in the USA and
the reaction to it, especially in the press, to indicate the context in
which film-makers were operating when framing their depictions of
drug use. I have concentrated on the USA because America took the
strongest and most influential line against drugs both domestically and
internationally. And, of course, the USA also developed the most influential and powerful film industry. The debate that ensued from about
1870 onwards both in the States and in England was far more complex
and multi-layered than I have space or need to detail – and often
involved comparisons and contrasts with the demon drink which generally worried Victorians far more than drugs.

As an unrivalled painkiller, opium was known across the ancient
world. It was first described in detail in the early third century BC, but
4,000 years before that, in Sumeria, the image representing the poppy
in the Sumerian picture alphabet was constructed from the phrase 'joy
plant'. Because of its magical powers to relieve pain and suffering,
opium featured significantly in the mythology of ancient Greece. Fer-
tility rites were often associated with opium because the sleep of the
poppy was so deep that people appeared to be dead before they awoke
– the death and rebirth links to the growing seasons and crop culti-
vation.

Opium was carried eastwards by traders and reintroduced back into
Western Europe by Crusaders who had learned of its powers from Arab
doctors. Originally confined to the world of potions and sorcery, by the
early sixteenth century its value as a medicine was rediscovered. In 1520
Paracelsus, the foremost medical authority of his day, concocted a drink
made of opium, wine and spices – a drink to be praised, which he
named 'laudanum'. For the next 400 years, most opium would be consumed in this way. Opium retained its pre-eminence all the way down
the centuries because medical knowledge was slow to develop. In 1680

the English doctor Thomas Sydenham wrote: 'Among the remedies which it has pleased Almighty God to give man to relieve his suffering, none is so universal and so efficacious as opium.' Even in the nineteenth century doctors underwent the minimum of textbook training and had no idea of hygiene, infection or any notion of the genesis of diseases and could do little to relieve suffering other than to turn to barbaric practices such as blood-letting with leeches. The most distressing symptom for patients was pain, and for that there was opium. It was prescribed especially for women, for everything from masturbation to hiccups, although it was childbirth and the aftermath that led 'more ladies to fall into the habit than all other diseases combined'.[1]

Paradoxically, the modern era of opium use in the West began with the English passion for tea. By the end of the eighteenth century the demand for what was fast becoming the English national drink was growing to the point where new sources had to be found. The answer was to begin extensive trading with China, which harvested the best tea. The trouble was finding a commodity that the Chinese would want. They already had the best drink, tea, and the best cotton, silk and fur; they also had wallpaper, china, porcelain and many other luxury goods that Western traders could only drool over. We had nothing to offer that the Chinese would want. Then in 1773 the British gained control both of Bengal and the monopoly on trading in Indian opium. As one historian put it, into the hands of the British 'had accidentally fallen abundant supplies of a product which any keen merchant might be forgiven for regarding as the answer to his dreams – an article which sold itself, since any purchaser who has acquired a taste for opium always comes back anxiously for more, cash in hand'.[2]

But surely China had its own opium? What about all those Fu Manchu movies with inscrutable Chinamen luring unsuspecting white girls into the grip of the opium den to smoke opium and kiss goodbye to their virtue? Didn't the Chinese have the drug thousands of years before anybody else? No, they didn't. Opium was introduced into China by Arab traders – the Chinese word for opium, 'a-fu-jung' means 'foreign medicine'. For hundreds of years after, it was used simply as a painkiller and a remedy for dysentery. Opium smoking had only come in on the back of the tobacco smoking introduced in the seventeenth century. But the British-owned Indian opium which now flooded into the country in exchange for tea and silver created a much more entrenched fashion for opium smoking.

While Britain was trading opium to China, large quantities of the drug were being imported into Britain from Turkey. Opium was the key ingredient for the array of patent medicines that came on to the market, allowing ordinary people who could not afford doctor's fees to self-medicate to relieve pain and to keep children dosed and quiet. One druggist in Manchester mixed his own brand of 'quietness' and sold five gallons of it a week to women who had to leave their children with a minder while they went off to the factories. In the main, opium was consumed in quantity by working-class people as a culturally sanctioned practice. Even De Quincey's salutary tale raised very little dust with the majority of the population, few of whom would have ever heard of it, let alone be able to read it.

The story was repeated in America when Boston traders broke the British monopoly on opium exportation previously led by the British Levant Company out of Turkey and the British East India Company out of China. At first the Americans traded across Asia, but supplies found their way back to the States in ever-growing quantities. In 1840 around 24,000 pounds (10,000 kilogrammes) were coming in every year, rising to half a million pounds (227,000 kilogrammes) by 1870, earning the government around $1.2 million in tax revenue. America's patent medicine industry was worth some $80 million a year by the end of the century, many preparations containing large doses of opiates and cocaine.

In 1803, while Britain was expanding its empire on the back of opium, a German drug clerk, Friedrich Seturner, first isolated an alkaline base in raw opium that turned out to be the main active ingredient. In honour of the Greek god of dreams, Morpheus, Seturner named his new compound 'morphine'. But there was no great rush by doctors and druggists to give up opium in favour of morphine even though the purity of opium could differ from batch to batch, whereas morphine crystals were consistent. Morphine could only be produced by a chemical process, so it was more expensive than opium and doctors, being traditionalists, were also reluctant to try anything new. This changed in 1856 with the perfection of a device (the prototype of which was developed by Christopher Wren) to deliver the drug directly into the bloodstream – the hypodermic syringe.

German chemists were also the first to synthesise heroin from morphine in 1898 and then market it (among other things) as a cure for morphine addiction – and also cocaine from coca leaves. Cocaine became a staple ingredient for a whole variety of cold and hay fever remedies, tonics and pick-me-ups. America's main manufacturer of cocaine from imported coca leaves was Parke-Davis, which in 1883 promoted cocaine to doctors with assurances that cocaine was efficacious well beyond the needs of clinical medicine in that it would 'make the coward brave, the silent eloquent' as well as 'free the victims of alcohol and opium habits from their bondage'. By 1906 80 million Americans were drinking and hoovering up 11 tons of cocaine a year. To this day, Coca-Cola deny that their product ever contained cocaine, but this is fully documented. The company was even threatened with court action under the new American laws about drug labelling enacted in 1906 that if their product did *not* contain cocaine (which by then it didn't) they couldn't call it Coca-Cola.

Back in the mid-Victorian era there were now two main routes into opiate use: first, the multimillion-dollar patent medicine industry, which through its advertising clout kept many newspapers afloat – a valuable insurance against any adverse publicity. Second, with the hypodermic syringe, doctors had an effective means of administering morphine, a powerful new weapon in the fight against pain, bringing almost instantaneous relief and a much-needed fillip to the professional reputation of doctors everywhere.

The most public display of opium use came during the American Civil War. It has been estimated that 10 million opium pills and more than 2 million ounces of other opiate products were distributed to the Union forces alone. Opium was swallowed and rubbed into wounds as an anaesthetic, and towards the end of the war morphine injections became common.

It was later claimed that so many soldiers became addicted to morphine through treatment for battle injuries that addiction became known as the 'soldiers' disease'. Yet military records of the time hardly ever mentioned any condition of the troops that could be interpreted as addiction, and autobiographical accounts of battle-derived addiction were few and far between.[4] But whatever the truth of veteran addiction, the end of the war marked the beginning of a new attitude to the use of drugs.

Opiate use in America and England was virtually unregulated – what laws were in place had hardly any impact on availability. However, concerns were raised in the pages of the medical press about excessive use of what we now know to be potentially harmful drugs. For example, there were cases of youngsters accidentally overdosing on the soothing syrups administered by parents, and more generally those who had become dependent on their medication were in a debilitated state. These were clearly reasonable concerns. But the public health agenda was overlain by a moral argument which suggested that those who had a drug habit were not simply ill or weak but morally degenerate and in some cases downright evil. The argument coalesced into an anti-drug campaign forged from a loose coalition of organisations and individuals who made up the social reform movements in England and America.

In England, the argument was most stridently expressed by the Society for the Suppression of the Opium Trade (SSOT). It had long been suspected by reformers that working people used opiates not only for medical reasons but for the same reason as they drank to excess. The SSOT regarded the issue of drugs and moral turpitude not simply as inappropriate use by working people, but constructed a definition of the addict (whoever they might be) as one who has taken a willing course to self-destruction, discarding all moral responsibility on the way. In other words, and in a very real religious sense, addiction was evil. The SSOT, founded in 1874, was a Quaker-based pressure group that regarded the opium trade with China as morally indefensible and agitated for half a century to get the trade stopped, but it succeeded only at the point where trading had become commercially non-viable. Although the moral case against opium chimed perfectly with middle-class Victorian sensibilities, it is doubtful that the organisation had much impact on the eventual legislative framework controlling drug use in England, which ultimately was much more the consequence of our obligations under new international agreements.

The situation in America was very different. Here, a very powerful coalition of social and moral reformers and political and religious fundamentalists created such a climate of condemnation against drug users that it led inexorably to draconian drug laws and a world view of drugs which (given America's dominance of international diplomacy) still sets the global agenda.

The drive towards morally based social reform in America had its roots in the progressive wing of the Republican Party. They claimed to speak for the white, rurally based majority who identified the nation with evangelical Protestant values which were seen to be undermined first by the Civil War and then by urban growth fuelled by rampant immigration. The followers of the Progressive Movement, as it became known, combined rising middle-class consumer power, rural ideology, women's rights and professional entrepreneurship (as middle-class professionals like doctors and pharmacists struggled to establish their credentials) with a WASP morality code. Together they looked on in disgust and outrage at the post-war creation of formidable seats of power in the new cities, bringing in its wake political corruption and spectacular wealth in the hands of a few alongside horrendous poverty and degradation in urban slums.

The reform movement to clean up the cities took many forms: the Women's Christian Temperance Union; the lobby opposed to the legalisation of prostitution; the National Consumer League; the League for the Protection of the Family; and the National Vigilance League. Links were forged between the Protestant and Catholic Churches in support of alcohol prohibition, and these same forces secured the outlawing of abortion, which had been allowed up to the Civil War.

In the light of medical concerns about addiction, doctors (many of whom were also active in the reform movement) began to modify their use of opiates – and after a honeymoon period (roughly 1884–1904) also turned their back on cocaine other than as a local anaesthetic. Heroin, first synthesised again in Germany in 1898, enjoyed an even briefer sojourn in the pharmaceutical sun. Even when the sales of these drugs in their pure form over the counter were still legal, pharmacists, taking the temperature of the water, began to withdraw from the trade. But the demand die was cast: from 1905, in Chicago for example, their reluctance to sell pure cocaine created a supply vacuum immediately filled by illicit dealing nearly ten years before legal sales were officially banned in 1914.

The patent medicine industry, too, was dealt a mortal blow by the Pure Food and Drug Act passed in 1906 as the result of Progressive lobbying against large corporations. Through press exposure, they were revealed to be distributing contaminated food and filling their medicine bottles with dangerous drugs. The act forced manufacturers to divulge the contents of their potions on the label. And once the public made the connection between their favourite nostrums and hair-raising accounts of addiction in the press they soon stopped buying them.

But there was also a third battle to be fought, one that proved far more intractable. It was realised that another group of drug users was out there – not the unwitting victims of unscrupulous companies or irresponsible doctors and pharmacists, but people who actually wanted to take drugs, wanted to get high, enjoyed the experience and were prepared to take the risks. This generated outrage on at least two counts.

First, there was a morally based vilification of euphoria as totally against the best interests of a spiritually and economically robust society. America was a young country that had reached the limits of its physical horizons once the west coast had been reached and linked with the rest of the USA by the railways. But it had aspirations to broaden those horizons, to make an impact on the international stage, and for that it needed to be strong in its religious and moral beliefs and its industrial and military strength. Euphoria and addiction threatened that vision – the addict was a non-productive parasite. Drugs also threatened the highly cherished ideal of individual freedom; the addict was a slave to drugs – and hadn't the Republicans fought a bitter and bloody war to free slaves? On the other hand, some thought that the very drive to 'tool up' for the future glory of America was itself a contributory factor in the seemingly universal desire to escape the pressures through alcohol and drugs. A doctor warned in 1881 that Americans were 'Essentially a nervous people, prone to go to excess in everything, gladly welcoming narcotics and stimulants, we go to a very decided excess in all matters of this kind'. The *Quarterly Journal of Inebriety* lamented, 'We live too fast; we do as much work in a day as our forefathers did in a week . . . We eat too fast; we think and read and even take our leisure at a high rate of speed.'

Linked closely to the idea of America's future was to invest that future in the wellbeing of young people, the belief that the nation would be revitalised by the wholesome vigour and endeavour of the young. Anything that might pose a threat to the health of the nation's youth (especially if it undermined the military effort) would be shown no quarter. And that threat could also come from within the ranks of young people themselves. 'Adolescent' was first coined by a psychologist in 1912 to indicate criminally inclined youngsters or juvenile delinquents.

Recreational drug use in America came to public attention in the furore over opium dens. Enter the world's first media mogul, William Randolph Hearst. If the Progressives provided the ammunition for the purity movement, Hearst fired the first and loudest shots: he took on the drugs war as a personal crusade and through his press empire created much of the media vocabulary of drugs we still have today.

From the get-go, Hearst knew exactly what his readership wanted. He was expert at milking stories for all they were worth, finding the most salacious and juicy angle and spinning the tale out for days or weeks at a time 'in the public interest' (of course) but accompanied by satisfyingly soaring circulation figures. The public wanted heroes and villains, they wanted scapegoats, people to blame for everything that went wrong in their lives, they wanted sex, depravity, mystery and murder. Hearst quickly realised that drug stories could provide the lot.

In the drive for profits and power, Hearst played directly to the less honourable aspects of the reform movement. Inevitably, a white purity crusade such as this was bound to be driven by xenophobia and racism, especially as immigration was identified in 1874 by an evangelical theologian, Josiah Strong, as one of the key perils facing the nation. And it was drug use by immigrants and minority groups that provided the catalyst for all drug users to be eventually condemned by the Progressives and society at large as delinquents and social deviants.

In the mid-nineteenth century, thousands of Chinese labourers had been brought over to the west coast of America to work in the gold mines and on the railways for wages that no white man would accept. As long as there were plenty of jobs for all, there was little hostility between the Chinese and white communities. But the completion of railway-building in the 1870s coincided with an unexpected economic depression, and jobs became scarce. The Chinese community then became the scapegoats of the west coast's employment problems, targeting anything alongside physical appearance that made the Chinese visible. One of these was the institution of the opium den brought from the Chinese mainland. That the Chinese smoked opium was bad enough; use of the drug other than for medical purposes was a sure sign of moral degeneracy – and foreign, strange immorality at that. But worse still, the exotic, slightly mysterious and dangerous atmosphere of the opium den was encouraging white artists, Bohemians and denizens of the white underworld to sink further in their depravities by consorting with heathens. The ultimate outrage was reported by a San Francisco doctor: 'the sickening sight of young white girls from 16 to 20 years of age lying half-undressed on the floor or couches, smoking with their lovers. Men and women, Chinese and white people, mix indiscriminately in Chinatown smoking houses.' Here were all the ingredients of the classic shock-horror drug story: young white girls . . . drugs . . . foreigners . . . miscegenation . . . sex.

Like Ella O'Neill, none of these individuals was a threat to law and order, but in 1875 San Francisco – home to the largest Chinese community – passed what was in effect the first law against recreational drug use, banning white people from frequenting opium dens.

The Chinese community fanned out across America, but with work scarce and faced with constant hostilities many earned their living providing 'leisure services' to eager white customers: gambling and opium dens. Many other cities and states followed the lead of San Francisco, but still the practice continued; in 1881 the *San Jose Mercury* declared that opium smoking had to be 'rooted out' before it could 'decimate our youth, emasculate the coming generation, if not completely destroy the whole population of our coast'. And once whites got a taste for the pipe, the practice soon spread to ordinary homes and private premises beyond the reach of the law.

After a long campaign of badgering his multimillionaire father George Hearst, William Randolph, newly expelled from Harvard, took over the San Francisco *Examiner* in 1877. He modelled the paper on Joseph Pulitzer's New York *World,* aimed straight at the masses, infused with a strange blend of sensationalism and idealism, plugging murder and scandal. New Yorkers thought it cheap and vulgar; Hearst thought it was so brilliant that it made other papers look antique. Under Pulitzer, the *World* circulation shot from 15,000 to 250,000, bringing in its wake enormous profits. Hearst viewed himself as the Pulitzer of the west, leading the *Examiner* in a crusade for the purification of California.

Hearst turned the paper upside down, introducing huge banner headlines and bringing on board top writers like Ambrose Bierce. He also took on Winifred Sweet, who arrived in San Francisco as a chorus girl in a touring theatrical group. Writing as either Annie Laurie for the west coast or (as Hearst's empire spread nationwide) Winifred Black elsewhere, she became queen of the sob stories, ramming home the anti-drug message to a readership only too willing to believe. When she arrived at the paper, Hearst told her to imagine a railwayman on the night shift, idly picking up his paper in a spare moment: 'think of him when you are writing a story. Don't write a single line he can't understand or wouldn't read.' A fervent and energetic campaigner, Winifred Black churned out hundreds of pieces for Hearst rags on a daily basis for over 20 years under classic headlines like 'Paradise Alley Is Fetid Hell-Hole of Lost Souls in Grip of Deadly Drug', 'Underworld's Pet Drug Makes Youths into Thugs and Slayers' and even 'Mussolini Leads Way in Crushing Dope Evil'. A Hearst headline writer was a specialist in condensed shock, 'seizing on the most fantastic facet in any story and compressing it into a capsule jolt'.[5]

The demand for shock by Hearst publications was relentless, an endless daily pressure felt by every editor and reporter. 'Staff men were under continuous tension, seeking the angle, the slant, the gimmick that would transform ordinary news into something stupefying'.[6]

Equally dramatic were the illustrations. As part of his campaign to persuade his father to let him take over the *Examiner,* William Randolph wrote to George Hearst from college in 1885, detailing the myriad faults with the paper including what he thought of the illustrations:

[They] are a detail, though a very important one. Illustrations embellish a page; illustrations attract the eye and stimulate the imagination of the masses and materially aid the comprehension of an unaccustomed reader and thus are of particular importance to the class of people that the *Examiner* claims to address. Such illustrations, however, as have heretofore appeared in the paper nauseate rather than stimulate the imagination and certainly do anything but embellish a page.

In other words, so that the proles get the message, make sure that your pictures unequivocally drive home the point. Once in control, Hearst hired the best graphic artists he could find to create the arresting images of the drug menace which adorned his newspapers and magazines. When Hearst bought the New York *Journal*, he poached the whole staff of Pulitzer's *Sunday World*, including the cartoonist K. F. Outcault who created an immensely popular cartoon, 'The Yellow Kid', chronicling the adventures of an engaging street urchin who gave his name to the 'yellow journalism' most associated with Hearst. However, Hearst's most notable illustrator was Winsor McCay, enticed away by Hearst from the *New York Herald*, who created in excess of 3,000 editorial cartoons including the timeless sensationalist images of drugs – the serpent of temptation, the dragon, the vulture, the bat, Satan, the Grim Reaper and the vampire.

Hearst popularised the tabloid template for drugs that everybody followed: youth in peril from heartless pushers giving away free samples; foreigners to blame; the promise of tough laws to stamp out the evil; each new drug declared to be more addictive and dangerous than anything which had gone before; all users mad, sad and bad; society in danger of imminent collapse. The game plan was to take some kernels of truth around the undeniable dangers of drugs – the addictive potential of morphine or the anxiety and paranoia of chronic cocaine use – and magnify them through a prism of racism, nativism and fear. All the lines of attack we still see today in the media were in place before 1914.

On the back of San Francisco's anti-opium laws, Hearst began an all-out attack on the Chinese – the 'yellow peril'. The opium den and opium smoking came to embody everything that right-thinking, honest people should fear about their innocuous, peaceable neighbours.

Another target was the black community of the southern states. Cocaine had been given to black slave workers by plantation owners and New Orleans harbour masters to reduce fatigue and hunger – more hours' labour for less food. Because many of the southern states were 'dry', cocaine often substituted as a recreational drug or might be added to whisky for an extra kick. Once slaves were freed, they were perceived by the white majority as an angry subhuman horde who would seek their revenge in the most heinous way – the cocaine-fuelled rape of white women. In support of the hate campaign against blacks, any statement by doctors or law-enforcement officials that 'proved' black coke addicts were responsible for most crime was given maximum publicity. Similarly, the alleged cocaine-inspired crimes of black people were used by anti-drug campaigners as proof of the dangers of cocaine.

Campaigners and journalists worked together to raise public fears and anxiety that would help create a climate for the control of all forms of drug use. Hamilton Wright, a research doctor, was one of the main architects of the Harrison Act of 1914 which effectively outlawed opiate and cocaine use and criminalised users. He wrote to the editor of the Louisville *Courier-Journal* in 1910: 'a strong editorial from you on the abuse of cocaine in the South would do a great deal of good [but] do not quote me or the Department of State.' That same year he was the main author of the first international report on opium in which he claimed that cocaine 'has been a potent incentive in driving the humbler negroes all over the country to abnormal crimes' when there was no evidence that black males used cocaine any more than whites. The press campaign against the black community reached its most absurd point in 1914 when the *New York Times* solemnly reported that some southern police departments had demanded an upgrade in bullets from .32 to .38 on the basis that they needed increased fire-power to stop a cocaine-frenzied black man. The predictable headline to the story ran 'Negro Cocaine Fiends Are a New Southern Menace.'

Wright and other campaigners needed the press to stoke up the pressure about drugs, to marginalise and demonise all drug users, but especially non-medical use by the working classes and immigrant groups, so that the public would be only too ready to accept the controls being worked out in the corridors of power. Nationwide, there were increasing numbers of books, pamphlets, medical articles, lectures and meetings on the drug menace – and in William Randolph Hearst the reformers had their most reliable and unscrupulous press ally. But Hearst himself had another role to play in the history of drug control, less direct, but equally influential.

Hearst was nothing if not opportunistic; he was happy to help foster a climate of hatred against the Chinese community but also put his full weight behind an attack on the government, which was accused of doing nothing to protect Cuba from its oppressive Spanish rulers. There was a rebellion; the papers were full of alleged Spanish atrocities. Then the American battleship *Maine* exploded in Havana harbour. It was either an accident or the work of Cuban rebels trying to secure American aid. If the latter, then it worked; Hearst papers went on the attack to such an extent that President McKinley was forced to declare war against Spain in 1898.

America lost 341 casualties in the war and gained Puerto Rico, Guam, control of Cuba for many years and the Philippines, where it discovered, to the horror of the new administrators, that the islands had a huge opium problem. Disgusted with the other European powers in the region for letting this happen, and anxious to flex its muscle internationally by taking the moral high ground, the Americans convened an international convention – the first time a group of nations had come together to consider a social and moral problem. Trouble was, back home the Americans had rampant drug use and hardly any laws or regulations. Thus began a chain of events which ultimately led to the passing of the Harrison Narcotics Act in 1914 and ushered in the modern era of US drug control whereby to be a user or prescriber of any controlled drug, whatever the circumstance, was a criminal offence.

Overnight, thousands of otherwise law-abiding citizens found themselves outside the law. They lined up alongside those less bothered by the law – those living on the fringes of society: criminals, prostitutes, artists, juvenile delinquents, minority groups and immigrants, the unemployed, the 'sporting crowd', musicians, the moral outlaws.

Together they were the 'drug fiends' that the press and all the campaigners, with their leaflets, articles, books, meetings, lectures and seminars, had worked so hard to create over the previous 40 years – criminalised in law and condemned as pathological liars and semilunatics who would do anything for a shot and do anything to convert non-users to the needle. It was now up to the new engine of massmedia entertainment – the cinema – to enshrine these stereotypes on celluloid, although for the likes of Hearst, even though he became a movie mogul as well, the pen was always mightier than the camera. As he once told Douglas Fairbanks: 'Movies aren't that powerful really. You can crush a man with journalism but you can't with motion pictures.'

2

Children of the night: early drug cinema

As one form of popular escapism was being controlled, another was waiting in the wings. In America and Europe the race was on to find a way of making still pictures move as a form of popular entertainment. Like computers, the Internet and mobile phones, once the first break-throughs were made, progress was swift. And like scientific endeavour generally, individuals were working independently on similar ideas. The ultimate victor would be whoever could transform a salon or side-show novelty into a commercial business. Such a man was Thomas Alva Edison, who, having failed to come up with his own system, set his employees the task of plundering the ideas of others and then pat-enting them.

Edison's kinetoscope debuted at the first Kinetoscope Parlour which opened up on Broadway in April 1894 featuring 40 or 50 seconds of Wild West show, prizefighting and the riveting spectacle of *Fred Ott's Sneeze*, the world's first copyrighted motion picture. People were fasci-nated by pictures that actually moved and willingly dropped pennies in the slot by the thousands to watch *Train Arriving at Station* or *Workers Leaving Factory* as well as some of the more risqué material of the 'What the Butler Saw' type, such as *Doloria in the Passion Dance*. Nobody then, least of all the inventors, thought they had anything more than a new and profitable optical toy. The idea of moving pictures as a medium of artistic expression, like literature or painting, did not occur to anybody.

As popular as the 'peepshows' were, the big problem was that only one person could view the films at a time. The key to cracking this was to come up with a viable projection system so you could show the same film to many more people at once and charge them more money. Like Bill Gates and his initial response to the Net, Edison misjudged the future – he thought of the kinetoscope only as part of a home-enter-tainment kit to go along with his recently invented phonograph – and found himself with a lot of catching up to do. Others, especially in

France, picked up the challenge of projection. But eventually Edison got with the programme, bought somebody else's invention, gave it a new name, the vitascope, and claimed the invention for himself. The big leap forward was not just the ability to project on to a screen from a distance, but a device called the Latham loop which eased the tension on a film so it didn't break after a minute or so as most film did up to then. Now film-makers could shoot more than a hundred feet of film and create real movies with proper stories.[1]

Koster and Bial's Music Hall on 34th Street and Broadway played host to the first public demonstration on 23 April 1896. True to form, as Edison didn't have enough films of his own, he pirated those belonging to the French Lumière brothers and showed them in between the live vaudeville acts. Motion pictures, as they quickly became known, took off big time. Entrepreneurs, including a number who would become the movie moguls of Hollywood, took over vacant stores and opened Nickelodeons showing half-hour films for 25 cents. The first one opened in Pittsburgh in 1905; by 1908 10,000 had opened up across the USA – in New York alone there were 200,000 daily admissions. In the era before the First World War, and on the back of these new inventions, thriving movie industries grew up in England, France, Italy, Denmark and Sweden as well as America.

With drug stories headlining in the popular press and film companies desperate for stories, it was inevitable that the early film-makers would want to cash in on the interest, but not always hanging on the coal-tails of yellow journalism. By definition, the pioneer film-makers were unconventional experimenters and risk takers not entirely wedded to the prevailing moral ethic of the day. Many of the early opium movies were comedies, light-hearted digs at those funny Chinamen and their weird habits or explorations of the funny things people might do under the influence of drugs. A young Scot, W. K. L. Dickson, Edison's laboratory head and creator of the kinetoscope, made *Chinese Opium Den* in 1894 for the penny arcades and went on to head up Edison's American Mutascope and Biograph Company, where in 1905 he made *Rube in an Opium Joint*, one of the earliest extant drug films. Rather than dens of vice and depravity, opium dens were often just tourist traps, some especially set up to give the gullible (rubes) a taste of the mysterious East and have some fun at their expense. Many similar films were made in the pre-war period but were often the same film retitled, such as *Deceived Slumming Party* (1908), set in New York's Bowery district, which might be the same as Dickson's film. *Lieutenant Lilly and the Splodge of Opium* (1913) and *Winky's Ruse* (1914) were two British examples.

Probably the most bizarre drug comedy of the period was *The Mystery of the Leaping Fish* (1916), written by the later cult horror film director Tod Browning and supervised by D. W. Griffith. With producer Thomas Ince and Mack Sennett, Griffith had formed the Triangle Corporation following the success of *Birth of a Nation*. In this Triangle production, Douglas Fairbanks Snr starred as Coke Enneyday. While ostensibly trying to bust an opium smuggling gang, Enneyday spent the whole film ingesting every substance he could lay his hands on – mountains of coke (of course), tins full of opium and a belt full of needles for that busy detective who needs to inject and go. In fact, Fairbanks was fanatical about healthy living. But he was also up for a good practical joke. Most biographies of Fairbanks omit any reference to this film.

As well as using drugs as a backdrop (or even the centrepiece) for comedy, film-makers capitalised on opium-derived hallucinations and dreams to show off their expertise at creating special effects. French film-makers like Georges Méliès and Leon Gaumont (an early pioneer of synchronised sound and image) were particularly fond of the drug special effects film. In 1906 the *Biograph Bulletin* described Gaumont's *Dream of an Opium Fiend* (1906) as 'An Oriental phantasy of bewildering gorgeousness' where the smoker first enters hell to be plagued by demons, imps and witches and thence to an 'Oriental heaven where he is surrounded by voluptuous and enticing beauties who beckon him, but are forever always out of his reach'. Isn't it always the way? *Variety*'s review of Gaumont's film ends on an interesting note which reflects the early cinema's eagerness to be regarded as an art form and not just a cheap novelty for the ignorant masses: 'The elaborateness of the production can only be compared to some of the greatest spectacles of the Metropolitan Grand Opera in New York.'

Censors were certainly at work, but in the early days it wasn't depictions of drug use that concerned them so much as sex. The Danish film *Opiumsdroemmen* (1914), which enjoyed great success in the States, graphically demonstrated the bliss of the opium state, but was apparently banned in Denmark because of the kissing scenes.

Of course, most drug movies were simply animated versions of Hearst-style yellow journalism. The Californian chief inspector for pharmacy had to stop a Chinese tour guide in San Francisco from paying a gang of 'derelict dope fiends' a dollar each to shoot up in front of the camera. *The Narcotic Spectre, Morphia the Death Drug, The Devil's Needle* and *The Devil's Assistant* all told a similarly lurid tale of morphine addiction and death, although according to film historian Kevin Brownlow the last title was a rather more compelling and sober drug film than most of the others, which were little more than crass melodramas. By the time this film was released in 1916, *Variety* had had enough of the drug film, observing wearily 'there is nothing left for it'. The reviewer was very sceptical of the happy ending in *The Devil's Assistant* where the hero gets off drugs just by going away to the country for some hard labour in the fields. This was at a time when it was widely believed that the only way out of addiction was either death or some poor prognosis of long-term, intensive medical care. Since then it has long been established that many chronic opiate users actually give up drugs without any treatment at all and that removing yourself from the drug environment can be a very important first step along the way.

The Drug Traffic (1914) was released in the year the Harrison Act came into force. The druggist sells illicit morphine and cocaine over the counter to selected customers while a fat cat pharmaceutical boss counts the profits from the sale of his TB cure heavily laden with morphine. Naturally, anybody remotely vulnerable and innocent becomes hooked and dies, although a happy ending was allowed in *The Derelict*, released in the same year – a habit is broken and a marriage saved. The premise of *The Secret Sin* (1915) was the battle of one sister to save her twin from morphine addiction acquired first through frequenting opium dens and then at the hands of a doctor.

Rarely for drug movies, the audience watching *The Dividend* (1916) was allowed a glimpse at the true antecedence of an addiction – rather than something stumbled into through weakness or the ministrations of a careless or evil doctor. John Steele, a widower with an only son, Charles, is a wealthy cutthroat landlord too obsessed with money and his business even to attend his son's graduation. The serious-minded son asks his father for a job; the father ridicules him, gives him some money and dismisses him. Over time, the son visits opium dens, becomes addicted and, when his father finds out, is thrown out of the house. Says his son Charles: 'If you had been a real father to me, I wouldn't have become a dope fiend. Did you ever give me any encouragement?' But the father refuses to mend his ways and continues to ignore his son, who eventually dies in a street brawl. The media even to this day often appear to wonder why it is that those who have every material comfort can become dependent on drugs. This film, from so long ago, shows that emotional deprivation (no mother, unsupportive father) can be equally devastating to vulnerable individuals however much material wealth is on tap.

The evils of cocaine were mapped out early on in a 1912 film by D. W. Griffith showing a side of cocaine use very different from his *Leaping Fish* four years later. The *Biograph Bulletin* outlined the plot of *For His Son*: 'A physician through love of his only son, whom he desires to see wealthy, is tempted to sacrifice his honor by concocting a soft drink containing cocaine, knowing how rapid and powerful is the hold by cocaine . . . The drink meets with tremendous success . . . but his son cultivates a liking for it. The father discovers his son's weakness too late, for he soon becomes a hopeless victim of the drug.'

The drink was Dopakoke, 'For that Tired Feeling', but it does more than combat tiredness. The son dies and as for the father – the final title sums up the plight of the would-be patent medicine manufacturer once the public knew what was in the bottles: 'He did not care whom he victimized until he found the result of dishonor at his own door.'[2]

Cocaine Traffic (1914), otherwise known as *The Drug Terror*, was described by *Variety* as 'six reels of misery'. A cocaine user, Spike, persuades his former boss, Andrews, to become a coke dealer. Meanwhile Spike's wife leaves him and he becomes a drifter. Needing a new source of supply after a police raid, Spike turns to Andrews whose daughter is about to marry Mr Hastings, who frequents high society. Spike manages to hook Hastings on cocaine, and Hastings in turn hooks Andrews' daughter, his new wife. Hastings loses everything and becomes a skid row bum. On the hunt for drugs, he has a showdown with Andrews in a derelict house that burns down, frying them both.

The trade press, led by *Variety*, condemned these films as simply exploiting prurient and morbid interest, with the added risk of encouraging the young to experiment. The film-makers responded with claims that these were educational films produced in the public interest. It became a feature of these films to seek on-screen endorsement from a worthy public servant. *Cocaine Traffic* was written 'with the assistance and approval of the Director of Public Safety and the Police Department of the City of Philadelphia'. Often such endorsements came at a price. For using his name in connection with this film, a Dr Robinson was promised five per cent of the gross.

Back in those days, cocaine was really a slum drug, with none of the glamorous associations of later years. And before anybody had heard of marijuana, it was cocaine that was pegged as the 'gateway drug' through which young people passed on the way to hell. Writer John Noble read a story about messenger boys taking cocaine to stay awake on the job and becoming addicted and he penned *Black Fear* (1916) as a result.

Most of the films depicting addiction focused on the plight of the middle classes – businessmen, doctors, society people and the like and their hapless wives and daughters led into ruinous drug habits by members of their own family. The newspapers were full of stories of drug depravities in the big-city slums, but the mainly working-class audiences of the early days of cinema were much more interested in the tragedies that befell those higher up the social scale where virtue was rewarded and vice invariably punished. And for those from the middle classes who began to be drawn into the new opulent cinemas from 1914 onwards, such films acted as a warning to be aware of the drug dangers that lurked nearby.

But the most stereotypical depictions of the drug scene were found in the stories of opium smuggling, a lucrative trade into the States across the Canadian border, once a ban was imposed in 1909 on importing opium for smoking. In these films, all smugglers were foreign and devoid of an ounce of humanity, not only trading in the all-enslaving opium but also luring white girls into slavery. Denmark was undoubtedly the trendsetter in the history of early drug movies. *Morphinisten* (*The Morphinist* (1911)) was one of the first movies to deal with drug addiction – a stockbroker heads for the morphine bottle every time the market falls – and the Danes also started the trend for linking drug trafficking with prostitution in *The White Slave Traffic* (1910).

Already by this time, because of the social disapproval of drugs, many doctors and pharmacists were retreating from the prescribing and retailing of drugs, creating a vacuum for gangsters to move in. Legendary American producer Carl Laemmle remade *White Slave Traffic* in 1913, followed by the British and the French, who all weighed in with several variations on the same theme. The archetypal arch-demon of the drug trade was Sax Rohmer's Dr Fu Manchu, in equal parts inscrutable and evil, as depicted in the 1921 British production, *The Yellow Claw*, and several other spin-offs and remakes.

But in among all the banal melodramas and crass racism of the opium movies, one movie stands out for its compassion and sensitivity. *Broken Blossoms* (1919), directed again by D. W. Griffith, presented a Chinese opium smoker in a very sympathetic light, contrasting favour-ably with *Birth of a Nation*, where Griffith was accused of uncritically absorbing the racial prejudices of the Revd Thomas Dixon, on whose novel *The Clansman* Griffith's film was based. Although Griffith himself was Jewish, he became so totally assimilated into the life of the southern gentleman he aspired to that he was thought of by some to be anti-Semitic.

In a neat twist on the imperialist theme, *Broken Blossoms* opens in China, where a young idealistic peace-loving man (known throughout the film as the Yellow Man) decides on a mission to England to preach the peace of Buddha to the savage, violent Anglo-Saxons. He settles in Limehouse, in London's East End, to be faced by the reality of brutal slum poverty. Disillusioned at his failure, he turns to the opium pipe; 'he huddles against the brick wall outside his shop hunched forward in a caved-in posture while hugging both sides of his chest, and reflecting a melancholy gaze in his drug-hooded eyes'. While he is in the opium den, a title card asks: 'In this scarlet house of sin, does he ever hear the temple bells?'

Meanwhile we are introduced to 15-year-old Lucy, the much-beaten and abused waif-like daughter of a prizefighter, conceived during one of his many drunken liaisons with a succession of 'loose women'. Both Lucy and the young Chinaman are framed together in the film as unwanted outcasts from a cruel and hostile world, setting up the common ground from which their relationship develops.

Lucy often passes the Yellow Man's shop window: he notices her and is struck by her beauty. He starts to follow her, eventually finding out where she lives. While Lucy is serving her father his dinner, she accidentally scalds him and is whipped mercilessly. She escapes and collapses in a heap outside the Chinaman's shop. The man sees her, but, still in an opium fog, he believes she is just a drug-induced vision. Realising this is no dream, he brings her inside and showers on her 'the first gentleness she has ever known'. He lovingly tends her wounds and offers her shelter while she recovers. He dresses her in Chinese silks and ribbons. His kindness and warmth prompt her to ask 'What makes you so good to me, chinky?' He doesn't respond, but simply catches moonlight in his hands, showering the rays on the girl as she sits up in bed.

While he is out, somebody hears movement above the shop and spies Lucy. Her father is informed, and after a bruising fight he goes to reclaim his daughter. The Chinaman returns home to find a scene of chaos and Lucy gone. Back at her own house, Lucy's father kills her in a frenzied drunken rage. The Yellow Man enters the house, discovers Lucy's dead body and empties a gun into her murderer. In his grief, he assembles all the icons of their love around her body: flowers, Lucy's favourite doll from the shop, burning incense, an altar and a small temple bell. 'As he smiles goodbye to White Blossom, all the tears of the age rush over his heart.' And then he plunges a knife into his chest and dies.

Finally, film-makers plundered classic literature for ideas and turned up yet more drug elements to include in their pictures, some more oblique than others. One of the earliest adaptations of this kind was the British version of Dickens' unfinished novel *The Mystery of Edwin Drood*, released in 1910 – the mystery being that Drood drifted off to opium dens whenever he got the chance.

That Sherlock Holmes was both a morphine and cocaine user was revealed to fans in *A Scandal in Bohemia*, published in 1886, although with cocaine only recently available, Doyle confused the effects of cocaine with morphine when he wrote about 'the drowsiness of the drug' and 'drug-created dreams'. *The Sign of Four*, published in 1888, was much more accurate, to the point where one researcher suspected that Doyle had more than an academic interest in coke.

Watson describes Holmes taking his bottle from the mantelpiece and the syringe from 'its neat moroccan case. With his long, white nervous fingers, he adjusted the delicate needle and rolled back his left shirt-cuff. For some little time his eyes rested thoughtfully upon the sinewy forearm and wrist, all dotted and scarred with innumerable puncture marks . . .

' "Which is it today?" I asked. "Morphine or cocaine?"

'He raised his eyes languidly from the old black-letter volume which he had opened. "It is cocaine" he said, "a seven per cent solution. Would you care to try it?" '

Dr Watson takes the opportunity to warn Holmes of the dangers: 'Surely the game is hardly worth the candle. Why should you, for a mere passing pleasure, risk the loss of those great powers with which you have been endowed?'

Holmes replies that he only uses drugs to fight off boredom, but Conan Doyle, picking up on growing popular unease about cocaine (especially when his books started selling in the States), suggests that Holmes's growing obsessive paranoia about the evil Moriarty was cocaine-induced. Dozens of Sherlock Holmes movies were made during the silent era but only some depicted his drug use, which was not fully acknowledged until Nicol Williamson played the part in the 1976 film *The Seven Per Cent Solution*, in which Holmes is persuaded to meet Sigmund Freud to overcome his cocaine addiction. The irony here is that Freud was a very early advocate of cocaine as a new wonder drug, not least as a cure for morphine addiction. He revised his views after recommending cocaine to his friend Fleischl, who was struggling with a morphine habit. Freud gave cocaine to Fleischl in the spring of 1884. By January 1885, Fleischl was injecting a gramme of coke a day and remained a chronic user until his death in 1901.

Studios had a technological field day with Robert Louis Stevenson's *Dr Jekyll and Mr Hyde* devising ways of executing the transition from one to the other. The most common interpretation of the book was that it reflected the Victorian love affair with the new techniques of psychiatry and psychoanalysis that unpeeled the human psyche for medical gaze. But it is documented that Stevenson may have been under the influence of cocaine as a cure for TB, because in an appalling state of health he none the less managed to write two drafts of the book totalling 60,000 words in six days. Could Hyde have been Stevenson in a rabid cocaine frenzy?

But perhaps the horror story has made a more subtle contribution to the history of drug cinema. To examine this more closely, we need to look at German culture just after the end of the First World War and the artistic movement known as Expressionism.

Germany underwent a collective madness after the war, first because they lost the war, totally undermining the nation's self-belief as a major military power and bringing them face to face with the collapse of the imperial dream. Then came the crippling humiliations of the Versailles Treaty and the war reparations imposed by the Allies. When Germany defaulted on payments, Belgium and France occupied the German industrial heartland of the Ruhr. The final blow was rampant inflation that destroyed the currency; workers were bringing home their wages in wheelbarrows. A million marks was worth just one US dollar.

Nowhere was this madness more apparent than in Berlin, whose artistic, Bohemian and aristocratic communities spent at least the first half of the 1920s at one long party of unbridled hedonism and alternative lifestyles. Berlin nightclubs were the most uninhibited in Europe. Homosexuality and transvestism were very public and highly visible. As one outraged observer noted: 'In the darkened bars one could see high public officials and high financiers courting drunken sailors without shame. Even the Rome of Suetonius had not known orgies like the Berlin transvestite balls, where hundreds of men in women's clothing and hundreds of women in men's clothing danced under the benevolent eyes of the police. Amid the general collapse of values, a kind of insanity took hold of precisely those middle-class circles that hitherto had been unshakable in their order. Young ladies proudly boasted that they were perverted; to be suspected of virginity at 16 would have been a disgrace in every school in Berlin'.[3] The critic Kenneth Tynan described Berlin at this time 'as decadent as it's humanly possible to be.'

Berlin was an irresistible draw for the young creative spirits of the Weimar Republic, like Bertolt Brecht, who said Berlin was 'a place for the ambitious, the energetic, the talented'. Like Hollywood, you went to Berlin to become famous, and it was a city that never slept; 'we needed little sleep and we were never tired. It was a city of crooks and cripples, a city of hot songs and endless talk.'[4] The city represented a state of mind, a sense of freedom and exhilaration. Yehudi Menuhin

said: 'Berlin had an advanced, neurotic society . . . based on extrava-
gance, brashness, show . . . Everything became possible. Everything
became Experience, with a capital E – and a capital X.'[5] He could have
been describing New York, Los Angeles or London in the early 1980s.
In both times, this brashness and show were underpinned by seemingly
limitless amounts of cocaine. And 1920s Berlin was awash with the stuff
– hardly surprising as Germany was the major European producer of
cocaine and morphine. Germany's neighbours wanted border security
tightened to stop drugs flowing across the frontiers. Inside Germany,
Berlin was the main centre of recreational drug use, with an estimated
6,000–10,000 cocaine users in the mid-1920s. One speaker at the 1923
meeting of the Berlin Medical Society noted that use was especially
prevalent among artists and actors, and the police were 'in a quandary
for a method to suppress the drug at after-theatre parties in private
homes' while cocaine was readily available in 'bars, low dives and even
on the street'. Cocaine users had 'special resorts throughout the city
where restaurant keepers and waiters sold the drug'.[6] Apparently, the
women who looked after the public lavatories were also a good bet for
top-quality blow. There were plenty of scams as well. When he first came
to Berlin, the playwright Carl Zuckmayer was penniless and took a job
as a pavement hustler for one of the many after-hours clubs. One night
his boss decided to add cocaine to Zuckmayer's street hustle, or rather
paper wraps of cooking salt and aspirin.

While the country was in the grip of political, social and economic
upheaval, the German film industry was trying to regain the export
markets of the pre-war period and in the process enjoyed a golden age
of film-making from 1919–26, producing dark brooding movies whose
influence resonated down the subsequent years. The early German film
industry actually produced few films where drugs were a central theme.
One was Robert Reinert's *Opium* (1919), released during a brief interregnum when the authorities abolished censorship, opening the
floodgates to sex movies like *Hyena's Lust, Women Engulfed by the Abyss*
and gay films such as *A Man's Girlhood* and *Different from the Others*. *Opium*
was very popular and sold out at an expensive Berlin cinema for three
weeks. But although censorship was re-established, Berlin's drug problems remained.

There was substantial drug use among Germany's film industry in the immediate post-war period. The 1920s German film producer Walter Slezak was asked about the effects of cocaine. 'It makes you feel so clever, *so* clever. You start talking a lot and you think you are saying the cleverest things in the world . . . ' As one of several producers working flat out to rebuild the German film industry, he used drugs to fight fatigue, aches and pains in ever-increasing amounts. The actress Salka Viertal recounted that 'there was enormous addiction', and a number of her associates in film and theatre committed suicide.

Simultaneously, Expressionism emerged – an artistic style grounded in dreams, visions, ecstasy and nightmares of films like *The Cabinet of Dr Caligari* and *Nosferatu*. The German Expressionist movement in art, at its height in the immediate post-war period, reflected all the monstrous iniquities in life; it set out to be gloomy and disagreeable – the complete antithesis of Impressionism. This aesthetic was captured most vividly in the German film industry with very stylised set designs and artificial and dramatic light and shade – giving an external expression to the artistic sentiments of the period. The Expressionist films were populated by characters driven by strange urges and violent passions and haunted by nameless fears – movies of blood and unchecked impulses, of cynicism and isolation, wasting sickness, murder and suicide. The scenery, too, reflected altered mind states with tilted walls, crazy angles, distortion and unreality.

The Expressionists concerned themselves with images of the mind, not reality, they did not see, they had 'ecstastic visions', and in that respect, in the words of film historian Lotte Eisner, 'the ghosts which haunted the German Romantics revived, like the shades of Hades, after draughts of blood'. These films, their ambitious creators hoped, would appear 'endowed with many levels of meaning'.[7] One level reflected the dark drug-driven side of the new Berlin *Zeitgeist*, best captured by the image of the vampire.

The vampire and the 'drug fiend' are both children of the night, wandering the streets under cover of darkness to avoid detection. They are both addicts; one must have blood, the other drugs. They both enter people's lives and property uninvited and unwanted, one to rob, the other to kill – or even sometimes they both kill in order to satisfy their cravings. They recruit new members to their way of life – or death. The synergies might be closer still. One book on addiction was titled

Better Dead, often the sentiment expressed by the vampire who longs for peace but is destined to wander the wastes for all eternity. Vampires inject with teeth; addicts use needles. The vampire is often shown to be irresistible to young women; the air is charged with a heavy eroticism as the vampire approaches his victim. The woman bares her neck and swoons with ecstasy as the vampire sinks his fangs into her body. Those who inject heroin often say that the heroin rush is better than sex, and many female heroin users are first injected by their male partners. Both vampire and drug fiend carry a ghostly pallor, sunken cheekbones, a haunted look of despair and self-loathing. In the modern era, Abel Ferrara titled his 1995 vampire movie *The Addiction*; Ferrara's biographer Nick Johnstone stated bluntly, '*The Addiction* uses vampirism with which to address addiction', and throughout the film Ferrara's use of shadow and light, photographed in black and white, pays direct homage to Carl Dreyer's *Vampyr* and Murnau's *Nosferatu* – symbolic of the prison of addiction and dependency.

Sara Graham-Mulhall, an anti-drugs campaigner and former Deputy Commissioner of Narcotics Control for New York State, conjured up a different spectre in her book *Opium, the Demon Flower*, published in 1926, in the chapter headed 'The Opium Vampire's Victims'. The vampire in this case was a woman, in Graham-Mulhall's view a very real manifestation of the film-based 'vamps' of the silent era who simply seduced for sex. Graham-Mulhall wrote:

> The various types of opium vampire present one of the most subtle and baffling studies in morbid psychology. Their stories were of two kinds: either they had become opium vampires through association of drug addiction in the 'underworld' or they were beauties of a dubious theatrical reputation who were opium vampires on the outer edges of crime. However, while not always beautiful, they were always attractive. Only in the final stages does opium destroy a woman's look. Often it improves them, which is one of the most dangerous influences among young women.[8] . . . They were usually pretty, young, clever with a half-innocent air which disarmed suspicion. They were all actresses in the great drama of opium . . .

Graham-Mulhall conjures up the image of the young vamp who is sent out by the evil drug barons to entrap young men, just as young men were lured by the beautiful but deadly harem of the vampire driven by the passion to increase the armies of the undead. 'A warning against the opium vampire is all that can be done to save the boys, the young men, from her entanglements, except to make the drug unobtainable. She is everywhere, in the flashy restaurants, at the exclusive private dances, in the movie theatres, on the stage, in the studios among those who create plays for millions to applaud them.'

The movie vampire and his minions are always elegantly dressed – Bela Lugosi in full evening wear and the harpies always in flowing gown. So, too, the opium vampire, 'among the women who are rich in idleness and money . . . they become drug scouts . . . Under the influence of the drug they stop at nothing in their adventures in opium; and those who are caught in the golden mesh of their drug nets find themselves dragged down to death with them.'

Sara Graham-Mulhall was writing in 1926. By then, the drug antics of the children of the night had been exposed to the cold light of day.

3

Scandals in Bohemia

The roisterers who lived in the Roman Empire weren't pikers at heart. They did the best they could, but were handicapped by the fact that chemistry and drugs had not been perfected up to the Hollywood stage.

Kansas City Star, 9 February 1922

In the early days Hollywood was little more than a hot, dusty village, five miles outside Los Angeles (population 250,000, mainly speaking Spanish), with one main street lined with palms and pepper trees and one hotel. The archetypal image of the silent film director striding about in trousers tucked into long boots became an affectation, but it was grounded in the need for protection against the fascinating variety of poisonous snakes inhabiting the world of the outside desert location.

When in 1910 the Nestor Company moved in to take over old barns and farm buildings, the locals were so alarmed that they banned further incursions. Most of what became known as the Hollywood film business had to set up elsewhere in Culver City, Santa Monica, Burbank – anywhere that would have them. But Hollywood rapidly became a state of mind, a symbol for the film industry even if very little of it was actually located there.

The phenomenon of 'movie stars' was unheard of until 1910, when Florence Turner took in New York as part of a tour to promote a song about 'the Vitagraph Girl', the company she had worked for since 1907.[1] The *New York Dramatic Mirror* wrote about Florence, calling her 'A Motion Picture Star', possibly the first time this idea had been aired in public.

The silent movie stars were the first mass-media celebrities. In the nineteenth century, Dickens and Mark Twain had spoken to adoring crowds on the lecture circuit, but they reached relatively few people compared with the potential audience for movie stars. The idea of celebrities also changed traditional interpretations of hero worship.

Previously, heroes were mythical or fictional characters or those who had really accomplished something, but whom the public knew little about because the mechanisms of mass communications didn't exist. According to film writer James Monaco, 'film fused two types: real people became fictional characters. The concept of the "star" developed – and stars are quite different from actors.'[2] In other words, whatever role Chaplin played, he was always known as the tramp, and Mary Pickford was typecast as 'America's sweetheart'. When she tried to change her public image, her career came to an end. Of Douglas Fairbanks, Monaco notes 'the most important role [he] played was not Robin Hood or Zorro but "Douglas Fairbanks" '.

Early on, the actors and actresses were regarded by the producers and directors as little more than celluloid fodder who would only ask for a rise if they became known individually. But the film-makers hadn't reckoned with a general public ever more gripped by movie fever and a thirst for knowledge about the faces they saw up on the screen, literally larger than life. Who were they? What were they like? What kind of lives did they lead? What did they do off screen? Very quickly the fan magazines started up, and individual stars became the subject of newspaper gossip and speculation. Gleefully reporting the activities of young, beautiful, rich people whose whole *raison d'être* was to be in the public eye was just too good a trick to miss for a sensation-seeking press.

And from those sets of questions asked by the fans about the stars came another, a question from 'out there' – one that pulled behind it a whole trainload of anguish and despair for the majority, tragedy for the many and, for the very, very few, international fame and fortune. The question was 'why not me?' They came in search of paradise, the bartenders, the waitresses, the music-hall acts, the wrestlers, the waifs and strays, because they had read that Fatty Arbuckle was a plumber's mate who happened to be in the right place at the right time when he unblocked producer Mack Sennett's drains. They had read about a host of other very ordinary (and often talent-free individuals) spotted in ordinary situations but with extraordinary good looks who had been transported into the land of dreams and make-believe. All you needed, it seemed, was a pretty face.

*

The same year in which Nestor became the first true Hollywood studio, 18-year-old Wally Reid had gone with his father, the playwright and film director Hal Reid, to the Selig Studio in Chicago. Wandering around while his father discussed plots and stories with studio executives, he became captivated with the idea of becoming a cameraman. Reid was something of a dilettante; he could paint, write poetry, play a variety of musical instruments, especially the violin, was well read and studied chemistry. Film historian Kevin Brownlow observed that Reid was 'the kind of young man immortalized by F. Scott Fitzgerald. He should have had a large house on Long Island and unlimited leisure.'[3] He also wanted to write and direct – and he did direct his father's own play, *The Confession*, for Vitagraph. He also had the lead part, yet acting was bottom of his list of dabblings. Reid had a very traditional 'man's man' view of the world and felt very uncomfortable putting on greasepaint to act. He told a close friend, Hearst journalist Adela St Johns, that something went out of his heart every time he did it. The trouble was that he was blessed (or, as he might have seen it, cursed) with good looks and a tall, strong physique. Movie producers could see what a box-office draw he could be and wanted him in front of the camera, not behind it.

An opening for an assistant director on $40 a week sent Wally Reid off to Hollywood, but the pressure to act was relentless and as a paid employee he had to do what he was told. Riding skills honed in Wyoming saw Reid in the saddle as a Western stuntman for Selig, and he began to appear in films opposite a 17-year-old starlet, Dorothy Davenport, whom he married in October 1913. During the course of 1914 he was partially won over to acting as an art form rather than something to be ashamed of by Geraldine Farrar, the opera star turned actress. He played her leading man in four films, by the end of which Wallace Reid was a star.

He was usually typecast as the debonair and dashing wealthy socialite with schoolboy charm and all-American presence. The image combined Tom Cruise and Leonardo Di Caprio with a dash of Pierce Brosnan. Fans projected their own fantasies and daydreams on to a very down-to-earth, open-hearted, extremely bemused young man. Women hid in his car, tried to get into his house or plagued him with letters and phone calls. Today we would call them stalkers.

According to Adela St Johns he couldn't understand why any red-blooded American should get any praise for the unmanly occupation of acting. His self-esteem apparently took another battering as he gave in to immense pressure from his family and the studios not to sign up when America entered the war in 1917. He was denied the chance to do his bit for the flag and it depressed him enormously.

If his self-esteem was bouncing along at the bottom, his bank balance was in seventh heaven. By 1919 he was one of the biggest box-office draws in America. The studio bosses had been right: as soon as it became apparent which stars were really making a difference to profits, salaries skyrocketed. Mary Pickford went from $175 a week to an annual salary in excess of a million dollars. Charlie Chaplin and Douglas Fairbanks were also in the million-dollar club, and the three became powerful enough to take charge of their own affairs through their own company, United Artists, formed in January 1919.

Like the rock and pop stars of modern times, a handful of young people barely out of their teens found themselves with more money than they knew what to do with. Silent film star Colleen Moore wrote in her autobiography in 1968: 'As more and more of us in Hollywood began earning bigger and bigger salaries, some of them pretty fantastic even by today's standards – and without today's tax bites – we splurged on homes and cars, and clothes and swimming pools, partly I suppose because our intensive work schedules didn't permit such luxuries as travel, partly because what started out as necessities or conveniences became status symbols, and partly because most of us had more money than sense.'[4]

Movie stars became the new royalty, but with a difference. Historically, kings and queens tended to be judged on their achievements (wars won, land captured, just rules passed) rather than how beautiful they were or how many possessions they owned. In any case, one expects royalty to live lavishly; it comes with the job and they would have been diminished in the eyes of their subjects if it were any other way. But here you had ordinary people being judged by their peers and their audience on some very shaky and temporary criteria – primarily looks (which fade) and the acquisition of consumer goods. J. B. Priestley wrote: 'A boy or girl could arrive here to land among the sudden splendours, the magical generosity, of an Arabian fairy-tale; but if the jewels and palaces appeared like Aladdin's, they could also vanish like

Aladdin's, leaving the youngsters that owned them stranded on the desert, listening to the howls of malicious invisible *genii*.'[5]

As Colleen Moore said, stars spent lavishly on 'things' because they worked so hard, that the only way to enjoy the money was to build a castle to escape to at the weekends and be pampered. Wallace Reid was acknowledged to be one of the hardest-working actors in Hollywood, doing several films a year. And while the money was big, the studio bosses had no truck with people phoning in sick. You worked until you dropped because the moguls did the same. Producer David Selznick's wife wrote that her husband's punishing work schedule was 'insane and only made possible by Benzedrine in increasing amounts'[6] and, if required, a studio doctor on hand to pump you full of whatever it took to keep you going. Drugs came into the pictures. Karl Brown, a cameraman on Reid's films, explained that the studio doctor 'goes where he's told, he does what he's told. At the moment he enters a studio, which is in effect a small principality with the vice-president in charge of production being the prince, whatever is required of him he does. Now that means everything from an injection of a forbidden drug to an abortion and all things in between.'[7] As the actor Sir Cedric Hardwicke observed: 'I had anticipated that Hollywood would be an actor's Eden. It proved to be a paradise only for the medical profession.'[8]

As early as 1916, when Douglas Fairbanks starred as Cole Ennyday, Aleister Crowley on a visit to Hollywood could condemn the community as 'a cinema crowd of cocaine-crazed lunatics'. It took a few more years before the press began to pick up on stories of drugs, sex and booze orgies at the palaces of the rich. Hollywood played as hard as it worked.

When Wally Reid got his first taste is unclear. Most likely it was early in his career after a riding accident badly injured his left leg. *Motography* (18 January 1913) reported that 'he was giving chase to a runaway on the boulevard' when his own horse lost its footing and fell with Reid under it. This injury continued to bother Reid for the rest of his life. In March 1919 the *New York Telegraph* reported during the filming of *Valley of the Giants* 'nearly every member of the Wallace Reid company was injured . . . when a train caboose, carrying the Reid company of players, jumped the tracks . . . and turned over'. Reid sustained a bad head wound requiring several stitches and then later in the year required yet more stitches in his scalp when a rock hit him on the head. His wife, Dorothy Davenport, later said that Wally was prescribed morphine at this time but denied this was the source of his addiction.

But by then Reid was in a particularly vulnerable state. He was doing a job he had no respect for and acquired adulation and riches he couldn't understand or deal with. He also found himself surrounded by a gaggle of spongers and sycophants, the proto-audience of the film business who abused his hospitality knowing he was always fearful of offending people and liked to portray the image of 'hail fellow, well met'. And because of the pressures of work, and Reid's own sense of obligation to do the best he could, there was no physical escape. So he found another form of sanctuary in drugs, not just those prescribed by doctors, but also delivered to his door by local dealers who also dropped by the secluded canyon house where he held court for his 'friends'.

Despite growing rumours around town, Reid kept his drug use pretty much under wraps. He carried on working, as did the actress Juanita Hansen, who wrote about her own battle against drugs for Hearst's *New York American* in 1923. She was keeping her drug use hidden from the public gaze at the same time as Reid, although, like him, it was only the drugs that kept her going through a punishing work schedule. Only when a dealer actually came to call at the house with a delivery (unlike Reid, Hansen usually went to collect her own supplies) did her maid realise what was going on.

But on 10 September 1920 the lid was taken off the secret world of drugs and the movies by the suicide of one of America's most popular young stars, Olive Thomas. With her classic girl-next-door looks, lucrative film contract and celebrity marriage to Mary Pickford's all-American brother Jack, she seemed to have the world at her feet. But the 20-year-old was found stretched out naked on a Parisian hotel bed still clutching a bottle of lethal bichloride of mercury.

Once her death was investigated, the 'mom's apple pie' image of Thomas and Pickford took a hammering when it was discovered that Thomas had been seen in some of the roughest dives of Montmartre. She was allegedly looking to score heroin for her husband, who was supposed to be a hopeless addict, and, having failed, killed herself. This unlikely scenario was followed by another story following the arrest of a US army captain named Spaulding on charges of cocaine dealing. One of his customers was listed in the ubiquitous little black book as 'America's Ideal Girl', which the press deduced was Olive herself.

Only nine days after Olive's death, actress Mildred Lee Moore was arrested for heroin possession along with actor R. Jay Belasco. Interviewed by the *Los Angeles Examiner,* Moore said that she had first taken drugs in New York and, having got hooked, decided to come to Los Angeles to sign up with a film company and 'get away from drugs. I was amazed after I had been here but a day or two when I learned that dope users are as common in Los Angeles as New York.' Whether being interviewed following arrest or writing 'tell-all' articles about 'my life in hell', movie stars were full of hardly credible statements like this one. After making her way in Hollywood and being a heroin user, Juanita Hansen claimed she had never even heard of cocaine when first introduced to it. All were keen to portray themselves as innocents abroad led down the road to doom and destruction by evil forces beyond their control – presumably in the hope of salvaging their careers. Neither Moore nor Hansen succeeded in the censorious moral climate of the day.

The net began to close on Wallace Reid. On 20 November 1920 *Variety* reported the arrest of Thomas Tyner with seven wraps of heroin on him. Tyner said he was 'delivering the dope to one of the best-known male picture stars on the coast and that it had been the second time he was engaged to deliver to the same star, whose wife, in the hope of having him break the habit, informed the authorities'.

Then, on 25 May 1921, police arrested one Joe Woods in the act of selling $1,000-worth of morphine at the home of 'a prominent actor in Hollywood' whose name the police refused to reveal.

Both instances involved Reid, and they belied his wife's assertion in articles written in December 1922, when the cat was truly out of the bag, that she had no idea what was going on.

Probably to get him out of the way until the heat died down, Reid's boss, Paramount studio head Adolph Zukor, sent him to New York in the summer of 1921 to star in the film version of the play *Peter Ibbotson*. It was here, Davenport later claimed, that Reid developed his morphine habit from medical prescriptions designed to combat insomnia. Reid didn't want to go, and by now was not a well man. Drugs were taking their toll, his work regime was relentless and his health problems were compounded by the extraction of nine teeth for which more pain-killing drugs were prescribed. Even so, Reid still thought he could handle the drugs. He had a lifelong interest in medicine (he once saved a road accident victim's life) and had a full-blown chemical lab-oratory installed in his basement. He almost thought of himself as a doctor. So he continued to work and party *in extremis*. But he was getting harder to manage, wheedling $1,000-a-day bribes out of directors to get him on to the set, where increasingly he was being propped up in front of the camera. He was also becoming cavalier about hiding his habit, once showing off a trick golf club with a syringe in the handle to director James Cruze, also a heavy drug user.

Meanwhile, Adolph Zukor had other worries. The biggest film scandal to break so far happened a year to the day following the death of Olive Thomas. On 10 September 1921 a young actress named Vir-ginia Rappe died in hospital after attending a party at the plush Hotel St Francis in San Francisco hosted by the hugely popular Roscoe 'Fatty' Arbuckle, who had a $3 million contract with Paramount. Fatty and his friends had decided to throw a party to celebrate Labor Day and motored up the coast in his new $25,000 Pierce-Arrow roadster to celebrate with a crowd of his cronies. Arbuckle checked in late Saturday night, commandeered three suites on the twelfth floor and the party took off. It was still going the next afternoon, an open house with people coming and going, boozing and doping. At around 3.15 p.m. it was alleged that Arbuckle inveigled Virginia, now very drunk, into one of the rooms and locked the door. What happened next became a matter of dispute, but she alleged that, having failed to have intercourse with her, Arbuckle had raped her with a bottle and then a shard of ice. The room was wrecked, Virginia had most of her clothes ripped off and she was taken in great pain to hospital, where she died from peritonitis. What caused this was only discovered when the deputy coroner received a strange call from the hospital following the post-mortem and went round to check up for himself. He had Virginia's sexual organs re-examined and discovered that her bladder had been ruptured.

The kiddies' favourite comedian was charged with rape and man-slaughter, and the case shook Hollywood to its foundations. Cinemas where his films were showing were trashed by audiences, the movies had to be withdrawn, costing Paramount at least a million dollars. The trial began in mid-November. Fatty's defence lawyers tried to portray Virginia Rappe as a good-time girl sleeping her way around Hollywood. Arbuckle himself claimed he had simply come across Rappe in a distressed state, moaning and groaning and tearing her clothes, and simply tried to help her. There was no direct evidence to implicate Arbuckle, and after much conflicting testimony the jury voted by ten to two for an acquittal. A mistrial was declared. Fatty Arbuckle was to be tried again.

Meanwhile, especially for the Hearst newspapers, it was open season on Hollywood, a glorious opportunity to combine moral outrage with prurience, of which the following was typical:

Nero, whose lurid orgies have been a byword of history, would have turned his head in shame at some of the modern-day ribald gatherings in which certain members of the Hollywood motion picture colony gave their passions and impulses unrestrained play.

Tearing down the curtain of secrecy that has veiled the spectacular conduct of a group known as 'the Live Hundred,' investigators have begun a sensational disclosure of 'parties' at which expense was not permitted to stand in the way of unmeasured excesses in drinks and drugs.

Detectives spying on one party saw 'an assortment of needles, opium pipes, morphine, cocaine, heroin and opium. Each guest hilariously helped himself or herself to liberal doses of drugs and selected needles or pipes as the individual desire demanded. With drunken caresses they injected morphine into one another or helped the next-seat neighbor to 'sniff' his or her selection. (*New York American*, 16 September 1921)

By the time the first Arbuckle trial had started, Wallace Reid was in hospital. Zukor had come under intense pressure from two sources to do something about Reid's addiction, now common knowledge around Hollywood but yet to find its way into the newspapers. The first was from Will Hays, who had been appointed to clean up both Hollywood's film content and its public image.* He had compiled a 'Doomsday' list of 117 Hollywood stars, writers and executives whose private lives had become too public and so were deemed 'unsafe'. Top of the list was Wallace Reid. The second source was a group of Hollywood personnel calling itself 'Federated Arts', set up with the express purpose of boycotting anybody who was bringing the industry into disrepute. They made representations to Zukor about the antics of Wally Reid.

The American drug laws had served to criminalise anybody using controlled drugs and any doctor who tried to help them by prescribing drugs to keep people off the streets and away from the dealers. Simply being a drug user was a crime, irrespective of how you came by your habit. Admitting Reid to a private sanatorium was an attempt to shift the perception whereby Reid was not a criminal but sick and in need of medical care. His health was bad, and he was now suffering from Kleig's Eye, similar to snow-blindness and caused by being exposed to strong studio lighting for hours on end. All the euphemisms about 'nervous exhaustion' were trotted out by his wife and the studio, but the truth was that Wally Reid was shut away in a padded cell to come off drugs.

With his major star hooked on morphine and out of action for an unknown period of time and his $3 million comedian having to face another trial for murder, Adolph Zukor could have been forgiven for thinking that things couldn't get much worse. And then they did.

On the evening of 1 February 1922, with Arbuckle's second trial just started, film director William Desmond Taylor was shot dead in his bungalow court apartment on Alvardo Street in the sedate LA district of Westlake. Taylor was the chief director of Famous Players-Lasky, a Paramount subsidiary, and if that wasn't bad enough, another of Zukor's big-money stars, Mary Miles Minter, and her mother, Charlotte Shelby, were both heavily implicated in the whole saga. Passionate letters from Mary to Taylor were found at the house, a story spiced up by a claim that her monogrammed nightgown or knickers (whichever story you believed) were also found by police. Charlotte Shelby was supposed to be against the match sufficiently for many to believe that she shot Taylor to keep him away from Mary.

Nobody was ever tried for the murder and to this day nobody knows

*The full story of Hays and Hollywood is the subject of the next chapter.

who did it or why. Consequently, over the years several articles and books have been written on the murder, and there is even an e-zine on the Internet called *Taylorology* devoted to picking through the evidence piece by piece.

Many people have skeletons in the cupboard, episodes in their past that have remained hidden from public view. But you can bet that once the press get hold of a story, little will remain hidden for long as hacks dig deep and those anxious for their 15 minutes in the sun come crawling out of the woodwork. And so it was that highly respected eligible bachelor William Desmond Taylor, dignified, cultured, *bon vivant* and art connoisseur, was actually William Cunningham Deane-Tanner, who suddenly disappeared from his Long Island home, leaving his wife and child. His brother Denis did exactly the same thing four years later and was never found.

The list of murder suspects fingered by the nation's press, from the *New York Journal* to the *Honolulu Star Bulletin*, was long and involved, but went something like this. Taylor was a notorious womaniser and died at the hand of a jealous lover. Those in the frame were actress Mabel Normand (about whom more below) and screenwriter Julia Ivers. He was murdered by a jealous man – including either Mack Sennett or Rudolph Valentino, who was in love with one of Taylor's girlfriends; he died at the hands of ex or current employees – including Edward Sands, who some claimed was Taylor's missing brother; burglars, black-mailers, crazed fans, disgruntled actors, bootleggers, anti-movie fanatics, the Ku Klux Klan, a soldier Taylor had court-martialled during the war; and relatives of spurned girlfriends – including Mary Minter's mother Charlotte.

But probably the one element in all the stories that came up most often was a connection between Taylor and the world of illegal drugs. Taylor had been seen at a number of 'hop' parties, where he was supposed to be gathering information for one of his films. Taylor was an addict himself. Taylor belonged to a secret cult of homosexual opium smokers whose trust he betrayed. Taylor was a dealer who used his connections to get young actresses hooked on drugs. These, and other outlandish stories about Taylor's drug connections, were often simply the invention of journalists or came from criminals seeking immunity in exchange for information or using the mystery surrounding Taylor's death to take revenge on a rival by naming him to the police. One convict named Hefner actually got an early release from Folsom prison because he claimed that the information he had passed over about Taylor's death would get him killed if he stayed in jail. He later admitted that all his 'information' about Taylor was false.

The most detailed stories connecting Taylor to drugs revolved around his relationship with actress Mabel Normand. She had risen to fame as a Mack Sennett comedienne and began an intense affair with the director which ended when she signed for Sam Goldwyn in 1917 in an attempt to get away from comedy. Her career stalled and then began to slide as she publicly defended her close friend Fatty Arbuckle. By this time, she was blotting out her disillusionment with Hollywood in drugs and alcohol, much to the distress of her new love, William Taylor. It seems that Taylor had been procuring drugs for Mabel in the hope of keeping her addiction secret, but could do little else for her.

The most popular drug story circulating was that in a desperate bid to cut off Mabel's supplies, he had gone to US attorney Tom Green in an attempt to gain support for a crusade against the dealers. It was also alleged that Taylor had physically thrown dealers off the Paramount lot and out of Mabel Normand's house. The endgame was supposedly played out when the dealers, fed up with Taylor's interference, had him killed. Tom Green gave three interviews on the subject, but there were discrepancies in each over some key issues, such as when and where Taylor and Mabel met, how much Mabel was spending on drugs and stories about Taylor confronting dealers face to face.

According to *Taylorology* editor Bruce Long, the problem with the drug-gang-as-killer story is that it did not emerge from local police stories or rumours from the local press or the film lots themselves, but from a New York pulp-fiction author writing speculative articles nearly a fortnight after the event. Of all the stories circulating about Taylor's murder, the drug gang theory was the only one that put both Taylor and Hollywood in a good light at a time when the press were really turning up the heat on what was increasingly seen as a decadent, dangerous and morally bankrupt industry. Lindsay Denison, writing in the *New York Evening World* (13 February 1922), said: 'Can Hollywood be morally fumigated? Or must it be wiped off the movie business map as a nuisance, as a farmer might burn down a vermin-infested barn before putting up a new one.' The likelihood is that the Hollywood PR machine picked up on the theory and played it for what it was worth, priming up movie-friendly newspapers and journalists to run with it as the most likely motive for Taylor's murder. It would help perpetuate the idea that Hollywood's drug scene was entirely driven by pushers and peddlers, keeping the doctor's role strictly off screen.

None of the evidence carefully detailed by Bruce Long points to a professional hit, and neither did the detectives working close to the crime believe that a 'dope ring' was involved. So who did it? A next-door neighbour, Mrs McLean, heard what she thought was a shot and went to the door, where she said she saw a man at Taylor's door. The man looked directly at Mrs McLean and then walked casually up the street, leaving her believing that the noise she heard must have been a car backfiring. But she was suspicious of this 'man' because he was 'funny looking', a view taken further by Mabel Normand herself, who later stated that her and many others thought the 'man' was actually a woman dressed up.

Although the drug gang theory is largely discredited, there seems to be enough circumstantial evidence to suggest that Taylor did have some contact with the drug world, because of his concerns for Mabel Normand. The theory seems to have been dismissed largely because of the evidence that this was not a professional hit, nor was there any direct evidence linking Taylor to a 'gang'. All of which may be true, but falls foul of the misleading notion that anything to do with drug dealing has to involve gangs and be organised and professional. This is a misconception which still exists today. Media drug stories are replete with 'drug lords', 'drug barons' 'and 'Mr Bigs', and crime dramas always have neat genealogies purporting to show the hierarchies of command within organised crime which are more likely a reflection of police command structures than the complex realities of drug dealing and trafficking. Taylor could easily have been the victim of a low-level street dealer with a grudge as much as any of the far more elaborate conspiracy theories that populate the still-unsolved Taylor murder mystery.

While the Taylor sensation was played out in the press, Fatty Arbuckle went through two more trials and was finally acquitted, although his career was in ruins. Wally Reid saw out 1922 in his padded cell.

More vitriol was heaped on Hollywood by the former editor of *Photo-*

play, Ed Roberts, in a collection of stories entitled *The Sins of Hollywood: An Exposé of Movie Vice,* published in May 1922. Although nobody was named and shamed, it is easy to work out who he was talking about, at one point implying that Wallace Reid deliberately turned young vulnerable people on to drugs.

Yet if the following article, entitled 'Happy Days in Hollywood', is anything to go by, published in *Variety* in the very same month as Roberts's sensational muckraking, there must have been a section of the Hollywood glitterati that thought itself fireproof against the white-hot glare of rampant anti-Hollywood publicity:

> With the brightening influence of spring there has been a distinct quickening of the social pace. Drugs are not much in evidence as during the more trying months of winter, but they still spread their genial influence at some of the more exclusive functions. Last week little Lulu Lenore of the Cuckoo Comedy Co. gave a small house dance for the youngest addicts. 'Will you come to my "Snow-ball" ' read the clever invitations. In one corner of the living room was a miniature 'drugstore' where Otho Everard kept the company in a roar as he dispensed little packages of cocaine, morphine and heroin. The guests at their departure received exquisite hypodermic needles in vanity boxes which have caused many heart-burnings among those whose were not invited.

During 1922, cinema audiences saw Wallace Reid on the screen in eight or nine films. But he was nowhere to be seen in public. As rumours of his fight grew, his wife decided to reveal all to the *Los Angeles Herald* in a four-part interview that ran from 18 to 22 December. 'I am opening the book on Wallace Reid's life so that the public will read and know the truth,' she said. A similar set of articles ran in the *San Francisco Examiner* from 31 December to 5 January 1923, in which Dorothy Davenport contradicted herself about the New York antecedence of her husband's drug problems. This time she hinted at parties that got out of hand, well before the trip to New York in the summer of 1921. She gave accounts of conversations with Wally in which she confronted him about drugs, with him promising to quit, addressing her as 'Mamma' as if to emphasise just how out of his depth and how vulnerable the man-boy star of American movies had become. Two weeks after the last article was published, Wallace Reid died, ostensibly from influenza, his weakened body unable to cope with the virus. He was 31.

The funeral took place at the First Congregational church in Los Angeles with the full panoply of Hollywood aristocracy in attendance – Charlie Chaplin, Pola Negri, Mary Pickford, Douglas Fairbanks, Harold Lloyd and Fatty Arbuckle – and thousands lining the streets.

Reid's was not the last drug-related Hollywood death of the silent era. In 1926 Barbara La Marr, dubbed prophetically 'too beautiful to grow old', died, aged 28, having worked her way through a whirlwind life-style, four husbands, umpteen lovers and mountains of coke. Like so many, her downfall was accelerated by drugs administered to her after a studio accident. Alma Reubens had co-starred in 1916 with Douglas Fairbanks in *The Mystery of the Leaping Fish*. But through much of the 1920s she was hiding a heavy drug habit until January 1929, when she was seen running down the street pursued by two men, who she claimed were trying to kidnap her. She stabbed one of them with a knife concealed in her dress. It turned out to be a paramedic; the other man was her doctor, trying to persuade Alma to go into a private hospital when she panicked and fled. Attempts at rehabilitation failed, and she died in January 1931, aged 33.

Mabel Normand managed to dislodge the monkey on her back, but after years of illness, adverse publicity and grieving for William Taylor, at the age of 38 she succumbed to TB in February 1930. She didn't live to witness the final degradations of her close friend, Fatty Arbuckle. With his career in ruins, he hit the bottle and died broke and broken on 28 June 1933.

With her husband gone, Dorothy Davenport, actress, transformed herself into Mrs Wallace Reid, anti-drugs crusader. She approached Hollywood producer Thomas Ince with an idea to do a drug propa-ganda movie sanctioned by the Los Angeles Anti-Narcotic League. Bessie Love, another actress from the Fairbanks coke movie, was chosen to play the suicidal addict Mary in what was first entitled *Dope*, then *Living Dead* and finally *Human Wreckage*, released in 1923.

The film (for which only a script remains) begins with the prologue: 'The Dope Ring, one of the most powerful and vicious organizations in American history, is composed of rings within rings, the inner ring including men powerful in finance, politics and society. But the trail to the "men higher up" is cunningly covered. No investigator has penetrated to the inner circle.'

Inevitably, the film did not actually follow through on its insights, but with reference back to the possible link between drugs and German Expressionism, the set design for *Human Wreckage* had a street of crazy-angled buildings specified in the script as 'something on the order of Dr Caligari's Cabinet [sic]'.

Jimmy Brown is arrested on a drugs charge but escapes prison, instead going to the narcotics ward of the county hospital. Jimmy leaves hospital supposedly 'cured'; meanwhile his overworked attorney, McFarland, dabbles in drugs to get him through and becomes hooked. McFarland's wife Ethel (played by Dorothy Davenport) has devoted herself to helping those less fortunate than her. It was she who persuaded her husband to take the Jimmy Brown case and now she has noticed that her neighbour's daughter Mary (Bessie Love) is not only injecting morphine but rubbing the drug on her breast to quieten her six-month-old baby. Ethel is outraged. Mary is taken to hospital and loses her baby.

Mary's pusher, Harris, is arrested and tricked into giving up the names of other dealers, including McFarland's, Steve Stone. However, as he is a dealer to the rich and famous, they ensure he has the best lawyer in town. And the best is McFarland. Stone gets off and sends the lawyer some morphine to show his gratitude. McFarland takes the morphine at home, falls asleep and Ethel discovers the needle and bottle. Ethel tricks her husband into believing she wants to try drugs as well and on that basis he destroys what's left of the morphine and vows to give up. Stone is a passenger in a taxi driven by Jimmy Brown. Both are killed when Brown drives the taxi full speed into the path of a train. Critical reviews were mixed. *Variety* thought it was simply an advert on how to use drugs, while *Motion Picture Classic* though it 'a profoundly moving picture handled with dignity and restraint'. In typically over-the-top mode, Hearst's *Los Angeles Examiner* declared it to be 'the most important picture ever made'. The film was so successful financially that it enabled Mrs Reid to take care of her family, set up her own production company and work towards establishing the Wallace Reid Foundation Sanitarium. She toured the country on speaking engagements and to her credit encouraged her audiences to think of chronic drug users as in need of help rather than punishment – and to drop terms like 'hop heads' and 'drug fiends'.

However, Mrs Reid's efforts to show the more responsible side of Hollywood was too little, too late. Since the first penny had dropped into a kinetoscope, the moral crusaders had the movies firmly in their sights. The parade of drug deaths and arrests, murders and sex scandals that dogged Hollywood in the early 1920s provided all the ammunition required to shoot the industry and all its galaxy of stars out of the sky.

4

Aaaaand cut!: the censors strike

In May 1980 drug historian Professor David Courtwright of the University of Florida interviewed Nick, a 71-year-old former drug user who grew up in New York just as the movies took off in popularity;

> I used to go out fooling around with a wild bunch of kids. They were mainly the sons of immigrants; Irish, Italian, German, Polish, Jewish. In them days we used to run up after the wagon – you know, they used to deliver the groceries and stuff in wagons. We'd get on the back of the wagon and get a couple of cases of tomatoes or whatever the hell was on there, then we'd go out and sell it . . . That's how we made our money to go to the movies and buy cocaine. You could buy it in a drugstore then. We could buy a half-ounce for 50 cents over the counter. After we sniffed cocaine, we'd just hang around and maybe go to a movie . . . We went in to see a show and we'd have cocaine.[1]

Nick's experience encapsulated everything that reformers in the Progressive movement thought was wrong with the movies. Young gangs of urban immigrants obtaining money illegally to buy drugs and sit in dark, dusty movie houses watching not just Keystone Cop comedies but movies which depicted (however tamely by modern standards) all aspects of sexual human relationships, including seduction, kissing, pregnancy, divorce and adultery. Even if many kids couldn't read the silent movie titles, a picture tells a thousand words and explains why the movies were such a hit with the millions of immigrants swarming into America at the turn of the century. There were even newspaper stories of cocaine on sale under cover of darkness in the cinema and all kinds of sexual shenanigans going on in the blackened back rows. A *New York Times* headline from 1914 read: 'Cocaine sold in theatres. Girls led into drug habit by men met at picture shows.'

The early days of cinema were marked by huge enthusiasms lined up against the moral reformers who saw cinema as yet further proof of the degeneracy of the big city. To be fair, there was some division of opinion here. Fervent Temperance campaigners viewed the cinema as a welcome diversion from the saloon, something to bring families together and prise father from the booze. In fact, bar owners and vaudeville and theatre managers joined the clamour against the movies because they were losing customers. But most within the reform movements were against it. The cinema was anathema on two counts.

First was the physical environment of the movie house. The Progressive movement was very much in favour of creating healthy outdoor opportunities for recreation and embarked on a huge urban park building programme; Chicago spent $15 million on parks between 1900 and 1910. Yet here was the movie business enticing young people away from the light and into the dark.

Second was the content of the films themselves in an era where there was no segregation by age – anybody could see any film. The Progressives were particularly concerned about the impact of urban living on family life and attacked anything they believed undermined traditional (for which read white, Protestant, rural) values. So immoral films became a new target alongside immoral books, magazines, plays, brothels, saloons and dance halls.

From the beginning there was a strong belief that cinema was such a powerful medium that impressionable young people would immediately act out what they saw on the screen – an argument which is still with us. In 1912 a YMCA official from Indiana had written in a letter to *Outlook,* 'Unless the law steps in and does for moving-picture shows what it has done for meat inspection and pure food, the cinematograph will continue to inject into our social order an element of degrading principle.'[2] British Church leaders, magistrates, educationalists and others, while also concerned about the impact of cinema on young people, were on the whole more measured and less hysterical in their responses. A wide-ranging and considered inquiry into cinema conducted by the National Council of Public Morals in 1917 found no link between film content and juvenile delinquency.

In America there was another, more sinister side to faith-driven reforming zeal. Canon Chase, a leading light in the censorship movement, labelled his colleagues 'Patriotic Gentile Americans' and claimed that the aim of his movement was to 'rescue motion pictures from the hands of the devil and 500 unchristian Jews'.[3] Anti-Semitism was the subtext of the whole anti-film, pro-censorship movement, led by the Protestants in the 1920s and the Catholics in the 1930s.

All the key figures of the new business were Jewish immigrants. Carl Laemmle (Universal) was born in a small village in south-western Germany. Adolph Zukor (Paramount) was born in another small village, this one in the wine-growing region of Hungary. William Fox was also Hungarian, Louis B. Mayer (MGM) came from Russia. Benjamin Warner left his wife and children in Poland to seek his fortune in the States. After two years mending shoes, he sent for his family and then earned his living selling patent medicines from the back of a wagon. The family eventually settled down in Ohio. His sons Harry, Sam, Albert and Jack bought a broken film projector and began the long road to a carrot-chewing bunny known the world over. And all those who were to grow powerful alongside and under them were from similar backgrounds: Irvin Thalberg (MGM), Harry Cohn (Columbia), Sam Goldwyn, David Selznick, Darryl Zanuck and a cast of thousands – producers, theatre managers, accountants and lawyers.

The Jewish movie pioneers knew instinctively what their audiences wanted to see – and they could see how much money they could make satisfying those needs. In turn, they were accused of undermining American values by the salacious, violent or subversive nature of the films they produced.

Yet they were also desperate to be accepted in their own right as respectable businessmen, running respectable businesses. At the same time as they were being accused of sabotaging the power structure, they urgently wanted to be a part of it. Neal Gabler, in his book about the Jewish domination of Hollywood, suggests that their embrace of America was 'ferocious, even pathological'. So keen were they to assimilate themselves and their enterprise into mainstream American popular culture that this handful of street-smart, power-crazy, workaholic, egomaniacal alien refugees from the ghettos and shtetls of Eastern Europe, ten thousand miles away from Los Angeles, screamed, shouted and bullied Hollywood into existence and fashioned the American dream on celluloid – hope, ambition, power, money, achievement, love, family life, tradition and land of opportunity.

Technological developments enabled the creation of full-length films with a strong narrative, more attractive to middle-class audiences. The studio bosses tried to present their business as art – resulting in a flood of historical adaptations in the early years of film and the much-heralded acting career of Metropolitan Opera star Geraldine Farrar, who helped inspire Wallace Reid to pursue *his* acting career.

Everything about Hollywood was a fantasy: the dream of going there and becoming rich and famous; the incredible lifestyle of those who made it; the relentless message of the studios that everything would be all right in the end, that good would ultimately triumph over evil. The industry sought to draw audiences into this fantasy by wrapping it up in opulent movie palaces that grew up out of the dust and dirt of the shopfront nickelodeons. This, too, was part of the drive towards middle-class acclamation (and, of course, increased profits) – to build on a scale to mimic the grandeur of the opera house.

The 1920s saw a frenzy of palace-building; hundreds of 1,000–5,000-seat cinemas sprang up in all the major urban areas, culminating in New York's 6,200-seat Roxy built on five storeys combining Renaissance, Gothic and Moorish influences. The ushers were drilled by an ex-marine, there was a music library, 25 Steinway pianos scattered around, washroom facilities for 10,000. Oh, and they showed films. Other cinemas encouraged families by offering free crèche accommodation.

None of this expenditure cut much ice with the reformers. If a movie was immoral, it was immoral, even if the film was based on historical fact – there was plenty in history that was unsuitable to be screened in front of children. In this, the moguls, for all their vision, were too profit-driven to accept the idea of segregated audiences where children would be excluded from some films. And as for the picture palaces, these could be condemned as even more enticing, inveigling young people to moral perdition. Young people and the working classes in general were still having their sexual and political passions inflamed by films depicting all the messiness of human relationships and those films suggesting that perhaps the interests of the working man and capitalism were not perfectly in tune.

The battle lines were drawn early on over censorship. The reformers wanted local, state or even federal regulations; the industry, not surprisingly, went for some form of self-regulation. Chicago became the first local authority to impose film censorship. In 1907 exhibitors had to obtain a police permit before any film could be shown. In 1915 Pennsylvania became the first state to appoint a state board to censor films and many others followed suit. From the very inception of public bodies to censor films, prohibitions on various aspects of drug use were in force. Maryland State Board of Censors prohibited any films that could be deemed as instructive in the use of 'opium and other habit-forming drugs'. Ohio banned 'scenes which show the use of narcotics and other unnatural practices dangerous to social morality', while in Massachusetts 'pictures or parts of pictures dealing with the drug habit . . . will be disapproved'.[4]

All legal challenges to censorship failed. Most damaging for the industry was the Supreme Court ruling on the Mutual Film Company suit against the Ohio Board in 1915 on constitutional grounds. In a shock decision, the Supreme Court said that the First Amendment on free speech did not apply to films because films were a business 'pure and simple' and were not expected to be in the business of expressing ideas that might have First Amendment protection.

What the industry feared most was a proliferation of censorship boards, each with its own views on what constituted unacceptable viewing, making film production a nightmare. In 1909 Edison's Motion Picture Patents Company, in collaboration with the People's Institute of New York, set up the National Board of Censorship of Motion Pictures. It was never that effective because the company didn't control all film production.

This became the National Board of Review set up in 1914. A liberal strain running through this body allowed films to be shown depicting prostitution and corruption. Not surprisingly, it came under attack from the moral guardians and did nothing to prevent more states establishing censorship boards. An example of the censorship lottery came from Pennsylvania, where films couldn't show a pregnant woman or even a woman knitting baby clothes. In Kansas, kissing was limited to a few seconds, while on-screen smoking and drinking were banned entirely.

Attempting to keep the self-regulation pot boiling, the industry formed the National Association of the Motion Picture Industry (NAMPI). In March 1921 NAMPI introduced the Thirteen Points condemning 'stories which make gambling and drunkenness attractive, or of scenes which show the use of narcotics and other practices dangerous to social morality'. But within a few months of this latest attempt by the industry to show it took content regulation seriously, the Hollywood scandals broke around the movie world, confirming the reformers' worst fears about the business.

The studios needed to act in a high-profile manner. NAMPI was disbanded and instead the Motion Picture Producers and Distributors Association (MPPDA) was formed, which in turn appointed the Postmaster-General, Will Hays, as its president. Hays was a close friend of President Harding and as chairman of the Republican National Committee had done much to get Harding elected. As Postmaster-General he had waged war on mail fraud and was known to be mad about the movies. He lobbied successfully on behalf of air-mail services, which were bringing down the prohibitive costs of film shipments. He looked like a wimp but was passionate about the causes he believed in. The film industry offered Hays $100,000 a year to disarm the industry's critics and derail the government's bid to censor the movies. He was the perfect choice, cosy with the President, a first-rate administrator and a country boy and Presbyterian Church elder with an unswerving moral code: 'What is immoral is always immoral,' he wrote in his memoirs. He firmly believed that the whole country would benefit from a solid dose of small-town values. He was the movies' spin doctor trying to present a better PR face to the public and encourage the studios to self-censor. On his appointment in March 1922 and to show he meant business in pledging to clean up Hollywood, he banned all Fatty Arbuckle movies and all screen references to drugs.

However, he made an exception for Dorothy Davenport and allowed the production of *Human Wreckage* to go ahead. As we saw, the film was well received as a decent drama in it own right, but the scene showing Bessie Love preparing to inject herself with heroin proved too much for the British censors, who in January 1924 banned the film from being shown in the UK.

The power to censor films in Britain was enshrined in the Cinema Act of 1909, through which local authorities gained the power to grant licences to cinemas. As in America, there was a clamour against the cinema as a darkened den of vice, and like America the film industry attempted to head off opposition with the formation of the British Board of Film Censors (BBFC) in 1912. Its first rules were no nudity and no depictions of Christ, and they introduced two categories of film – U for universal and A for over-16s only – but this was not compulsory. Rubrics against drugs swiftly followed, but for different reasons from those in the States. Over there, the country had a manifest drug problem, plastered all over the newspapers, which the movie censors wanted to pretend wasn't happening. In Britain the motivation was different. The 1915 report of the British censor listed those things which could not be mentioned, including 'references to controversial politics' and 'relations of Capital and Labour' but also 'the drug habit, e.g. opium, morphia, cocaine etc.' on the basis that 'It is claimed for such films that they serve to warn the public against the dangers of the abuse of such drugs, but the Board decided that there being no good reason to suppose that this habit was prevalent in this country to any serious extent, the evils of arousing curiosity in the minds of those for whom it was a novel idea far outweighed the possible good that might accrue by warning the small minority that indulged in the practice'.

The assessment that Britain had a relatively small drug problem at the time was quite true. The government did not introduce drug laws on the US model until 1920 and then primarily (as a global power) to set an example for the rest of the world. The main dent in British complacency came during the First World War. It was claimed that soldiers on leave in London were buying cocaine from prostitutes. Cocaine was sold on the streets of London, bought from chemists and traded on, but it was a glorious triple-whammy for the press of the day. Cocaine was a valuable export of the enemy, Germany, so obviously the plan was to undermine the stout British tommy; prostitutes were the source of the drugs, so a good sex angle – and, of course, there were the drugs themselves. But it wasn't only the street dealers selling drugs to the troops. Both Harrods and the pharmacists Savory & Moore were fined for selling cocaine and morphine in special packs advertised as 'a useful present for friends at the front'. The result was an addition to the wartime Defence of the Realm Act whereby in July 1916 it became an offence to possess opium and cocaine.

Then Britain was hit by its very first celebrity drug scandal. At the end of a Victory Ball in 1918, a young actress, Billie Carleton, aged 22, apparently died of a cocaine overdose. The *News of the World* lamented: 'Admired by thousands, loved by many, her picture in hundreds of albums . . . light-hearted, gay and apparently happy . . . Today she lies in the cold, dark tomb, her butterfly existence cut tragically short, her brief life ended.'

In fact, from the scant medical evidence available it seems that a sleeping pill, Veronal, actually did the damage, which her doctor admitted prescribing. However, one of her boyfriends, Reggie de Vielle, was jailed for conspiracy to supply cocaine, although acquitted on manslaughter charges. Billie's death was held up as a warning to the increasingly liberated young women with a newly acquired franchise, who frequented the dance halls and nightclubs that opened up in the post-war period. The message was that they were really too frail to cope with the big wide world, and perhaps it would be better if they stayed at home like their Victorian ancestors. But however that message was carried, it would not be through the silver screen; an attempt to dramatise Billie's life, *The Case of a Doped Actress*, was banned. Once the Hollywood scandals broke, the BBFC had another reason to act against drug movies.

The British film company Astra made *Cocaine* in 1922 and presented it for preview to the BBFC, who promptly banned it. The producer, Herbert Wilcox, was furious because in order to try to compete with the Americans, British film-makers were spending high on production values and expected some encouragement for their efforts. Wilcox had gone out of his way to make the film acceptable to the BBFC, but to no avail. Wilcox refused to accept the decision and tried to get the film shown in London, home to the nightlife shown in the film, but the London County Council backed the BBFC and supported the ban. Manchester, however, took a different view and allowed the film to be shown at the Gaiety Picture House, where it attracted large audiences. An advert in *Film Renter and Moving Picture News* (13 May 1922) sold the film to cinema managers: 'If you're down in the mouth, dull, depressed, and feel like nothing on earth, take a dose of COCAINE. It will buck up your box-office receipts. It will drive away depression.' *The Bioscope* (11 May 1922) announced the film as 'The biggest money-maker which has been offered to exhibitors this year'.

Fearful that censorship would break down, the Home Office wrote to the mayor of Manchester, but without success. Cardiff went the Manchester route, but then succumbed to government pressure and banned the film following a protest from the Chinese community about a leering Chinaman depicted on an advertising poster – a classic stereotypical view that if it was drugs, it had to be evil Chinamen, even if the drug was cocaine. But Manchester's defiance raised alarm bells about the dangers of being too rigid, and the film finally appeared as *While London Sleeps*.

No such reprieve for *Human Wreckage*. The opening homily that 'Dope is the gravest menace which today confronts the United States' couldn't persuade the BBFC to allow British audiences to see the film. But Mrs Davenport was not to be put off so easily. In order to pressurise the BBFC, she sent a representative to Britain to arrange a private showing of the film to public celebrities. This prompted the BBFC to write to the Home Office, both to alert them and condemn the film: 'There have been few, if any, films submitted to the Board since its inception which the examiners look upon as more dangerous than this film . . . and we see no possibility of altering it so as to make it suitable for public exhibition in this country.' And so the BBFC ban remained. No film with drug addiction as its major theme appeared on a British screen until 1956.

Meanwhile, back in the States, Will Hays was busy trying to impose self-regulation on the film industry. At a trade conference in New York in October 1927, Hays issued a 'Don'ts and Be Careful' voluntary regulation code which prohibited swearing, white slavery, drug trafficking and nudity and encouraged producers to exercise good taste when it came to violence and sexual relations. Drug trafficking was a 'Don't' and the use of drugs was a 'Be Careful'.

But this was not an attempt at serious film censorship and came nowhere near the demands of the more vociferous reformers for whom the changing social climate in America during the 1920s and early 1930s meant that the tempo of the moral crusade needed to be accelerated. The horrors of the First World War had served to distance the people from traditional values; there was a backlash especially among young people, who wanted to create a new world in their own image. This was the Jazz Age, where women especially strove to break out of their political, social, sexual and moral straitjacket. The old order was breaking down, women seduced men, Prohibition gangsters were heroes, unions fought against the bosses. All this, the studios wanted to write large on the big screen until they came up against a foe more organised and even more powerful than the Protestant reformers.

For much of the 1920s, the Catholic Church had kept silent on the issue of movie censorship. But once the talkies came and immorality found a voice, the Church had to be heard. The Catholic League of Decency was formed to scrutinise films for material likely to be offensive to Catholics which, when it came to films that dealt with human relationships, would be just about everything. Their leading light was Martin Quigley, editor of the film industry magazine *Exhibitors Herald World*, a staunch lay Catholic and another believer in industry self-regulation.

The Catholics were much more geared up to causing trouble for the industry than the Protestant faith groups. They were heavily concentrated in urban areas, better organised with a national press attracting millions of readers. A Catholic professor of literature and editor of a Catholic youth magazine, Daniel Lord, was brought in to draft a Church code for the movies. Not surprisingly, he was anti-abortion, birth control, theories of evolution and secular education, and he was anti-Semitic.

Lord's final draft, adopted by the MPPDA on 31 March 1930, was 'a fascinating combination of Catholic theology, conservative politics and pop psychology – an amalgam that would control the content of Hollywood films for three decades'.[5] About drugs, the code was unequivocal: 'Because of its evil consequences, the drug traffic should not be presented in any form. The existence of the trade should not be brought to the attention of audiences.' But if it was anti-drugs, it was also anti-Prohibition: 'The use of liquor should never be excessively presented . . . In scenes from American life, the necessities of plot and proper characterization alone justify its use.'

But in truth even the new code was hardly worth the paper it was printed on. Not until July 1934 would the code be given real teeth. Until then, there was a censorship 'interregnum' often called the pre-code era, where film-makers basically did what they liked under the cloak of a censorship code that was universally ignored. This coincided with the rise of the talkies that increased hugely the impact of film on ever-more sophisticated audiences, who wanted to see real people in adult situations. And so came a spate of movies with sex outside of marriage, marriage ridiculed, ethnic lines crossed and racial barriers ignored, economic injustice and political corruption exposed, vice unpunished and virtue unrewarded; 'in sum, pretty much the raw stuff of American culture, unvarnished and unveiled.'[6] Except when it came to drugs – an undeniable feature of urban life, much written about in the press, but hardly dealt with by the movies, and, when it was, with nothing like the sophistication and subtlety of other films dealing with life as it is lived.

Matthew Bernstein makes the point that censorship exposes 'the fault lines of differing political ideologies, class and religious affiliations and ethnicities'.[7] Which is true, except there was no fault line when it came to drugs except to divide those who did use drugs (and who had no power, political clout, representation or rights) from those who did not take illicit drugs – and had everything else on their side.

So where did movie-going audiences of the late 1920s and early 1930s encounter the dreaded spectre of drugs? An early talkie was *The Drake Case* (1929), concerning a high-society girl's morphine-fuelled decline and fall. Next year came *Big News* and *Conspiracy* (with Bessie Love from *Human Wreckage*), both dope ring investigations, and *Soldiers of the Storm* (1933), pitching goodies against the smugglers. *Behind the Mask* (1932) was the best of the 'narc and smuggler' movies with Boris Karloff as Mr X, a morphine distributor who uses a hospital as a front for his nefarious operation and stashes his dope in a graveyard. Edward van Sloan as the sadistic surgeon employed by Mr X to carve up the hero adds more Gothic overtones to the film, which overall was very similar in look to Universal's neo-expressionist films like *Frankenstein*, although this film was regarded as rather dull: '68 minutes of fog and shadow', as one critic put it. Doctors were generally fingered as being the drug rogues – possibly because film-makers were wary of highlighting the activities of out-and-out gangsters. Michael Curtiz directed lunatic drug fiends in *The Mad Genius* (1931) before going on to direct film classics *Casablanca* (1942) and *Mildred Pierce* (1945), while 'a narcotics tragedy' was played out in *Discarded Lovers* (1932). Often 'the drug fallen' fell from the heights of celebrity, wealth or power. *The Masquerader* (1933) featured Ronald Coleman as the politician with a penchant for pills, and in *Murder by an Aristocrat* (1936) the killer turns out to be the dope-addicted offspring of a wealthy family. And continuing the saga of evil Chinamen, opium dens, smuggling and white slavery ad nauseam, Edward G. Robinson dressed up in *The Hatchet Man* (1932).

Just about the only film to try to tackle the subject sympathetically was *Heroes for Sale* (originally entitled *Breadline*, 1933). Directed by William Wellman, the star was *Broken Blossoms* hero Richard Barthelmess. The film opens in the trenches of 1917, where Tom (Barthelmess) is not only badly wounded during a raid but has his heroic deeds credited to a cowardly comrade, Roger. Shot up with morphine by German medics, the guileless Tom thanks his benevolent captors with the words, 'That'll be a godsend, doctor', but becomes hooked. As we have seen, getting any drug theme past the censor was tricky. So at the very least the only route to dependency allowed in the movies was through doctor-derived pain relief.

Back home, Tom looks after his aged mother while employed as a bank clerk by Roger's father. But the monkey needs feeding and the evil pusher is asking for more money. Tom's addiction becomes public, and he agrees to enrol in the state narcotics programme in prison to get clean. Six months later, he is released, ostensibly cured, whereupon he goes through a whirlwind of different jobs, ending up as a labour leader and political activist on behalf of the workers' struggle.

In the pre-code era, film-makers were still able to get away with humour around drugs, like Harold Lloyd's *Welcome Danger* (1929), the first sound drug comedy where our hero plays Harold Bledsoe, a botany student and unlikely disrupter of a war between Chinese and American traffickers. It was Lloyd's first speaking role and fans flocked to hear what he sounded like. *Fall Guy* (1930) was adapted from a Broadway comedy about a low-level coke dealer who eventually outwits his employers and becomes a narcotics officer. Then there was the famous scene in Chaplin's *Modern Times* (1936) where Charlie is in prison and seated next to a coke dealer at dinner. The dealer spots the police coming round making enquiries and puts the coke in a salt cellar. Naturally, Chaplin then proceeds unwittingly to sprinkle coke all over his food, and in his subsequent frenzy single-handedly quells a prison break-out attempt and earns first a comfortable cell and then a pardon.

The movie business tried the patience of the Catholic reform movement to the limit. Eventually, in 1933 they threatened a boycott of the cinema. Not only could the studios not afford to ignore the spectre of 20 million Catholics staying at home, but the economics of the business were in a tailspin. The industry had invested heavily in tooling up the cinema chains they owned for the sound revolution. Then the Depression clobbered their profits and left them vulnerable to attack. On top of everything else, President Roosevelt's New Deal package hinted at federal censorship, and a reformist educational group called the Motion Picture Research Council published a series of reports linking bad behaviour to degenerate movies. Assailed on all fronts, the movie bosses had to act. They created the Picture Code Administration (PCA) which, instead of forming an overfamiliar relationship with on-site studio executives, was answerable directly to the board of the MPPDA and the New York moneymen who controlled the industry.

On 2 July 1934 the MPPDA empowered the PCA to enforce Daniel Lord's code. And to run the PCA, Hays appointed Joseph Breen, a former journalist and a highly active member of the Catholic movie reform lobby. As PCA chief from 1934 to 1954, he became one of the most influential figures in American culture.[8] When he died in 1965, *Variety* summed up his career, observing, 'More than any single individual, he shaped the moral stature of the American motion picture' and he applied the code with crusading zeal and administrative guile and obstinacy – a zeal underpinned by virulent and unremitting anti-Semitism.

From now on, the rationale of the studios was not to disturb the political and social status quo and not to disturb the income flow that had been badly disrupted by the Depression. Hollywood had an enormous stake in maintaining cultural prestige and approval over the long term. And because films cost fortunes to make, studios couldn't afford to alienate any segment of the audience – so they either avoided controversial subjects or presented them within a highly constructed framework that evaded larger issues. The MPPDA Studio Relations Committee and the Production Code Administration intervened in the writing of scripts and the shooting and editing of finished films – basically trying to second-guess the views of local censorship boards and the religious groups.

The judgement of Breen and the PCA was that cinema was simply an entertainment and nothing more. It had no mandate to raise social, political or moral issues because it was an extremely powerful medium of mass communication and therefore dangerous insofar as sexual or political passions might be aroused. This generally suited the studios because, despite the irritations of censorship or interference with individual films, adherence to the code helped keep powerful religious groups onside and deflected the clamour for dreaded government censorship. The audiences were happy – cinema audiences began a healthy rise in the mid-1930s (Hays took the credit for this) and in any case some of the strict moralists among the moguls like Louis Mayer actually thought cinema *had* gone too far.

The main battles were fought over depictions of sex, adultery, seduction and love outside marriage. For the movie business, human relationships were the stuff of life; they were what the audiences wanted to see along with some gratuitous violence. Having sex and fighting were what real, normal people did. Sex put bums on seats – drugs in the main did not. Drug users were not normal. People did not want to see movies about drugs unless there was a sex angle to the story. Later it was different; young people wanted to see films they could identify with, and one of the defining features of all youth culture since the mid-1960s has been drugs. If a film didn't get past Breen, it didn't get a PCA seal. No seal meant it could not be shown in the lucrative first-run cinemas. And up until the 1950s there are no records of rows between the major studios and the censor over drug content.

In the real world the Hollywood hierarchy continued its love affair with drugs. Because of its increasing rarity, opium became as fashionable as cocaine. Queen of the drug hogs was Tallulah Bankhead, who smoked, shot and snorted anything she could get her hands on. But everybody was very, very careful, and there were no major busts or deaths in the 1930s.

Once the Breen era kicked in, just about all references to drugs disappeared. Movies now had to be wholesome, family entertainment where all evil is vanquished and everything turns out right in the end. And how much more wholesome and winning could you get than *The Wizard of Oz* (1939), the apotheosis of morally uplifting movie-making? But wait a minute – nothwithstanding that even teenage Judy Garland was already on the chemical carousel that would kill her – should we look at this film a bit closer? 'Poppies, poppies will put them to sleep,' says the Wicked Witch of the West as Dorothy, Lion, Tin Man and Scarecrow drift into reverie. And how does the Good Witch wake them up? *Snow*.[9]

5

The Forty Thieves: drugs and the exploitation movie

Their names are forgotten today, and probably hardly known to the audiences who, from the late 1930s onwards, watched their films in cities, towns and hamlets across America. Names like Dwain Esper, Kroger Babb, Louis and Dan Sonney, Willis Kent, Samuel Cummins – known as the Forty Thieves, because they ripped each other off as much as any audience or cinema manager. They were showmen, they were rogues, they were chancers. Esper once sent out an FBI wanted poster of himself, warning of this dangerous confidence trickster. They could be ruthless, litigious and downright devious – descriptions that could fit any of the Hollywood moguls so far mentioned, or any of those who dominate the business today. In fact, the films these guys produced and directed paved the way for much of the highly profitable sex and violence we now see on our screens.

In the same way that the moguls differed in their desire to be accepted by America's elite, so these movie-makers differed in their career aspirations. Babb desperately wanted to be known as a respectable mainstream producer. Dwain Esper had no such ambitions; his career epitomised 'the aggressive spirit, crass sensationalism and reckless artistry that define the exploitation showman at his scandalous best'.[1]

But collectively there was a major difference between the Forty Thieves and a Louis Mayer or Jack Warner. Thieves' movies were never going to be shown in the plush picture palaces of New York or Los Angeles. Liveried ushers would not be showing patrons to their seats to see a Dwain Esper or a Kroger Babb. There would be no nursery facilities to assist those parents wishing to see a Willis Kent extravaganza. You'd be watching one of their films not in a 65,000-seat theatre dotted with Steinway pianos but in 'a squat of plaster between a drugstore and a shoe store . . . a rectangle of four walls . . . no balcony. No center aisle. No sculpture, no cherubs or open skies on the ceiling.'[2]

The crowds who trudged to these utilitarian main-street theatres sought a break from Hollywood make-believe. They came seeking reality in undiluted doses. What they actually found was a bizarre mixture of the two: saccharine morality tales interrupted by moments of raw, ugly truth that studio films would never touch. In other words – exploitation movies, Hollywood's hidden history, the soiled underwear beneath the fur coat of movie glitz. In fact, although the word 'exploitation' came to mean any sleazy low-budget film, the term was specific to a certain time and place in movie history roughly coinciding with the rise and fall of classic Hollywood and the studio system.

Exploitation movies (EMs) had three defining features. First, they covered all the topics forbidden by the Hollywood production code and its various predecessors – venereal disease, sexual intercourse, child-birth, abortion, prostitution, nudity and, of course, drugs. So one aspect of 'exploitation' was cashing in on the prurient interests of audiences, current 'hot topics' in the news, and the fact that Hollywood passed on such subjects. Not that Hollywood wanted to, but as we have seen they had to compromise with the juggernauts of moral reform in order to stave off serious attacks on their profit lines. The EM occupied a role on the margins or the underbelly of cinema history, but 'what is socially peripheral is so frequently symbolically central'.[3] Drugs, sex, nudity, prostitution and other 'transgressive' behaviours were played out on the screens: EMs shone a light on the way society feels and deals with these subjects.

Secondly, they were very cheaply made. Production-wise, they came in below even the so-called Poverty Row studios like Monogram and PRC, which made hundreds of B-movies. Many of the EMs were made after-hours using the facilities when the respectable film-makers had gone home, shot in a week on tiny budgets of a few thousand dollars. Tim Burton's biopic of film-maker Ed Wood gives a very good idea of what exploitation film-making was all about – low budget, low pro-duction values, making the best of virtually nothing, using unemployed technicians, freelancers, perhaps the odd has-been star on the slide. The rest were usually never have-beens, although Betty Grable and Victor Mature were two Hollywood stars whose early careers included

EM work. Cinematographer Ernest Laszlo, who shot *The Pace That Kills* for Willis Kent (see below), went on to be director of photography for films like *Stalag 17* (1953), for which actor William Holden received an Oscar, and Robert Aldrich's *The Big Knife* (1955), one of the best movies about Hollywood.

More typically was an account given by EM stalwart Timothy Farrell, who once acted in a film where the cinematographer and first assistant wore thick glasses while the second assistant camera operator was virtually blind. They spent the whole shoot falling over the equipment and each other.

Thirdly, EMs were independently distributed and invariably shown in cinemas not affiliated to the majors. Up until the late 1940s, when the studios were hit by anti-trust action, they owned not only all the means of film production but also the major cinema chains and could dictate what films were shown. Unlike the major studios, which distributed one copy of the film simultaneously to hundreds of cinemas across the country, the EM film-makers worked with a handful of prints, selling the rights to show them in different states to other distributors – known as States Rights distribution. Alternatively, they would hawk the films around personally like snake oil sellers – turning up in a small place, doing a one-off deal with the local cinema owner, known as 'four-walling', and then moving on. A film-maker who couldn't afford to make his own films might become a distributor to build up the funds to realise his dream and then sell his product into those areas he couldn't cover himself.

The term 'exploitation' defined the subject matter, but it also defined the mode of promotion. Without the marketing budgets of the major studios, the EM-makers had to improvise. Billboards were tied to trucks to ride around town like the circus announcing its arrival. There were window cards for shops and lurid poster campaigns. 'Nurses' were on hand to deal with upset patrons; lecturers and booklets accompanied the sex hygiene films; there were displays of drug paraphernalia and even a dead body supposedly killed by drugs, but which was actually the mummified corpse of a cowboy shot in a duel.

The exploitation movie came out of the early sex hygiene movies of the 1913–19 period. These were Progressive-style morality tales and generally welcomed by the movement. *Damaged Goods* (1915) was a classic of the genre and was reviewed as not parading evil 'in order that good may come out of it'. The plot line followed a typical pattern for this kind of film. Middle-class family man gets drunk, sleeps with working-class hooker, gets VD, passes it on to wife, who in turn passes it to unborn child, who is born with the disease. The message was clear, the presentation sober. However, into the arena came films depicting the gruesome details of the syphilis-ravaged body produced for medical students but shown to soldiers during the war to warn them of the dangers of illicit sex.

These were condemned, censored and banned both locally and by Hollywood self-censorship. Although the messages of these films were precisely those crude morality tales like *Damaged Goods* endorsed by the moral reformers, the presentation was totally unacceptable. The sex hygiene movie became the first to be added to a list of Forbidden Topics that grew in the years leading up to the full implementation of the production code in 1934. The EM-makers developed their own aesthetic, which in the words of EM showman David Friedman meant any subject could be tackled 'so long as it was in bad taste'.

And what distinguished bad taste was the degree of explicitness – how much bare flesh, how much kissing or sexual cavorting. This is what condemned the EM to the fleapit cinemas, even though they were often more morally correct than their Hollywood counterparts. Some of the pre-code Hollywood movies shamefully depicted virtue unrewarded or vice unpunished; the EM might have gone in for more prurient detail, but the wages of sin were invariably disgrace, dishonour and death.

For the drug film, the pattern of development was different. The disgrace of Hollywood in the early 1920s made it increasingly difficult to make any mainstream drug movie, whatever the content and however presented. Eventually, by definition a drug film was an EM because the subject was totally taboo.

In the same way that Hollywood tried to combat censorship in the name of art, so the EM-makers claimed to the local and state censors that their films were educational. Those films depicting childbirth may have had some educational value because information on such matters for women was either banned by law or sidelined by social squeamishness. On the drugs front, however, the films were entirely hopeless, crude propaganda even by the standards of expert knowledge of the day. This, as we shall see, was especially true of cannabis.

The die was cast for the drug movie right back at the turn of the century and the emergence of urban working-class young males as the new breed of drug users. They used drugs not because of over-prescribing by doctors but simply because it was pleasurable and, for some, helped to blank out the monotonous routine of their lives. And using drugs for pleasure was as outside the political *Zeitgeist* as it was possible to be (and still is). 'Increasingly associated with slothful and immoral "criminal classes" who degraded the nation's cities, narcotics use threatened to retard national growth with pauperism, moral degeneracy and crime. A consensus had emerged; the non-medical use of "narcotics" was a cancer which had to be removed entirely from the social organism.'[4]

Interestingly, however, although the younger users were invariably working class, the message of the films was very much directed at the middle class and their fears about the safety of their children. Nearly all the drug films of the early period mentioned in Chapter Three were variations on the theme of degradation and despair visited on the upper and middle classes through drugs. The genre played itself out by the end of the First World War but was revived in Hollywood by the death of Wallace Reid and the release of *Human Wreckage* (1923). Already by then, the drug film was under scrutiny from the censors: *Human Wreckage* required special dispensation from the Hays office. Heavy pressure by the film's influential producer, Thomas Ince, ensured that it was released ahead of a rival film with a similar plot, *The Greatest Menace*, even though that film's independent producer, Al Rogell, said his film was completed first.

The Pace That Kills (1928)

In the immediate aftermath of the Hollywood scandals and because the press and audiences were probably sick of them, drug films virtually dried up. By the time *The Pace That Kills* was released, the drug movie was firmly in the laps of the independent film-makers, even though the message of the films was entirely consistent with what had gone before. The film, written and produced by Willis Kent, opens with what was called the Square-Up – a piously worded homily as to the dangers of drugs and part of the credibility kit put together by EM-makers to persuade the censor that this film was only produced in the public interest:

> Since the dawn of creation, race after race has emerged from the dim shadows, flourished, then faded away into the mists of obscurity. History teaches that each nation, each race perished miserably when they ignored their problems and failed in their struggles against debauchery and sin. Today we – the highest civilization the world has ever known – are faced with the most tragic problem that has ever confronted mankind – a menace so threatening, so all-embracing that if we fail to conquer it our race, our people, our civilization must perish from the face of the earth! What is this octopus – this hideous monster that clutches at every heart? Creeping slowly, silently, inexorably into every nook and corner of the world? It is the Demon Dope! In its slimy trail follow misery, degradation, death; and from its clutching tentacles no community, no class, no people are immune regardless of birth, training or environment.

Eddie leaves his idyllic life down on the farm and his childhood sweet-heart, Mary Jane (probably no hidden joke there), to go off to the evil city in search of a better life and to look for his sister, Grace. Mother had received a letter from an old friend offering Eddie the chance of a job but knew, as the title card said, 'So many good clean boys leave home and never return'. As if to emphasise the threat of the city, modernism and the wild ride Eddie would shortly endure, Kent takes us through a montage of high tech to denote Eddie's passage from rural innocence to urban danger – the spinning car wheels of Uncle Caleb's motor taking Eddie to the station give way to train wheels and finally the wheels of the city tram. In reality, it's the pace of city life that kills as much as any drug.

Eddie's job is in the packing department of a store where he meets Fanny. She gently mocks him as 'country boy' and leads him into bad ways, with little snorts of cocaine passed off as 'headache powder' – the main effect of which causes him to straighten his shoulders and adjust his tie. She whisks him off to a nightclub, where he sees his sister in the company of the 'king of the underworld'. He approaches her, but she refuses to acknowledge who he is. Eddie goes to parties with Fanny where Snowy, the thin weaselly-looking pusher, turns up with the joy powder, much to the delight of the ever-more-agitated group awaiting his arrival. The pair start stealing from the store to pay for the coke, lose their jobs and from there it's downhill all the way. They meet up with Grace in an opium den, where she is arrested for killing the gangster. Matters go from bad to worse, Fanny sells herself to pay for the drugs, gets pregnant and drowns herself. When he finds out what's happened, Eddie joins Fanny in her watery grave. Apparently, the original plot line had Eddie cured after a torturous spell in hospital.

Unusually for a drug EM, the film actually suggests something that shocked patrons can do about this awful situation: 'Write to your senator and lend your support to the Porter Bill for the segregation and hospitalization of narcotic addicts – the greatest constructive measure ever offered for the abatement of the narcotic evil.'[5]

There are some points to note from this, the first of the true exploitation drug movies. First, cocaine is indicted as the stepping-stone drug for young people, the 'kid catcher', as the film describes it. And, indeed, they start with cocaine and move on to injectable morphine, opium and then heroin. The notion of a 'gateway drug' was soon to be transferred to marijuana demonstrating that so-called escalation theory where unsatisfied users move from one drug to the next in search of kicks had little basis in pharmacological fact. By the 1970s cocaine had become a 'hard drug' right at the opposite end of the spectrum from where young people might begin their drug careers.

Secondly, we see the man as the main victim of drugs, rather than the woman, who actually is the real pusher here. Not only does she introduce him to drugs, but in the nightclub she adds alcohol to their non-alcoholic drinks in violation of Prohibition laws. With most of the EMs, it is the woman who is the victim of men's unchecked sexual appetites. She is raped or violated, she, not the man, becomes a prostitute, gets pregnant, has an abortion, becomes diseased and is disgraced or dies. But in *The Pace That Kills* women and drug dealers conspire to reduce a productive, upright young man to an unemployed drug fiend. This was central to the Progressive movement's nightmare of drugs.

Finally, despite the tabloid stories of drug degradation in the urban slums, this was not the angle adopted by any of the exploitation drug movies. Instead, they focused on either the corruption of the rural dream or the dangers posed to urban middle classes by the corrosive depravities of the city. Eddie and Fanny's fellow party guests were all smartly dressed middle-class types and, while portrayed as a 'lowlife', the dealer wasn't exactly a scruff.

The Pace That Kills sold into exactly the kind of main-street grind-house theatres described above. Their reputation within the industry was cinema for the plebs – small and poorly maintained and patronised by those from the wrong side of the tracks. Reviewing the film, *Variety* suggested smugly that it 'will only be patronised in the main-street houses where they can feature a lobby display of hop-cooking utensils. They could give away needles as door prizes.'

Narcotic (1933)

Dwain Esper entered the fray with *Narcotic,* which harked right back to the early days of drug movies and a turn-of-the-century doctor who begins smoking opium to relieve the pressures of his job. He becomes addicted and attempts to pay for his habit by inventing a patent medicine. To deal with pain after a hit-and-run accident, he takes to heroin, his wife leaves him, he tries to sell his patent medicine on the road and eventually shoots himself.

Esper had a run-in with the censors in Boston over *Narcotic.* Not only did the censors turn the film down, but they wanted to confiscate the print and have Esper arrested on morals charges and incitement to criminal acts. Fortunately, the wily film-maker was a friend of the mayor. He dashed over to the mayor's office, conned his way in and told his story. The mayor was straight on the phone to secure both the print and the seven-day permit to show the film. Not only that, he arranged for the film to be shown that Friday and sorted out the advertising. Esper claimed that eventually the film ran for nearly five months with no bother from anybody, although anything like that for an exploitation movie would have been a rarity. A few days was usually all you got before you had to move on.[6]

The film was promoted in classic exploitation style, as described by Dwain Esper's wife Hildegarde:

I made a display to put in front of the theater. I faked how they packaged all the different kinds of drugs, and it was behind glass – just made like a great big picture frame, three by five. I would stand in the lobby. And you know that people would come and stand there for an hour looking at things? We would drive by every night where our picture was on and people would be standing looking at those boards and they wanted to know what dope looked like. It was so good, the police came and took it out of the lobby and thought it was real. When they got it down to the police station, was their face red![7]

Narcotic was the last of the drug films for a while to focus on addiction in adults; primarily the films dealt with the perceived threat to young people. At the *de rigueur* party scene, the doomed well-to-do of *Narcotic* are seen smoking the latest devil drug on the block, one that heralded some of the most famous drug exploitation movies of all time – marijuana.

Although hemp was a valuable cash crop going back to the earliest days of white settlement, and small groups of urban Bohemian types smoked hash in the late nineteenth century, there is little evidence for cannabis smoking for pleasure in the States until the early years of the twentieth century.[8] It was popularised in America by Mexican refugees on the run from the Mexican civil war, crossing the border into the south-western states. American soldiers in the frontier forts cottoned on to cannabis – likewise the inhabitants of New Orleans' red-light district courtesy of visiting soldiers and sailors from Africa.

One of the very first warning articles about cannabis was published in the *Pacific Drug Review* in 1905 which describes marijuana as 'one of the most dangerous drugs found in Mexico . . . Its wonderful powers as an intoxicant have long been known to the natives and many are the wild orgies it has produced.'

Cannabis crossed the border with its reputation for allegedly causing insanity, violence and death already in place, linked as it was to the 'lower orders', juvenile delinquents and mercenary soldiers. An article that first appeared in a New York medical journal in April 1912 compounded the mythology of marijuana as the drug of madness by suggesting that its other name was 'loco weed'. This may have been a confusion with the datura plant or thorn apple, which had the nick-name Jimson weed after soldiers stationed in Jamestown became very confused and agitated after ingesting the plant, which could be smoked.

Marijuana was not controlled either by the Harrison Act or by the UK's Dangerous Drugs Act of 1920. But at an international level, the Egyptians and the South Africans were making dramatic and unsubstantiated claims about the insanity potential of the drug sufficient to convince their League of Nation colleagues of the need for some controls. Back in 1894, the British had conducted a substantial inquiry into cannabis in India, after similar claims that its use drove smokers mad. The massive seven-volume report of the Indian Hemp Commission concluded that in moderation the drug was relatively harmless and despite interrogating hundreds of witnesses could not substantiate the horror stories. But this was politics and, as a leading nation on the diplomatic scene conscious of the need to set a good example, Britain outlawed cannabis in 1928.

In America the stories linking marijuana to atrocity crimes began to grow. The Hearst newspapers ran with classic Winifred Black/Annie Laurie tales: 'Marihuana makes fiends of boys in thirty days'; 'Hasheesh will turn the mildest man into a blood-thirsty murderer'. Smoking cannabis was for adults the 'short cut to the lunatic asylum' and 'sure death' for children. California was the first state to ban cannabis as early as 1913 with many of the rest following by the early 1930s. As with opium and the Chinese, some of this legislation was directed against the Mexican immigrant population – the premise being that as the immigrant mind was already degenerate, it could easily be turned by the effects of 'loco weed'. But many states, such as Montana and Nebraska, banned the drug where there were no Mexicans or any evidence that the drug was in use there. This is mainly explained by the rise of a new class of professional bureaucrats who, prompted by Progressive and Prohibitionist sentiment and the general anti-drug environment, simply enacted a pre-emptive strike against cannabis. However, although there were a number of local and state ordinances banning the drug in America, the federal authorities had yet to intervene.

While the nations of the world were still deliberating in the 1920s, marijuana made its film debut in the western *Notch Number One* (1924), where cowboys commit mayhem and murder under the influence of the weed. *High on the Range* (1929) starred Yakima Canutt, a famous stuntman who had appeared in hundreds of films, including *Ben Hur.* In the first part of the film, *The Weed of Death,* Chick, who constantly smokes dope and is therefore the villain, gives some to the ranch owner's beloved son, Dave (played by Canutt). Tom, the foreman, spots this and tries unsuccessfully to warn Dave off. Meanwhile, Chick gets the sack for kicking the horses and is knocked to the ground by the boss, who vows to stamp out dope smoking on his ranch. Dave gets progressively more stoned, and Chick gets his revenge by shooting the boss. For some unknown reason, Tom decides to take the blame for the boss's murder and is hunted down by the other ranch hands. The rest of the film is lost, so we'll never know what happened. Shame.

Even into the 1930s, the public at large knew little of marijuana – which might explain how references to the drug slipped past the Hays office. In the 1933 comedy *International House,* Cab Calloway and his Cotton Club Band sing 'Reefer Man', while the musical murder mystery *Murder at the Vanities* (1934) includes the song 'Sweet Marihuana Brown'. Even Bela Lugosi gets in on the act. His 1933 film *Night of Terror* contains one scene where he asks the detective guarding him if he can smoke. The policeman not only agrees but takes one himself and lights up. He sniffs the air and asks, 'Hey, what kind of cigarette is that?' 'It is an *oriental* cigarette,' says Bela as the policeman falls asleep.

But dope songs and dodgy cigarettes shortly vanished from the screens, as would all other references to drugs. The existing anti-drug sentiments became part of a general 1930s moral backlash against the hedonistic 1920s. In the aftermath of economic collapse, the Depression and threatened civil disorder, the nation was looking for a period of economic calm and stability, a window of opportunity to push the moral agenda of restraint and responsibility. The popular press were restating the virtues of family values, the need to uphold decency and self-control in a time of adversity. Condemnation of illicit sex and drugs became part of America's soul-searching for the causes of the Depression, which some saw as the retribution of an angry God. And while some yearned for the innocence of the past, others saw the future as the chance to break away from the corruptions of the past, start again, the clean break, modernism, healthy living. In neither myth-ology was there any room for drugs or the people who used them. The primary aim of the Production Code was to ensure that film as entertainment did nothing to 'degrade human beings or to lower their standard of life and living'. What the studios produced, what had the cash tills ringing, what the people wanted coming out of the Depression was fantasy and escapism. Cinema itself became the new drug, the opium of the masses, keeping the studios on the right side of the code. And just as the full force of the Production Code kicked in, so did America's latest drug scare – and we enter the era of reefer madness.

With the collapse of Prohibition, the government turned its attention to the 'war against drugs' and in 1930 established the Federal Bureau of Narcotics under the control of Harry Jacob Anslinger. Anslinger was a career bureaucrat. He had been a high flier at the Treasury and before the drugs job had been Assistant Commissioner of Prohibition. Although vehemently anti-drug, his role as the demoniser of cannabis must also be seen in the light of the head of a government department wholly dependent on Congressional money for survival in a hostile funding environment.

When he first came into the post, he was lobbied by local politicians, doctors and other concerned citizens who pushed for federal laws against cannabis. Anslinger refused, knowing he had few agents in the field and also because there was no obvious control mechanism. There had been some legal challenges to the Harrison Act over the years, and Anslinger was wary of adding a new drug to the list. It had also been agreed in Washington that it would be difficult constitutionally simply to add cannabis to the Harrison Act, which controlled heroin, mor-phine, opium and cocaine, because the act had been drawn up under the terms of the International Opium Convention of 1912 which did not include cannabis.

Anslinger was a realist; he was not looking to establish an expan-sionist bureaucracy. What he wanted was for the states to look after marijuana and small-time dealers and users and leave the bureau to concentrate on the big traffickers. So he attempted to persuade the states to sign up to a Uniform Narcotic Drugs Act. But by the end of 1934 only ten states had signed up, the rest complaining about red tape and other potential difficulties. It was at that point that Anslinger went on the offensive against cannabis to improve the take-up of his new law.

He began to build the case against marijuana, compiling files of all the murders allegedly committed under the influence of the drug. This was the essence of reefer madness – not that it damaged physical health or that it was the stepping-stone to other drugs (that would come later) but that it drove otherwise sane people to insane acts of violence.

The Hearst press could be relied on to keep up the pressure with sensational stories, and Anslinger also enlisted the help of powerful groups like the Women's Christian Temperance Union and the General Federation of Women's Clubs to spread the gospel of reefer madness.

However, he found one route for anti-cannabis tirades blocked. Whatever the supposed dangers of the drug, and however much it might have been seen as a public service to broadcast them, the Hollywood Production Code meant that no anti-drug film would be produced by the main studios or shown in their cinemas. So was forged a strange alliance between exploitation film-makers and the government, which lent its support by supplying footage and public endorsements to exploitation movies about drugs.

Assassin of Youth (1935)

Made by former D. W. Griffith actor Elmer Clifton, the title was taken from an article written by Anslinger. Joan is set to inherit her grandmother's wealth on condition she fulfils a morals clause in the will and behaves herself. Failure to do so means her cousin Linda gets the loot. Linda tries a number of tricks to set Joan up in compromising situations to besmirch her reputation, including getting her and her younger sister Marjorie into dope. Meanwhile, Arthur, a young reporter, is sent to the town by his boss to check out stories of rampant marijuana use among the young people there. He insinuates himself into the local scene and eventually rescues the heroine from the clutches of the local 'reefer' pushers. They are all exposed and the happy couple marry.

Unless the title was meant to convey that marijuana takes away the innocence of youth, the only real victim of the film is Marjorie, who goes mad at a party and tries to stab a girl. Her doctor diagnoses her as suffering from 'marijuana addiction', 'the third case I've seen today' – suggesting a clinically infectious disease. Strangely, though, she seems to engage with only marijuana twice. Once, when Linda is handing it around, Margie is told there is none left for her – Margie asks for something stronger and is given an unidentified pill. The same thing happens later at a party when she asks Linda for something stronger than dope and again is given presumably the same unidentified pill.

Spliced into the film (shown to the cub reporter by his boss) was part of a lecture by Dr A. E. Fossier from New Orleans, who in 1931 had read a paper before the Louisiana State Medical Society entitled 'The Mariahuana Menace [sic]'. In it, he claimed that the word 'assassin' derived from 'hashish' in support of the alleged violence-inducing effects of the drug. The myth derived from the cut and thrust of competing Muslim sects told to Marco Polo over 150 years after the event when all written records had been destroyed. The Assassins were actually named after their leader, al-Hasan ibn-al-Sabbah, or Hassan for short. The Hassan group became confused over time with the fable told to Marco Polo of the Old Man of the Mountains, whose acolytes were called Ashishin. They were allowed to enjoy all their hearts' desires (women) in their master's elegant palace before being given a drink that put them to sleep. When they awoke, they would believe they had been dreaming. Then the old man would command them to do his bidding, including murder, on the promise of another trip to paradise when they returned.[9]

The boss also shows Arthur footage of a young woman lying dead on a Chicago sidewalk having jumped from a window. The voice-over intones, 'Suicide to most people, but to me it's murder by marijuana' – and another clip portraying an axe murderer claiming that he had to kill his family before they killed him. This clip was not shown in all the versions of the film that circulated and doesn't actually mention that the murderer had been smoking cannabis.

An attempt was made to get a Production Code seal for *Assassin*. No chance. One of the Production Code administration employees commented: 'In my opinion, this is a tawdry, poorly done feature which should not be shown on any screen. It is the worst picture I have seen since I have been on code work. Moral value: none; direction: poor; acting: terrible.'

Marihuana – Weed with Its Roots in Hell (1936)

In Dwain Esper's tale, we follow the story of Burma White, an upper-middle-class high-school girl (who like all the 'high-school kids' in drug EMs looks about 25) who lives with her mother and sister Elaine, who is engaged to the wealthy Morgan Stewart. Burma is cheesed off because Elaine attracts all the attention, so Burma starts hanging out with the fast crowd at a dance hall, where she meets Tony, a gangster and drug dealer. Tony holds a beach party where everybody goes nude bathing, smokes dope, laughs hysterically and generally has a good time. Except that stoned Burma and her equally stoned boyfriend Dick make love on the beach and Burma becomes pregnant. Dick goes round to remonstrate with Tony for getting him stoned. Tony's response is to give Dick some dope to sell. Next day, the dope sells the dope and is killed escaping from narcotic agents.

Burma leaves home, moves in with Tony and becomes not only his main dealer but a heroin addict to boot. Tony persuades Burma to give up the baby for adoption, but unknown to Burma he gives the child to her sister Elaine. Burma is selling heroin and cocaine to ex-marijuana users but wants more money quickly. The ludicrous plan is to kidnap her sister's child to scam money from her rich husband. The child is kidnapped, but Burma leaves the child and goes out (which of course you do, having stolen a child for money). In her absence, the police arrive, take the child and Burma's stash, and the whole ridiculous scenario ends when the distraught Burma takes an extra-big shot of the Big H and dies.

Although these movies could play without a Production Code seal, they still had to pass muster with the state censors, who routinely differed in their ideas as to what should be cut. *Marihuana* was rejected outright in Maryland and Pennsylvania – always a tough state for censorship – and was also banned in New York (where it was submitted under the title *Sinister Weed*) but allowed to show with some cuts in Chicago and Ohio. But they weren't the same cuts. In Chicago, the nude bathing scene had to go, plus scenes showing how drugs were used and transported – one of the dealers hides his stash in the heel of his shoe. The Ohio board also vetoed the nude bathing, but allowed the drug scene. But they demanded a number of cuts to the story line about Burma's 'love child' and the plot to kidnap the child. Also cut was the newspaper headline 'Federal Authorities Powerless to Suppress Marihuana Traffic'.

Reefer Madness (1936)

Dwain Esper also purchased the rights to *Tell Your Children*, also entitled *The Burning Question* but most famously shown as *Reefer Madness*. Like *Assassin*, an expert lectures on the dangers of the drug. This is Dr Carroll telling the Parent–Teacher Association that cannabis is 'more dangerous than all the drugs'. He then takes them through Anslinger's gory file of cannabis axemen.

Two suspicious-looking city types in suave suits with two 'bad' women in tow start hanging around a soda fountain frequented by some more of those elderly high-school students. The youngsters are enticed up to an apartment and to the accompaniment of some manic piano playing (apparently pounding the ivories like a lunatic indicates dope psychosis) are lured into smoking reefers. Bill takes a few puffs and is immediately seduced by one of the women. Bill's sweetheart Mary turns up and is groped by a dealer. Bill sees what's going on and fights with the dealer, who accidentally shoots Mary dead. Bill is framed for Mary's murder and is sentenced to death. The prosecution wheel in Dr Carroll to give expert testimony on Bill's sanity. 'In the middle of a perfectly serious discussion of *Romeo and Juliet* he suddenly broke into an hysterical fit of uncontrollable laughter.' Well, there you have it – clearly a homicidal maniac.

Meanwhile, Bill's mate Ralph, who has spent the whole film chain-smoking dope, finally flips and kills one of the pushers. He is shipped off to the lunatic asylum, and as for the two 'loose women', one is jailed while the other kills herself.

Buoyed up with the box-office success of *Marihuana*,[10] Esper milked the theme still further with *Sinister Menace* (1937), a documentary short using footage Esper claimed was supplied by the Egyptian government to the bureau and given to Esper by Anslinger. The film purports to show the degradation caused to young Egyptian men, who begin the film flexing their muscles in the sun, shortly to become hollow-eyed unkempt addicts, slaves of a drug not actually mentioned. It was probably not hashish, the popular form of cannabis in Egypt, because we are told that the 'dope peddler' cuts his drugs with 'crushed human skulls' – which, as any drug-adulterating skull crusher worth his salt knows, is white, while hash is brown.

By the time Esper's short was doing the rounds, America had banned cannabis – not through the adoption of a Uniform Act but the Marihuana Tax Act of 1937. Anslinger was in a bind. He couldn't get the states to sign up to the Uniform Act, so he had attempted to shame his countrymen through the international route. His plan was to persuade an international Conference for the Suppression of Illicit Traffic in Dangerous Drugs, held in Geneva in 1936, to include cannabis in any treaty that came out of the conference. This would force the US into passing federal laws against cannabis. Unfortunately for Anslinger, the other countries refused to play ball. Instead, the legislators came up with a tax law. This put a very low price on the cost of cannabis for legitimate users, mainly birdseed manufacturers, but a large premium for any unauthorised trade, effectively banning the drug for recreational purposes. The bill passed through Congress with very little discussion – one Congressman actually asked another what marijuana was, to which the reply was 'some sort of narcotic'.

With the act in place, Anslinger cooled off on the anti-cannabis propaganda through the 1940s, otherwise it would now look as if the bureau couldn't cope.

As much as Anslinger was anxious to hunt down drug dealers and big-time traffickers, he was acutely aware of the publicity value of arresting those in the entertainment industry. For most of his time in office, Harry Anslinger had a particular beef against jazz musicians, accusing them of being the main conduits for drugs between those on the margins of society – the peddlers, the criminals, the lowlifes and Bohemians – and innocent young people swaying into depravity to the beat of wild jungle rhythms. He kept files on all musicians suspected of using drugs, arrested a number of unknown players, but unsuccessfully tried to engage the music business in a wide-scale sweep of the industry to rid it of drug-using musicians. What he really needed was star busts, but his only success was drummer Gene Krupa, who was arrested on marijuana charges in 1943.

So when the rising, young, handsome, Oscar-nominated star of *The*

Story of GI Joe (1945), Robert Mitchum, was arrested on a marijuana charge in August 1948, Harry must have thought Christmas had come early. Mitchum was a new kind of star, laconic, cynical, uninterested and sexy, appealing to men as much as women. In the immediate post-war period, Mitchum was the essence of cool and his arrest was probably one of the most sensational Hollywood drug busts of all time.

On 3 August 1948 Mitchum, then aged 31, and a Los Angeles real-estate agent, Robin Ford, visited a house in Laurel Canyon Hill near Hollywood rented out to a wannabe starlet, 20-year-old Lila Leeds. For reasons that are not known, the house was under observation by the police and federal narcotics agents. As they watched, they saw Mitchum and Ford enter the house. The actor wanted the house lights turned off. 'They hurt my eyes,' he said. Off went the lights, and the feds said they then heard Lila mention 'reefers'. She lit one and passed it to Mitchum; she lit another and passed it to her friend who was staying at the house, a 25-year-old dancer, Vicki Evans. Ford, too, was smoking marijuana.

At that point the police swung into action. Led by Detective Sergeant Alva Barr, they went in through the back of the house. As they forced their way in, the joint fell from Mitchum's lips and Ford dropped his on the sofa. Barr picked up the offending cigarettes along with fifteen more from the coffee table and took two partially smoked joints from Lila.

All were arrested and when one of the officers asked Robert Mitchum his occupation, he replied gloomily, '*Former* actor'. When the inevitable posse of reporters showed up, he told them, 'Sure, I've been using the stuff since I was a kid,' adding, 'I guess it's all over now. I'm ruined. This is the bitter end.' However, producer David Selznick, part-owner of Mitchum's contract, was more upbeat, telling reporters he was sure that his star would emerge from his troubles 'a finer man'. Mitchum later insisted he'd been set up. The four were released on $1,000 bail each.

In reporting the details of Mitchum's arrest, *Time* magazine felt the need to add a note as to exactly what marijuana was. So what does this tell us about the impact of Anslinger's cannabis campaign? Perhaps, like politics, the only people who were really engaged over anti-drug hysteria were politicians and the media. Although there hadn't been a

Hollywood drug scandal for over 20 years, *Time* magazine's assessment of the Mitchum arrest was nothing less than apocalyptic:

'The most self-conscious city of a self-conscious nation was in for a first-rate scandal, and it hated and feared every whisper of it . . . Hollywood's laboriously contrived self-portrait was once again in danger of looking like a comic strip – and an ugly one. For years, the world's best press agents have been plugging the theme that Hollywood is . . . a wholesome little community . . . The fact [is] that under the klieg-lit, high-pressure, high-paid strains peculiar to Hollywood, some of its supertense citizens sometimes volatilize and take to drink, adultery or dope . . . Speaking for the whole industry, MGM's Dore Schary pleaded with the public not to 'indict the entire working personnel of 32,000 well-disciplined and clean-living American citizens'.[11]

The studio hired top entertainment lawyer Jerry Geisler, who had successfully defended Errol Flynn on rape charges and Charlie Chaplin for taking a minor across a state border in contravention of the Mann Act. Although publicly Geisler was telling everybody to withhold their judgements until the trial, the word around Hollywood was 'if you're guilty, get Geisler'. Sergeant Barr was in no doubt of his mission: 'We are going to clean the dope and narcotics sellers out of Hollywood. And we don't care who we have to arrest.'

On 8 September the Grand Jury heard the evidence and all four defendants were indicted on possession of marijuana and conspiracy to possess. The only evidence offered was the testimony of Barr; Mitchum, Leeds and Ford were all found guilty. The charges against Evans were reduced to 'visiting a place where marijuana was used'. She was tried later and acquitted. The three defendants were released on bail pending sentence, during which time the conspiracy charges were dropped.

On 9 February 1949 Mitchum and Lila Leeds returned to court without Ford, who was in jail on another charge. Mitchum entered a submission for probation, saying he had only occasionally used the drug in the company of others, was not a 'confirmed' user of marijuana and never bought it. He went on to say that he had found it had only mild sedative effects and was helpful to release tension 'when I was overworking. It never made me boisterous or quarrelsome. If anything, it calmed me and reduced my activity.'

The judge, unimpressed, told Mitchum that as a star he had a responsibility to his thousands of fans and sentenced him and Lila Leeds to a suspended sentence of a year in jail plus two years' probation with a condition that they served the first sixty days inside.

While Mitchum's plea had cut no ice with the judge, he had accurately described the effects of cannabis, which were very different from the horror stories of violence portrayed in the press and on screen and promoted by the Bureau of Narcotics. While such stories appear ridiculous today, they didn't even pass muster when matched up against official reports of the time.

What the public were handed by way of information about marijuana were the highlights from Anslinger's files where people who patently had serious mental illnesses to start with had gone on the rampage with axes and knives, murdering their loved ones under the influence of marijuana. It was clearly unwise for a mentally ill person to smoke dope, and if regular and powerful enough may have led to further instability. But what the propaganda suggested was that perfectly normal people could be driven mad by cannabis, not simply the already 'degenerate' minds of immigrants but the impressionable and vulnerable children of ordinary white middle-class families.

The first official American inquiry into cannabis was conducted in 1925 at the request of the governor of the Panama Zone acting on reports of increasing use of the drug by American soldiers stationed in the region. The governor convened a committee of doctors and other civil and military personnel and also requested laboratory studies of the effects of cannabis.

Despite widespread use of the drug, the committee found no evidence in the military files on the 'deleterious effects of marijuana'. The laboratory tests were equally unremarkable. Four doctors, an army lieutenant and the chief of police all took part. Only one of the six showed any marked effects: 'mental confusion and loss of appreciation of time and space.' The chief of police smoked seven joints but did not experience any subjective or objective physical or mental symptoms. The slight rise in pulse was accounted for by 'the large cigar he was smoking at the time'. More tests were carried out, again showing little out of the ordinary.

The committee concluded that 'cannabis was not habit-forming in the sense in which the term is applied to alcohol, opium or cocaine or that it has any appreciably deleterious influence on the individuals using it'. While the tests may have been scientifically naive by the standards of today, taken with the lack of evidence from the medical files at the very least they undermined notions of cannabis being 'a weed with its roots in hell' or 'assassin of youth'.

The second blow to anti-cannabis propaganda came in 1945. By then, not only had the bureau toned down its anti-cannabis hysteria, but the more thoughtful periodicals and magazines suggested that cannabis did not seem to be any more dangerous than alcohol, even though nobody suggested repealing the law. The more benign profile of cannabis was underlined by a report of the mayor of New York published in January 1945. Mayor Fiorello LaGuardia had always been sceptical of the fuss over cannabis and in 1939 had commissioned a panel of experts to look into the drug. After six years of study, their report not only challenged all the major assumptions about cannabis but recommended that 'marihuana and its derivatives and allied synthetics have potentially valuable therapeutic applications which merit further investigations'.

The Mitchum case had a curious ending. In September 1949 the district attorney, William Simpson, moved to reopen the case, and on 31 January 1951 Mitchum pleaded not guilty. The case was quietly dismissed with no publicity from either the studio, the police or the Federal Bureau of Narcotics. The court ruling read: 'After an exhaustive investigation of the evidence and the testimony presented at the trial [remember, Sergeant Barr's was the only evidence heard], the court orders that the verdict of guilty be set aside and that a plea of not guilty be entered and that the information or complaint be dismissed.' What happened? Is it possible that the court decided that somehow Mitchum had been set up? Why, for example, were the police and narcotics agents watching the house in the first place? Perhaps they'd had a tip about Lila Leeds, who like her fictional counterparts was the immediate source of the dope Mitchum smoked. It is also possible that this was a warning shot from Anslinger across the bows of the studios to demonstrate that nobody was immune from the feds. Anslinger had gone to see Louis Mayer at MGM in 1948, the year Mitchum was busted, to suggest that Mayer lay down the law to Judy Garland, Peter Lorre, Errol Flynn, Humphrey Bogart and Orson Welles, who were the subjects of federal narcotics investigations.[12] The joke here was that at least in respect of Judy Garland, if she had a drug problem it was entirely the fault of Mayer and MGM. From the age of 16, she was told she was too fat for the movies and fed amphetamines to keep her weight down and barbiturates to go to sleep after heavy shooting schedules, all given by studio doctors. Although Mayer was a conservative Republican and family man, Anslinger may still have felt the need to show what he could do. Here was one control freak showing another who was boss. Having made the point, he may then have been happy to let the matter drop.

Mitchum went on to a glittering film career. Not so Lila Leeds. MGM dropped her. But as EM-maker David Friedman said, 'She was news; she was blonde; she was a natural for an exploitation picture'. Fresh from the success of *Mom and Dad* (the most popular sex hygiene EM ever), Kroger Babb decided to have a crack at a drug movie.

She Shoulda Said No! (1949)

The Square-Up for *She Shoulda Said No!* claimed once again official sanction: 'We wish to publicly acknowledge the splendid cooperation of several of the Nation's narcotic experts and Government departments, who aided in various ways the success of this production. This is the story of "tea" – or "tomatoes" – the kind millions thru ignorance have been induced to smoke. We are proud to bring to the screen this timely new film about Marihuana. It enables all to see, hear and learn the truths. If its presentation saves but one young girl or boy from becoming a "dope fiend" – then its story has been well told.'

When the film was first shown under the original title *Wild Weed*, it totally bombed because audiences were fed up with dope pictures. Babb changed the title to *The Story of Lila Leeds and Her Exposé to the Marihuana Racket*. Another flop, so finally he chose *She Shoulda Said No!* with a still of Lila posing in a scanty costume under the strapline 'How bad can a good girl get . . . without losing her virtue and self-respect?'

Although the sexy shot of Lila Leeds launched *She Shoulda Said No!*, it never played more than one day at any cinema. To fend off censorship and raise the ante on the shock value, strict age restrictions were placed on many of these films, with under-21s excluded, something mainstream Hollywood refused to countenance. Apart from age restrictions, there would be special one-off midnight showings of films. First this would help demonstrate that the cinema was serious in keeping young people out. But it was also a 'come-on', daring the audience to walk on the wild side, suggesting a film be seen only when all decent people were tucked up in bed. The owners could also charge more for a late-night film. Kroger Babb's press book for *She Shoulda Said No!* claimed that the one-off shows were part of an arrangement with the authorities to ensure the film circulated around the country as quickly as possible to warn of the menace. David Friedman had an alternative rationale for the one-off performances – the film was so bad that Babb needed to clean up and get out of town as quickly as possible.[13]

In this, the last of the classic dope exploitation movies, Babb himself does the Square-Up, declaring that the film will 'lift the veil of ignorance from your eyes'. Clearly, Anslinger hadn't done enough of an assassination on cannabis, as perhaps *Time* magazine's footnote on the Mitchum case indicated.

The film starts cheerily enough: young kids buy dope from Markey, kids crash car, most dead, one loses both legs. Rita comes to Markey's place for dope and brings her friend Ann, played by Lila Leeds. More parties, more bad piano playing, people freaking out. Ann becomes a dealer, and when her brother comes home from college to find he's got a pusher for a sister, instead of tackling her on the subject his curious solution is to hang himself. Ann gets busted for dealing and jailed. Haunted by voices calling her a 'kid killer', Ann joins the rest of us in losing the plot and is hospitalised. Eventually released, she tips off the police about a big bust and salves her conscience. We end on violin music and the final reassuring words 'no one seeing this film could be easily tempted to so wreck their mind and body'.

The major marijuana scare movies differed from press reports and magazine articles and lectures. The message of the printed word was undeniably racist in tone, linking the cannabis menace to Mexican immigrants and the dregs of society. None of this got to the screen.

What the audiences saw instead was young, white, middle-class kids having a good time and paying for it. This was much more likely to draw in Mr and Mrs Middle America than sordid tales of foreign habits. There was nothing scary about marijuana or any other drug, unless it was going to 'infect' *your* son or daughter. Unlike the warning tales of the doctors and police, the drug's alleged capacity to turn a sane mind to mush was not always a theme, but the stepping-stone theory was often highlighted – that cannabis was a gateway drug to harder substances. This went against the tone of the bureau's stance. It did not suit Anslinger's purposes – he kept the gateway theory out of the articles he wrote and lectures he gave and denied it during the Marihuana Tax hearings in May 1937. He needed to have the drug demonised in its own right in order to convince the politicians on the need for control.

But there was a commonality. The headlines and plot lines were anti-drug, but the subtext was anti-pleasure: Judaeo-Christian morality meets Protestant work ethic in outrage at the thought that young people might want to hang out, be unproductive and, perhaps most disturbing of all, not consume, in an emerging society where the imperative to produce had been replaced by the requirements of consumption.

It is also worth noting how these and other drug films were routinely promoted. Nobody tried to entice audiences in with the promise of seeing people giggling inanely, shooting up, getting stoned and falling asleep, because any film director knows how boring that is. If anybody needs convincing, try watching Warhol's *Trash*. No, the demented promise of the posters both in their visual imagery and wording was the sex and depravity that drug use caused. So we got:

Devil's Harvest – sin, degradation, vice, debauchery, a vicious racket with its arms around your children.

The Burning Question, aka *Reefer Madness* – 'dope-created ecstasy avalanching into frightful perversions'; 'drug-crazed abandon'; 'A shot kept her beautiful and alive . . . it killed her soul.'

Marihuana – Weed with Its Roots in Hell – 'weird orgies, wild parties, unleashed passions'. A syringe with the word 'misery' inscribed on its barrel.

Narcotic – 'Women crave for it. Men will slay for it. Both will die for it.'

Another version of the poster for the same film using the day-to-day of tabloid journalism for its credentials . . .

'Blasted from today's headlines! It rips the lid off the "dope" racket!'

'One night of bliss for 1,000 nights in hell.'

'Can they take it just once . . . and then quit forever?'

Cocaine – the thrill that kills – 'Strips the soul bare. Inflames the senses' across a poster with a half-naked woman and another in the early stages of a rape.

The posters were often more interesting than the film, majoring on the striptease aesthetic, partial revelation and maximum suggestion. The promise of the poster was that marijuana caused sexual abandon, whereas the police propaganda was that it made you go mad and kill people. The Prohibitionists were not in the business of publicising marijuana as a gateway to ecstasy, any more than modern-day government and health officials acknowledge the pleasure that many drug users derive from taking drugs.

After *She Shoulda Said No!*, the drug film business went very quiet, until another bust even more sensational than Robert Mitchum's – when Frank Sinatra and Otto Preminger busted the Production Code wide open.

6

Junkie goes to Hollywood: heroin in the 1950s

Serious films about drug addiction only began in the 1950s because the constraints of the Production Code began to weaken and because of the influence of the Italian post-war school of neo-realist films on American film-makers. By contrast, movies about alcoholism were already more advanced.

Up to the 1950s, the alcohol movie had four staging posts.[1] The first might be called the moral model. This was a temperance, Victorian view of drinking which prevailed in the movies up to the 1920s, where alcoholism was regarded as a personal weakness, a moral flaw and a sign of spiritual degeneracy. During this period, the supernatural and diabolical metaphor was reserved for the substance – the demon drink. For drugs, the evil was resident in the user – the dope fiend – suggesting that the drug user was much more likely than the drinker to spread addiction through society by preying on the weak and vulnerable.

By the mid-1930s the concept of alcoholism as a disease, not an indulgence, was vigorously promoted by the newly founded Alcoholics Anonymous. Alcoholics were now to be regarded as genetically different from everybody else and so not to blame for their addiction. To this was added a psychological model which saw alcoholism as a condition of the diseased mind, or more in tune with the psychoanalytical view, resulting from some unresolved childhood trauma. Finally, research during the 1950s began to investigate cultural differences in drinking patterns – and also a different view was espoused that anybody who drank enough could become dependent as a response to external factors. For drug addiction in the 1950s, popular perceptions were still very much stuck in the dope fiend, personal weakness mode. The three most significant heroin movies of the period discussed below tried to break through the stereotype.

The late 1940s and early 1950s were awash with newspaper stories, articles and cheap novels purporting to tell the story of heroin addiction in post-war America. The best, like William Burroughs's *Junkie* (written under the pseudonym William Lee in 1953), were not the fake stories of clean-cut youth led down the rocky road. Those tall tales, the ones fashioned into all the dope movies of the 1930s, were simply propaganda to engender a sense of fear into the middle classes, who would be the most likely to lobby their senator or congressman to keep up the funding of the Narcotics Bureau.

To discover some of the reality of drugs in America you had to travel to the underbelly of American society, to the 'mean streets' of New York, Chicago, Los Angeles, and hook up with the gamblers, musicians, whores, pimps, gangsters, writers, poets, small-time crooks and vagabond romantics. This was the heartland of writer Nelson Algren,[2] whose book became one of the most famous films about drug addiction.

The Man with the Golden Arm (1956)

Algren's major work, *The Man with the Golden Arm*, was published in 1949. Set in Chicago, where Algren spent most of his life, it told the story of Frank Majcinek, or Frankie Machine. The arm was golden thrice over: Frankie was an ace card dealer, he had aspirations to be a jazz drummer – and he poured money into his veins to feed a drug habit. Frankie has two burdens on his back: the drugs and the guilt he carries over his wife, Sophie, whom he crippled in a car crash while driving in a drunken stupor. She is wheelchair-bound, nags him constantly, won't let him practise his drums and drives him both to the arms of his ex-girlfriend, a stripper named Molly, and to Louie, the ex-user turned drug dealer. Frankie accidentally kills Louie in a fight, and as the police close in he commits suicide. The book was a best seller and in 1950 won the first ever National Book Award for fiction.

Independent producer Bob Roberts approached the Production Code Administration with the idea that he would adapt the story for the screen. Not surprisingly, he was told that the film broke every aspect of the code on drugs. He persisted and they said they would consider his ideas, but warned him of the problems he would face from the Bureau of Narcotics and every state and local censorship board in the land.

Undaunted, Roberts pressed on, bought the rights to the novel and asked Algren himself to write the screenplay. Algren, however, had little time for either films or Hollywood, criticised Roberts as a 'phoney' and openly supported writers blacklisted in Hollywood in the wake of the McCarthy hearings into alleged Communist infiltration. But Roberts hung on, despite being followed around Hollywood by the FBI, only because he found a soul mate in the actor signed to play Frankie, John Garfield. The film, however, was in trouble because Roberts could not find the money or the distribution for a story about drug addiction written by a Communist sympathiser. Garfield, too, was being harassed over his political views, and then in 1952 he suddenly died of a heart attack and it seemed the project had died with him.

By 1955 the world had moved on. McCarthy and his House Un-American Activities Committee had been discredited and the rights to the film were now in the hands of producer-director Otto Preminger. The Austrian-born Preminger had already clashed with the censors over an innocuous comedy, *The Moon Is Blue* (1953). Tame even by the standards of the day, the film was none the less refused a seal by the PCA because the words 'virgin' and 'seduce' were liberally sprinkled through the dialogue, and generally because it dealt frivolously with the subject of adultery, even though no adultery actually takes place in the film. Backed by the studio United Artists, Preminger took the unprecedented step of releasing the film without a seal. What was thought to be economic suicide turned out to be a $5.5 million return on investment. It demonstrated that it wasn't just the art-house crowd watching new-wave Italian neo-realism who could make their own minds up about whether or not to go and see a non-seal movie. So who better to get Algren's novel to screen than somebody who had already defied the PCA and won and cared even less about the Catholic League of Decency and the Federal Bureau of Narcotics?

What Preminger did was to ignore Algren and devise his own script. The adaptation made some critical changes to Algren's story, all aimed at making Frankie more sympathetic and the film more acceptable to cinema audiences. Frankie's wife becomes the female villain of the piece; not only does she fake her car injuries to keep Frankie tied to her, but it is she, not Frankie, who accidentally kills the dealer and then throws herself from the apartment building as the police come to arrest her. In the book, Frankie's ex-girlfriend Molly is half-black; in the film she is played by blonder-than-blonde star Kim Novak. That Louie is an ex-addict himself is suppressed. He appears throughout as a well-dressed parasite, profiting from Frankie's misery, accentuating the difference between the user and the pusher. And in the end, Frankie does not commit suicide. He goes through the agonies of withdrawal at Molly's place and cleans up. But Preminger avoided the saccharine ending. In the final scene, Frankie looks at Sophie's body lying on the pavement and, though he has survived and is with Molly, he walks off with a look on his face suggesting that his problems are far from over. Why go to such lengths to distort the story, making Frankie more sympathetic? Because Frankie was played by Frank Sinatra, one of the biggest stars in the world.[3]

Sinatra was the first singer to attract hordes of screaming teenage girls. He may have cultivated a persona of vulnerability, but the knickers that flew on to the stage in the 1940s from the bobbysoxers had little to do with wanting to mother him. Once the war ended and the soldiers came home, Sinatra cleverly reinvented himself as a 'man's man', trilby on the slant, cigarette slouching out of the side of his mouth. At the height of the McCarthy era, he wasn't afraid to make public statements about tolerance while rumours began to spread about his association with gangsters.

Alongside his illustrious singing career, Sinatra had already scored on the screen as the rebellious soldier Maggio in the multi-Oscar-winning war epic *From Here to Eternity* (1953). Sinatra had wanted the part of Terry Molloy in *On the Waterfront* (1954). Producer Sam Spiegel and director Elia Kazan wanted him too, but Harry Cohn at Columbia was putting up the money and he wanted Marlon Brando. Sinatra was not best pleased, so when the chance came to beat Brando to the punch, he jumped at it. Preminger sent 50 pages of the *Golden Arm* script to both actors with a note apologising that it wasn't finished. Through his agent, Sinatra sent the script back inside 24 hours and, much to Preminger's bewilderment, said he'd do it. Brando's agent hit the roof, because he'd decided not to show his client the script until it was finished.

Preminger knew he had the right man; he'd seen Sinatra play no-hopers at odds with the world both in *From Here to Eternity* and in his portrayal of Barney Sloan in *Young at Heart* (1954). Preminger's plan for the movie was to start shooting on 1 October 1955, wrap it up in a month, edit in November and have it on the screens by Christmas to head off any other attempt to produce a low-budget quickie about the drug problem.

In making the film, Preminger said he wanted to challenge the idea that you could take drugs for fun:

> *That* is what I wanted to emphasize, that people think they can take it for kicks, as they call it, and suddenly leave it alone. As Frankie says in the picture, 'I thought I could take it or leave it and suddenly I noticed that I couldn't leave it any more' – *there* is the danger. I also tried to show in the picture that the psychological cause is really what keeps the man on narcotics. The physical cure is comparatively easy today if you take it in hospital with the help of drugs and doctors. But the psychological cure is very hard. Statistics show that people fall back into the habit in alarmingly high numbers, because of mental unhappiness.[4]

And that, of course, was the whole tragedy of Frankie Machine. Addiction to heroin is not inevitable; Frankie found he 'couldn't leave it any more' not because a bit of fun had turned bad, but because none of his problems had been solved. In the same way that people try to rationalise their debts so they only have one creditor, so Frankie collapsed all his problems into one – heroin.

Like Preminger, Sinatra failed to understand why drugs could not be discussed on screen. 'The system's crazy,' he said. 'Every manner of things have been seen in the movies, but about drugs everybody's supposed to stick his head in the ground.' He saw the role as a chance to do his bit in the anti-drug effort. Recalling his New Jersey youth, he said, 'There were a couple of older guys on the block who acted kinda funny and later I found out they were on junk. In poor, tough neighbourhoods like that, one peddler can ruin a lot of lives.'[5]

The film was submitted to the PCA, now headed by Geoffrey Shurlock, who rejected it. Shurlock had been Joe Breen's assistant during the row over *The Moon Is Blue* and thought his boss had gone over the top in banning a film which he had seen on stage and thought was 'a lot of fun'. He actually believed that the Catholic Church needed to get its head out of the sand when it came to 'sin' on the big screen, but he didn't have much choice with Preminger's latest offering. Depicting the grim reality of drug use in the graphic style adopted by Preminger was in flagrant violation of the code. End of story as far as Shurlock was concerned. The film passed to the Board of the Motion Picture Association of America, based in New York, Shurlock's bosses, who also refused to grant a production seal. When *The Moon Is Blue* was refused a seal, United Artists, determined in the wake of *The Miracle* decision that the studios should have the right to provide adult entertainment, resigned from the MPAA. They rejoined, only to leave again when the seal for *Golden Arm* was refused. Nor could the press understand why such a 'powerful condemnation of the use of narcotics' as *Variety* put it, should not be shown. The film was 'gripping and enthralling'; Sinatra's performance as Frankie described by the *Saturday Review* as 'virtuoso'.

It was a brave decision on Sinatra's part to play a chronic drug user, however much a victim he appeared. Sinatra was an international star who had made his name as a singer, the heart-throb of millions of girls and admired by men for his studied coolness. It is probably true to say that while other stars have played drug users such as Al Pacino, Matt Dillon and Ewan McGregor, all found fame subsequent to these roles, or in McGregor's case as a result of it. Nobody at the peak of their fame has played a drug addict. For his performance as Frankie Machine, Sinatra received an Academy Award nomination.[6]

Harry Anslinger's opinion was as predictable as the fact that he condemned the film without having seen it. One reason was his personal hatred of Frank Sinatra because of his associations with dope-smoking musicians, the underworld and for his views on McCarthy. To make a point about his influence, Anslinger told the industry trade paper *Variety* that where he had prior knowledge of 'dangerous' themes scheduled for radio or television, he made his views known to the station and the offending programme was not aired.

Although the bureau had no powers to censor or ban movies, Anslinger wielded considerable individual power, and as well as pledging himself to clean up the entertainment world he also fought against the distribution of any film he thought contained objectionable material. He issued an unofficial ban on a prizewinning Canadian documentary, *Drug Addict* (1948), on the grounds that he opposed 'propaganda on the dangers of drug addiction because it "advertised" the use of drugs and stimulated curiosity about their effects'. The film was a serious attempt by playwright Richard Anderson to portray the heroin user as an individual and not a criminal stereotype. No wonder Anslinger disapproved.

On Anslinger's recommendation, the US government had a 'friendly word' with their Canadian counterparts to ensure that the film was not shown in the USA. Of course, Anslinger was more than happy to endorse drug propaganda when it suited him – 'reefer madness' in the 1930s, and now in the 1950s the promotion of the good work of his department with 'narc as hero' movies like *To the Ends of the Earth* (1948).

If the film censors and Anslinger were out of touch with public opinion, surprisingly the Catholic League of Decency was not. They took careful note of the reviews for *Golden Arm*, observing that nobody condemned the film as immoral. The view was that in the light of this film and the studio's reaction, the drug prohibition of the code would have to be amended, so it would be pointless to give it the all-damning C rating. They gave it a B, meaning cinemas could book the film without fear of Catholic-led demonstrations. The film did good box office in all the major cities; in Chicago it played to packed houses at the Woods Theater for a month.

There were still some battles against censorship to be fought, although there was far less resistance than expected. Some states demanded minor trimmings, and United Artists took the Maryland State Censorship Board to court over its demands for cuts to scenes showing Frankie shooting up. The Baltimore City Court confirmed the censorship, but it was overturned by the Maryland Court of Appeal on the grounds that the film did not breach the state censorship laws which banned films or scenes that *advocate* drug use. Simply *showing* somebody using drugs or discussing the problem was not enough to warrant censorship. In fact, the court thought the film would have 'a beneficial effect as a deterrent from the use of narcotics' – a view on drug films the exploitation-movie-makers had been trying to get acceptance on for years.[7] Except, of course, their films were rubbish and *The Man with the Golden Arm* was not.

When the film was shown in Holland, it received a special award which allowed the cinemas to refund to patrons the tax they had paid as part of the ticket price.[8] The Home Office advisers to the British Board of Film Classification raised no objections to the film either. By the mid-1950s they were quite relaxed about drug films so long as their moral values were 'sound' and no scenes appeared where drug use was shown to be attractive or financially profitable for the dealers. The film was given an X certificate with four minor cuts, only one of which was to do with drugs, where Frankie gets his shot from Louie and the dealer leans forward towards Frankie's face with the needle. The others concerned the beating Frankie gets when, as a card dealer, he is caught cheating. The final decision awaited the arrival in London of Otto Preminger himself, who persuaded the BBFC to keep the shot with Louie in exchange for another shot of Frankie cooking up his heroin on a heated spoon.

In the light of previous BBFC policy on drugs, some local authorities in England queried the decision to allow the film. The BBFC director, without mentioning Home Office involvement, defended the decision by saying:

> Sordid and grim though the story is and concerned as it is with the serious vice of drug addiction, the film throughout consistently stresses moral values and would certainly have the effect of deterring anyone, in the most powerful manner, from any temptation to drug addiction.[9]

Back in 1915, the justification for banning all drug films in Britain was the absence of a problem. By the late 1950s this was no longer the case. Or rather, Britain did not have a drug problem, simply drug users, not all of whom were taking drugs as a result of doctors prescribing them. In stark contrast to the USA, although Britain had drug laws, it was not a criminal offence to be a drug user. Indeed, as a measure of last resort, a medical committee had decided that a doctor could prescribe morphine or heroin to a drug user in support of his or her habit. American doctors were in admiration of what they called 'the British system' as something radically more humane – especially as during the 1950s American drug law became progressively more draconian. Estimates of the extent of heroin use in the USA put the figure at around 60,000 regular users, which counted only those known to the police and the prison system. In the UK the number of users known to the Home Office in 1955 was a mere 360. Some American experts suggested that it was the British system that kept the British figures so low, but the huge difference was accountable by the desperate poverty experienced by so many living in America's major cities.[10]

American television undoubtedly played its part in taking the sting out of films with drug themes. One of the most popular US programmes of the mid-1950s was the crime series *Dragnet*. During 1956, 13 editions dealt with drugs and nobody objected. When *Dragnet* producer Jack Webb went to the PCA with a drug-related movie script, it was rejected. But change had to come. In 1956 the outright ban on any mention of drugs was lifted. Justifying Preminger's speedy production schedule, the major studios responded quickly to the success of *Golden Arm* with a spate of drug movies, mostly second-rate thrillers like Columbia's *The Tijuana Story* (1957) and Warner's *Stakeout on Dope Street* (1958).[11] More noteworthy was Fox's *A Hatful of Rain* (1956), directed by Fred Zinneman and the first drug film to benefit from the amendment to the Production Code.

A Hatful of Rain (1956)

The film told a familiar story of a soldier caught up in addiction after being treated with morphine for war wounds. All the clues for Fred Zinneman's film are laid in the first ten minutes. A father comes to visit his sons, Johnny and Polo. He is greeted by his daughter-in-law Celia, who lives with Johnny in a comfortable apartment. She is busy preparing a dinner to celebrate the visit. But all is not well. When Celia answers the phone, it goes dead. This isn't the first time. Johnny was not at the airport to greet his father as arranged. They meet in the street and, as they ride off in a taxi to get brother Polo from his bouncer's job at a bar, Mr Pope remarks how tired his son is looking. Later, he asks for the money Polo said would always be there for him as he wants to open a bar and restaurant in Palm Beach. But the money is all gone with no explanation. The explanation is that Johnny collected himself a Korean War drug habit – and the dealer, called Mother, wants yet more money. Matters come to a head, the secret is revealed and Celia drops a dime to the police: 'I want to report a drug addict'. A light appears at the end of the tunnel as Johnny prepares to face the treatment.

Don Murray played the ex-Korean War vet. He was an accomplished actor, who the previous year received a Best Supporting Actor Oscar nomination for *Bus Stop* starring Marilyn Monroe. Michael Starks noted: 'it is almost painful to watch as Murray bares his emotions and inability to deal with them.'[12] Equally accomplished in the film were those playing his family, desperately trying to come to terms with the tragedy in their midst. Eve Marie Saint, fresh from her role in *On the Waterfront*, played Murray's wife; Tony Franciosa re-created the part he played in Michael Gazzo's original stage play. Gazzo was asked to write the screenplay, but although the dialogue was vivid, Zinneman thought the structure was too flabby and called on the talents of Carl Foreman, shamefully in exile as a result of the McCarthy-inspired Hollywood blacklist. Foreman was living in London; he spent a few days in Mexico with Fred Zinneman and a few days later submitted a revised script with (in Zinneman's words) 'a fine dramatic structure'.[13]

The narcotics division of the NYPD took the director and his lead actor around to New York's main drug haunts. Zinnemann and Murray also found doctors prepared to talk to them who illegally prescribed drugs to users. The director recalled: 'A most harrowing experience was seeing patients at the corrective hospital on Riker's Island . . . where the hard cases were treated.' Zinnemann called *A Hatful of Rain* 'the grimmest of all the films I ever made' and was very impressed with the bleak visual poetry of Joe MacDonald's camera work accentuated by shooting in black and white, a crucial element in the film's style. Composer Bernard Hermann, famous for his *Psycho* score, devised another atmospheric soundtrack, but as Zinnermann lamented 'the only trouble was nobody came to see it'. The success of *The Man with the Golden Arm* was vested in the presence of Frank Sinatra and Kim Novak, whereas *Rain* had no major stars.

Monkey on My Back (1957)

This film completes the trio of 1950s movies about addiction involving regular guys who hit rock bottom and can't pull themselves out. *Monkey on My Back* is based on the true story of Barney Ross (Barnet David Rasofsky), one of the greatest Jewish boxers of all time. During the 1930s he became the first boxer to hold both the lightweight and welterweight world titles. He quit boxing in 1938 and went on to become a Second World War hero, receiving a Silver Star for bravery at Guadalcanal. But Ross was already dealing with a major gambling habit. As a world-champion boxer, he had money to burn. Once he retired from the fight game, he was bankrolled by a bookie so he could open his own bar. But he gets overwhelmed by debt; the bookie takes over the bar and leaves Barney with nothing. The war seems to be his salvation. His sweetheart finally says yes to his proposal of marriage after years of doubting that he was a safe bet. She has a daughter and they both adore Barney. But his wartime heroics leave him in an army hospital with malaria, and he spends weeks dosed up on morphine. He returns to the States for a hero's welcome and is offered a plum job with the PR company run by the father of the comrade whose life he saved at Guadalcanal. But he now has a morphine habit he cannot shake. Life begins to unravel again – he loses his job, is in hock to the dealer and his wife thinks another woman is the reason for Barney's nocturnal disappearances. All is revealed when the dealer is arrested and Barney volunteers to go into treatment. He re-emerges to start again as the words 'The Beginning' end the film.

Why did our three heroes get into a drug mess in the first place – or perhaps, more crucially, why did the habits continue? In Frankie's case, he says he just tried it for 'kicks', but then found he couldn't stop. On the surface, both Barney and Johnny could simply blame access to limitless wartime supplies, albeit for a short period. But all of them had pain in their lives – and all found morphine to be the best cure in the world.

Before prison, Frankie carried the guilt of the car crash and a general sense that he wasn't amounting to much. After prison came despair as his dreams evaporated and the world closed over him.

For Barney Ross, a real person, the background that was distorted or left out by the film made his cinematic slide into addiction almost incomprehensible. At 14 he had witnessed his father's murder at a grocery store, the doting mother of the film had a nervous breakdown following his father's death and Barney had to leave home to live with a cousin. As a teenager, he was often in trouble with the law and was a one-time messenger boy for Al Capone. In the film, morphine treatment for war wounds is the catalyst, but in an important moment a doctor tells Barney that the roar of the crowd was Barney's drug and once he quit fighting he couldn't cope without it. Barney suffered the sense of fraud that many people who are successful feel – a vague uneasiness that they don't deserve all the accolades or wealth. Barney says he was only as good as the legs that got him out of trouble when he had his back to the ropes.

Johnny Pope's situation is more complex still. Beneath the apparent bonhomie between father and son, there is much bitterness. Pope brought up his sons when his wife left, but emotionally he was an absent father. He comes across as overbearing and controlling while at the same time disappointed in the lives his sons have made for themselves. Polo works in a deadbeat bar, while Johnny has quit night school, although like Barney he is a war hero. Both sons are desperate for their father's approval – and for his military heroics Johnny does better on that count than his brother. Many patients treated in hospital with morphine will develop a mildly unpleasant physical dependency easily dealt with. But to develop a psychological craving indicates larger forces at work.

Absent fathers loom large in many stories of real-life drug problems for men, whether absent physically or just emotionally. When Polo cannot come up with the money for his father's new bar and refuses to say why, Mr Pope lashes out: 'You're a bum. You always were and you always will be.' 'If I didn't love him, I'd kill him,' says Polo to his brother as he hits the bottle. In fact, Polo's drinking is actually more obviously damaging to himself and to his family because it's so obvious – while Johnny's habit is hidden from all except Polo. All three films had subsidiary addictions in the plot. Apart from Polo's drinking, Barney's troubles start with gambling, and Molly's boyfriend, whom she takes up with when Frankie goes inside, is an alcoholic. Ironically, Frankie despises him not simply because he hangs around Molly, but because he sponges off her and appears to have no ambition other than to get drunk.

Apart from their habits, Frankie, Barney and Johnny share a character trait that turns up time and again in the 'pathology' of addiction – the childlike desire for instant gratification – infantilism – whether to satisfy a pleasurable want or to relieve a painful hurt. Jim

Morrison wrote, 'We want the world, and we want it now' – and to some extent all of us want to skirt around the 'no gain without pain' homily. Some carry this further: one part of addiction is an escape from the pain altogether. We see examples of this in all three films. As Molly escapes from Frankie in a taxi, she has hardly pulled away when he turns robot-like and heads straight for Louie's flat. Barney is like a boy who has just found the key to the sweet factory in his profligacy with money spent on gambling and his eagerness to be 'mine host' when running his bar. When Johnny's problem is exposed and he goes into withdrawal, Celia cradles his head like an adoring mother.

Although Barney and Johnny spend some time on the streets searching for a regular supply, neither they nor Frankie are part of a street drug culture. Frankie is more 'of the street' than the other two; he dresses more shabbily and lives less well, but none of them is destitute, homeless or hungry. A street drug scene was very evident in New York and Chicago during the 1950s, primarily involving young gang members, but this isn't the world of our three heroes. They are all adults who have established a one-to-one with a regular supplier (who makes house calls and even helps them shoot up) while they try to carry on with their chosen occupations. Frankie and Barney are both in the entertainment business, supplier of more than its share of heavy drug users. Johnny had a regular job until he lost it. They don't relate to the world of the junkie, viewing their predicament as an unfortunate accident. Their habits don't appear to be that onerous. At one point Barney says to his dealer that he hasn't seen him in a week and none of them exhibits much in the way of 'junk sickness' until the craving hits, the shivers start and that hunted look crosses their faces.

All three have women who care for them and want to help them get well within the framework of a stable relationship. Molly, Kathy and Celia are all appalled at what is going on. Being streetwise, Molly knows all along what the problem is; Kathy and Celia assume another woman is involved. And in a sense, they are right. Although the users in these films do not romanticise their relationship with dope, many users do. After all, Lou Reed sang about heroin, 'it's my life/it's my wife'. Frankie's relationship with his wife Zosh, on the other hand, is anything but mutually supportive, held together as it is by lies, guilt and her own crushing dependency.

The message about treatment is ambiguous. Frankie was able to detoxify easily and was eager to follow his doctor's advice about staying away from old haunts if he wanted to remain drug free. But it doesn't take much for him to relapse. Once again he clears the drug out of his system, but at the end one is left with the impression that while morphine might be out of his body, it isn't out of his mind. Barney appears to be able to face the world again, but there is no way of knowing how things will turn out for Johnny. The overall sense of the films is that these men have succumbed to drugs through individual weakness – the old Victorian temperance explanation of alcoholism – while some of the underlying psychological reasons are well buried from the viewer.

Frankie, Barney and Johnny are basically 'good guys gone bad'. In his desperation, Johnny almost turns to crime but doesn't. They all want to do the right thing by those who love and care for them, but they can't. The look on Frankie's face at the end suggests that he could easily slide back because he knows no other environment than the world of illegal gambling and cheap bars and dives. Unspoken, of course, is the likelihood that if he had made it as a musician the temptations would have been just as great. With more stable backgrounds, the outlook for Barney and Johnny (whose wife is pregnant) appears more optimistic.

These were the first films to deal in an adult way with a serious subject. Undoubtedly, the perspectives on addiction were overwrought. But they were still streets ahead of most of what had gone before in challenging the press, police and political image of the addict as criminal as opposed to somebody who needed help. With that in mind, what exactly was the impact on audiences of seeing a film like *The Man with the Golden Arm*? Would it deter use, as the British censors suggested and as many a drug movie-maker had pleaded to stony-faced censors? Sociologist Charles Winick tried to find out. He conducted before and after (seeing the film) tests with around 1,000 16- to 17-year-old New York school students with a mix of race, gender and class and the degree to which they were more or less adjusted to their environment. Winick was trying to establish whether or not exposure to the film would change attitudes towards the subject of addiction. The main finding was that every attitude shift towards a more permissive view of drugs was associated with the action of Frank Sinatra in the film. This was especially true of those whose tests showed them to be relatively less adjusted, for whom Sinatra 'has become a kind of folk hero, who is a romantic symbol of total sexual expression and adventurous living'.

As well as the teenagers, Winick interviewed 50 drug users contacted through Narcotics Anonymous. Most enjoyed the film very much, feeling that at last they were seen as being part of a social problem, rather than just criminals. Not surprisingly, having nobody to represent their interests or care much about what happened to them, the users seemed pretty desperate to have their situation legitimised. Having Frank Sinatra in the lead role played straight to the expressed beliefs of users that many stars are secret users – a 'fantasy' realised in the many biographies of later years. Overall, those interviewed felt that their addiction was vindicated and even 'glorified' by the film.

Winick did not explore whether or not seeing the film had any impact on the current or potential drug use of those young people interviewed. But he perceptively observed that 'the film would be only one of a very complex series of interrelated triggers which might have some relation to a person's attitudes towards drugs. Seeing a "problem" film may initiate a learning process, but not change basic attitudes.' Here was Winick back in 1963 quoting a source from 1948 on an issue which we are still caught up in today when it comes to informing, educating or entertaining young people (as in films or television) about drugs. As far back as 1948, it was recognised that basic attitudes, values and mind-sets cannot be changed by simple exposure to the media. This is the fundamental flaw in all censorship of drug films and educational films and videos attempting to warn young people about the dangers of drugs.

In his conclusion, Winick points out that some 25 million people saw *Golden Arm*, and since then more films about addiction have been allowed. He suggests that this indicates a greater acceptance of the subject, and perhaps a greater sympathy with those in trouble. Yet at the same time he points out that drug laws in America during the 1950s became harsher and treatment facilities were actually reduced in number.

The Connection (1962)

One film about heroin addiction which emerged from a very different tradition was Shirley Clarke's adaptation of the Jack Gelber play *The Connection* (1960). Shirley Clarke, who died in 1997, started out as a dancer, and her early independent films focused on this theme. Her work in the early 1960s, *The Connection* and the documentary about Harlem street drug gangs, *The Cool World* (1963), were landmarks of the American New Wave in film.

The film re-created a day in the life of a group of heroin users lounging around a New York loft doing nothing much. They are waiting for their dealer, Cowboy, to turn up, and a budding film-maker, Jim Dunn, has agreed to pay for the deal if the users will allow him to film it.

Dunn knows nothing about the heroin lifestyle and users and, expecting confessionals in front of the camera, gets angry because all they want to do is just sit around, play a bit of music[14] and generally hang out. He persuades them to talk to the camera about themselves. Some rant, some joke, some philosophise, some just clam up. Ernie, who has a massive chip on his shoulder about life, comes closest to a confessional when he starts talking about the father who made him work on a farm until he was 17 and gave him nothing more than a slap for his trouble. But the pain of the memory stops him short: 'I need to be high for this stuff.'

But Cowboy comes over the hill to the rescue like the US cavalry and they all get their shots. In the words of addict-writer Alex Trocchi: ' . . . the perceiving turns inwards, the eyelids droop, the blood is aware of itself, a slow phosphorescence in all the fabric of flesh and nerve and bone; it is that the organism has a sense of being intact and unbrittle, and, above all, *inviolable*. For the attitude born of this sense of inviolability some Americans have used the word "cool".'

The Connection feeds us another bit of drug scene reality when the director says he wants to meet 'The Big Connection – the man behind the man' – and Leach sits him down for a little lesson. Leach says: 'You will not see the man – the man behind the man – because there is no such man.' Sam chips in: 'I'm the man if you come to me. You're the man if I come to you.' Solly says: 'You are your own connection.' This serves to put a dent in the still-strong Mr Big theory of drug distribution by implying that most dealing on the streets is users selling to users.

Cowboy is better dressed than the others, but he is a current user, and if he does adopt a superior air it's the swagger of somebody who has just managed to get one rung off the bottom. In his book, Nelson Algren made Louie an ex-user. There is no sense of that in *Golden Arm* – Louie only admits to a candy habit. Nor do Johnny Pope's or Barney Ross's dealers look as if they get high on their own supply. They are 'on' the street, but they are not 'of' it.

Shot in black and white, *The Connection* has its connections to the film noir world of the Beats way down the other end of the street from Barney and Johnny or even Frankie. Those guys want to be part of the world – they have dreams, hopes and aspirations and lots to lose. The gang of jazz musicians and drifters who hang around Leach's flat have nothing to lose except perhaps their freedom. They are the alienated, the unloved (not a woman in sight), the irretrievable dope fiends. Everything revolves around scoring and using junk. They are (in Solly's words) 'hungry for a little hope', but that's just about getting the next fix. You sense some self-hatred but no guilt, apart from Ernie, who has pretensions to be a musician but has a suspicion hanging over his head that he pushed somebody who overdosed out of a window. There are no explanations or judgements made about their status, no 'models of addiction' underlying the text – it just is – and with no mention of coming off or treatment one assumes they always will be addicts until or unless death intervenes. Solly, the philosopher of the group, says they all fix 'to forget, to be happy, to be sad, to be . . . '.

Solly also proffers the view that 'it starts and ends here', suggesting that this group does have its destiny in its own hands. But although society may see them as a homogeneous group of junkies, they are in truth all very different. Ernie observes the truth of Solly's education – 'he can read Greek and Hebrew' – but cannot understand what Solly is doing on the scene: 'You don't even act like a junkie,' he tells him. But as for Sam, 'Sam will always be a junkie, he doesn't have a choice'.

None of them is the semi-mythical zealous junkie, wanting to turn other people on. But because Jim Dunn is hugely uncool and knows nothing about drugs (he's never heard the word 'pot'), and because they feel they are nothing more than a freak show to him, Cowboy decides the best thing is for Dunn to have a shot as well. Naturally, he is very apprehensive, but he takes the dare, throws up and just nods out for a bit. For Leach, however, the least 'cool' of the group, death nearly does intervene. He whines his way through the film about the boil on his neck, about the others messing up his 'pad' – and then when Cowboy comes he whines that he isn't getting high. Cowboy says that as a user himself, he has never been able to recapture that first buzz and, one suspects, like all the others in the room, has long ago reached the stage of taking heroin just to stop feeling sick. But with the junkie inner child peeking out once more, Leach moans on and on until Cowboy agrees to give him another shot – and it almost kills him. The others leave quickly, and Jim Dunn gives up filming altogether.

There were no 'messages' about addiction, no heroes or villains, no smartly dressed pusher preying on the innocent, no compensating moral values, nobody gets their just desserts, nobody gets the girl and lives happily ever after. And instead of the melodramatic, overdriven score of *Golden Arm* was the super-cool bebop of Jackie McLean, like many jazz musicians of the period, a user himself. The whole hip, jazz feel of the film underscored by the music prompted a review in *Jazz News* (28 June 1961) noting that of all the avant-garde American movies *The Connection* stood alongside John Cassavetes' *Shadows* as 'the most polished, the most convincingly made and the best photographed' and 'one of the truly important pieces of cinema to emerge from America since the war'. Writing in the *Village Voice* (2 October 1962), underground film activist Jonas Mekas said that the film, while apparently about nothing, peformed a 'sort of spiritual autopsy of contemporary man . . . his wounds opened', although other underground critics thought the film wasn't grisly enough and in that sense was too 'stagy'.

The Connection was slammed by the critics for having the audacity to show a real slice of heroin life. Yet the censorship arrows of the New York Board of Regents, who denied the film an exhibition licence, were not targeted at the drugs but on the use of words like 'shit', 'piss', 'fuck' and 'cocksucker'. When the ban was appealed against, New York State's highest court decided that while the words might be vulgar, they were not obscene because they were not used in their usual connotation but 'as a definite expression of the language of the narcotic'. None of which stopped Shirley Clarke from receiving an Academy Award and winning a prize at the Cannes Film Festival.

7

Altered states I: stairways to heaven

In the mid-1950s America's drug of choice was confidence. The country had come through the Depression, fought a world war and made a major contribution to the Allied victory, and fought again in Korea (even though the result there was inconclusive). Now millions of white middle Americans could enjoy their jobs, their cars, their houses, their TV and all the other accoutrements of stability and prosperity, safe in the sure and certain knowledge that God was on their side and, in the world of the Protestant work ethic, life was good. The twin fears of Communism and nuclear war still loomed large, but McCarthyism was discredited and most adults simply wanted peace, security and conformity. What they got were teenagers, juvenile delinquents, beatniks and eventually hippies.

Parents and kids have been falling out for ever. Three thousand years ago, an Egyptian priest warned that 'our world has reached a critical stage, children no longer listen to their parents. The end of the world cannot be far away.' Going even further back another two thousand years, the inscription on a Babylonian clay pot declared: 'This youth is rotten from the very bottom of their hearts. The young people are malicious and lazy. They will never be as youth used to be before. Our youth today will not be able to sustain our culture.' So even five thousand years ago, people were pining for the 'good old days', and somebody was so anxious about the state of things that he or she went to the trouble of carving their angst into clay.

Contrast this view of independence with the views of President Theodore Roosevelt and many of the Progressive reformers of the early twentieth century. They thought the wildness, recklessness and fighting spirit of young people could be harnessed for the good of the country, for the revitalisation of the nation – and especially channelled into efficient military action. In 1904 the American G. Stanley Hall was the first to describe the period from 14 to 18 as 'adolescence' and, in words that were to come back and haunt American adults, proudly stated that 'semi-criminality is normal for healthy boys'. Flash forward to 1953 when a Boston judge wrote: 'We have the spectacle of an entire city terrorized by one-half per cent of its residents. And the terrorists are children.' How had the foot soldiers of the nation's future become the barbarians at the gate?

The fear of adolescents by adult society began to grow in the 1920s when many (mainly middle-class and well-to-do) young people rebelled against the value system of the previous century. The Depression created an army of working-class kids loitering on the streets with nothing to do. And the war left large numbers unsupervised with dad away fighting and mum in the munitions factory – many of these kids now with cash earned from working in those same factories.

Post-war, in the white heat of new-found prosperity, young people with disposable income formed the 'teenage' market, a term first coined by 19-year-old Eugene Gilbert, who in 1945 established Gil Bert Teen Age Services to help manufacturers tap into the dollar lodestone. But from an adult point of view, a more worrying development was the teenagers who did not want to sign up to the Great American Dream. For whatever reason, this group felt alienated from the mainstream; they were bored with the greyness and conformity of 1950s America and wanted to shock and damage a society they held in contempt. When the war was over, they did not want to file back meekly into school or college. They wanted to live fast and, if necessary, die young. And they wanted to see it on the silver screen.

The major studios obliged with A-list teenage angst movies like *The Wild One* (1954), *Rebel without a Cause* and *Blackboard Jungle* (both 1955) – seminal statements of mid-1950s alienation, violence and tragedy. By contrast, the teenage drug movies of the same period came way down the cinematic food chain. In his book *Cult Movies 2*, Danny Peary said he was surprised that the picture of adolescent drug use portrayed in *High School Confidential* (*HSC*) (1958) didn't seem to have moved on from *Reefer Madness* over 20 years earlier in another time altogether. He shouldn't have been *that* surprised.

High School Confidential (HSC) (1958)

At one level *High School Confidential* was just another 'dope leads to heroin' romp. Fresh from his vertically challenged role in *Tom Thumb*, Russ Tamblyn plays an undercover narcotics officer who enrols at Santo Bello High School to suss out the drugs. Naturally, he is way too old to pass as a school student, but this is dealt with by saying that this was his third go, having flunked out before. The idea is to get in with the bad set and weed out the weed that is apparently rife in the school. He struts around flashing his wad, flirting with all the girls and the women teachers and informs the leader of the Wheeler Dealers gang, played by John Drew Barrymore, that he is the new boss. Barrymore's sidekicks include Charlie Chaplin Jnr and *Bonanza* star Michael Landon.

Barrymore turns out to be the link between the kids and the drugs, his girlfriend Joan and classmate Doris both hooked on marijuana and then heroin. Tamblyn pretends he is in the market for drugs but wants to meet Mr Big, played by child star Jackie Coogan, later the Munsters' Uncle Fester. Eventually, as you would expect, the goodies are saved and the baddies head for jail. There is the stock scene of the policeman reporting on the awful state of drugs in schools. He talks to a teacher but is actually addressing the audience, which serves to give the plot authenticity, allowing the film to be trailed as yet another drug story taken from real life. So far, so predictable. But there was a tension in the film.

Producer Albert Zugsmith said he was trying to produce a realistic movie, but MGM was under pressure directly from Anslinger to show the evil effects of marijuana. Anslinger also succeeded in having the classic prologue emphasising the dangers tacked on to some versions of the film. For his part, Zugsmith had been involved in some classy movies – *The Incredible Shrinking Man* (1957), one of the more intelligent 1950s SF films and no less a film than Orson Welles' *Touch of Evil* (1958). For *HSC*, Zugsmith talked to teenagers and went to Californian dope parties with beat poet Larry Lipton. And *HSC* was probably the first teenage drug movie to tap into rock'n'roll; Jerry Lee Lewis opens the film on a flatbed truck playing 'Boppin' at the High School Hop'. The net result is a bizarre mishmash of 1930s formula anti-drug stock, sexy blondes in tight sweaters, bucketloads of contemporary teenage slang and an eye-rubbing club sequence where a girl does a 'Lenny Bruce meets Allen Ginsberg' rap. Through a beat poem backed by jazz musicians, she drawls: 'Tomorrow is a drag man, man, tomorrow is a king-size futz. They cry "Put down pot, don't think a lot" – for what?' And so on. It was probably scenes like this, the upbeat soundtrack and the fact that nobody dies which brought criticisms that the message of the film was ambiguous. It may have been a cheap shot by a major studio trying to cash in on the teen film boom, but Zugsmith did seem to make some efforts to appeal to the audience – however camp and trashy the outcome. Yet, he couldn't resist the PR opportunity of claiming in the press that teenage marijuana use was like 'a cancer that can spread like wildfire'. Did Anslinger have Albert's arm up his back at that time? Probably not.

Other attempts to show the world of 1950s teenage drug use were similarly short on accuracy, but with some hints that young people were beginning to take control of their own destiny however badly that might turn out – while gulping down some of the new drugs on the scene.

The Devil's Sleep (1949) starred producer George Weiss' stock baddie Timothy Farrell pushing barbiturates ('goofballs') to school students. Farrell also runs a gym and supplies amphetamine to young girls who, in these new fashion-conscious times, want to lose weight. A judge blames herself when her daughter gets mixed up with pills, but rather than blaming evil pushers as well she tells a policeman that it is the pace of life that carries the can: 'Everyone's rushing nowhere, to get nowhere for no reason.'

Teenage Devil Dolls (1952) tells a routine anti-drug scare story but with some new twists. Unhappy at home with her mother swapping husbands like cake recipes, Cassandra (the Greek prophetess of doom) starts hanging out with the wrong crowd, a gang of bikers. She gets into barbs, then heroin, fails at school and drifts off into the drug life. At one point she is banged up in a detox ward and curiously goes through her withdrawals to the sounds and vision of boiling kettles. She heads off to Mexico in a stolen car with a dealer with darkened skin and a charcoal beard played by the writer, director, producer Bramlett Lawrence Price Jnr (who, with no expense spared, also cast his parents as

Cassandra's folks). Eventually, Cassandra is rescued by the policeman hero of the story who puts her on a train and sends her home. Are the train tracks a metaphor for a new life on the straight and narrow? Will she make it? As she rides off into the sunset, the narrator intones: 'Where most stories end, Cassandra's may only have begun.'

While the standard 'reefer madness' frame of reference is firmly in place, nevertheless this film nods to the future of teenage rebel movies. We don't see a perfectly happy, ordinary young woman get hooked for no obvious reason by an evil pusher hanging round the soda fountain. Cassandra is unhappy at home and chooses to run with a different pack. They're bikers: the bike became the icon of all movies about bad-ass juveniles, literally the vehicle of the road to be much travelled.

The old school exploitation hacks like Dwight Esper were still in the game with *The Pusher* (1955), but even here something new was happening. In previous dope movies, adults seemed to have no trouble in posing as students; in *The Pusher* the on-screen lecturer bemoans that the narcotics officer 'finds himself unable to mingle among the teenagers without arousing suspicion'. But *The Cool and the Crazy*, a real throwback anti-dope movie release, like *HSC*, in 1958, was a million miles away from the reality of the drug explosion that was just around the corner.

In 1960 historian Arthur Schlesinger wrote about 'the New Mood in Politics'. He felt the mood that had dominated America for a decade was becoming increasingly irrelevant. America may have been confident in the 1950s, but as a nation it was tired, lacking in purpose, dominated by the politics of fatigue, after the efforts of the Depression, the war and so on. Eisenhower was the perfect President for the times – he made politics boring at a time when people were tired of politics and the call to arms. Even the fear of Communism and nuclear war had not been enough to galvanise America, but now Schlesinger smelt something in the wind, the need to find a new sense of purpose, a yearning for something beyond passivity and acquiescence. He listed what he thought were the straws in the wind. Top of his list and most germane to this book was the rise of the Beat Generation, 'plainly the result of the failure of our present society to provide ideals capable of inspiring the youth of the nation'. He cited the religious boom sparked by Billy

Graham as indicative of 'the widespread yearning for spiritual purpose of some sort in life'. But had he written this five years hence (or perhaps known a bit more about the Beats), he would have seen that the spiritual quest was equally important for the generation coming up, but it had nothing to do with the established Christian Church. Instead, the search ranged through Buddhism, Zen and the religions of the East, the sects based on cults of personality, the worship of the road as a metaphor for spiritual freedom and the exploration of inner space and altered states of consciousness through drugs. But he was right on the button when he predicted that as America re-found its psychological balance, the 1960s would be 'spirited, articulate, inventive, incoherent, turbulent with energy shooting off wildly in all directions'. 'Above all,' he wrote, 'there will be a sense of movement, of leadership, and of hope.' What he could not have predicted was that hope would be incrementally hacked off America in huge chunks with the deaths of Jack and Bobby Kennedy, Martin Luther King, students at Kent State University, thousands of American soldiers in Vietnam and the unnamed black victims of ghetto riots, police brutality and the fight for civil liberties.

William Burroughs, Jack Kerouac, Allen Ginsberg, Lawrence Fer-linghetti and Gary Snyder – these were the madmen and outlaws venerated by the 1960s generation; the Beats who headed Schlesinger's list. They in turn had their 'secret heroes' (as Ginsberg put it): Charlie Parker, Dizzy Gillespie, the French poet Rimbaud, Dylan Thomas and the Californian anarchist poet Kenneth Rexroth. Kerouac had told fellow writer John Clellon Holmes that he felt himself and his friends 'a generation of furtives' largely because of their experimentation with a wide range of drugs. This thing called 'the Beat Generation' first came to public attention in a Sunday edition of the *New York Times* in November 1952, when Clellon wrote generically about the Beats without naming individuals. He characterised them as a cultural revolution in progress made by a post-war generation of disaffected young people coming into a Cold War era without spiritual values they could honour. Instead of obeying authority and conforming to traditional middle-class materialistic aspirations, they had their own 'will to believe'.

The rebellion could take many forms, although the key planks for the likes of Ginsberg and Kerouac were jazz and drugs, intimately tied to the passion for black culture encapsulated by Mailer's term 'white negroes'. George Mandel's novel *Flee the Angry Strangers* centred on the life of a white middle-class teenager who became addicted to heroin. But it was mainly marijuana smoke that drifted from the clubs, bars, dives and lofts of the Bohemian, artistic and literary twilight world and the black rent parties across to the white university campuses. By 1964 Allen Ginsberg was openly campaigning for the legalisation of marijuana. LSD, on the other hand, came in through altogether more elite circles: it remained locked up in clinical laboratories, military establishments and psychiatric hospitals for 20 years before it leaked out to the student campuses courtesy of Timothy Leary, Richard Watts and the other acid psychonauts of the period.

We can identify three sources of drug cinema in the 1960s, as the movies tried to deal with the seismic shifts in consciousness and liberation: drugs/sexploitation soft-core porn, the efforts of the major studios and, most significantly, the rise of the independents.

The first was simply an excuse to make soft-core porn movies that played on the mellowing properties of marijuana and the loss of inhibitions prompted by taking LSD. An era of on-screen permissiveness was beginning to dawn whereby the low-rent exploitation movie-makers dispensed with any pretence of producing educational films or films with a moral message backed up by booklets and lectures as part of the show. Although this was done simply to assuage the local censors, some of the films tackling pregnancy and abortion probably did provide information for women unavailable elsewhere. By the late 1950s, 'education' was ditched in favour of what were known as 'nudie cutie' films featuring as many naked women as wafer-thin plots would sustain. *Psychedelic Sex Kicks* (1967) and *The Acid Eaters* (1968) were typical of a legion of 'trip and grope' movies playing the sleazy emporiums of the period.

For the major film studios, the 1960s brought gathering storm clouds. The squalls began back in 1948, when the studios were indicted by the government on charges of Sherman Antitrust Act violations by colluding together as owners of the largest cinema chains to restrict fair competition. The case went all the way to the US Supreme Court, which upheld previous court decisions in favour of the government, leading to the studios divesting themselves of the cinema chains and breaking up an industry structure that had lasted since the earliest days.

Television made another incursion into the film industry's monopoly of mass entertainment and it came under more pressure when white families fled the cities for the suburbs in a time before the development of suburban multiscreen cinemas. As a consequence, box-office receipts declined from an all-time high in 1946 of 78 million a week to only 15 million by 1971.[1] Local urban theatres closed, studios reneged on star contracts. Some studios switched to TV production, especially when nationwide co-axial cable allowed national TV broadcasting to relocate itself on the west coast where much of the creative talent was based.[2] The once-mighty studios dominated by the Zanucks, Cohns and Mayers, and used to swallowing up minnows, were themselves sold to larger communications conglomerates. The success of *The Sound of Music* (1965) was actually the last gasp of the wholesome family entertainment movie for many years. Young people wanting a night out under cover of darkness were rapidly taking over as the audience sector of key importance to the industry. The new demographics of cinema combined with an increasingly moribund censorship code, more sexual freedoms and greater drug use among America's white middle classes focused the industry's mind on what ultimately became the driving force behind mainstream cinema – the viewing expectations of the youth market. The major studios wanted some piece of the counterculture film business to restore their sagging profits.

Nineteen sixty-eight saw the release of two films from the majors that made a pretty good fist of bottling the drug mood of the period. *The President's Analyst* from Paramount starred James Coburn as the PA who resigns from his job and is hounded by government agents and all manner of spooks. On the run, he hooks up with a group of hippies, makes love and does drugs. He tries some blue-dyed LSD, which in the early days of its street use often came in liquid form and could be blue either through oxidation or to disguise it as aftershave. The whole was an engaging mixture of black humour and sharp political satire – having a poke at everything from the telephone companies to bureaucracy, professional liberalism and fashionable therapy. The film neatly captured some of the paranoia of the times, not least the Establishment fear that the hippies really would take over the world.

I Love You, Alice B. Toklas is rated by some as Peter Sellers's best film. It told the story of a Jewish lawyer who gives up the rat race for dope and a chance with the lovely Nancy (catchword 'groovy') played by Leigh Young. Sellers's apartment becomes a 'crash-pad' for his new-found friends. According to Leigh Young on her website, she was pretty green when she auditioned for the part of Nancy and smoked her first joint on camera having been told it was oregano. *Toklas* was the first mainstream movie where dope smoking was portrayed against a backdrop of comedy and where the smokers suffered no horrible retributions for their sins. Co-writer Paul Mazursky went on to write, direct or act in such films as *Bob & Carol & Ted & Alice* (1969), Mel Brooks's *History of the World Part I* (1981) and *Down and Out in Beverly Hills* (1986).

Also in 1968 came *Head*, directed by Bob Rafelson. He had created the Monkees for TV, whose show began in September 1966 and ran for 56 episodes. Once their show came to an end, they were eager to shed their teenybopper image for something more streetwise. The script was written by Jack Nicholson, then a struggling actor in low-budget movies anxious to supplement his income.

Head, with its hippie/druggie aesthetic, was supposed to be the route to countercultural acclaim. Appearances by such disparate personalities as Frank Zappa, Rock Hudson and Ronald Reagan were spliced into this plotless, fragmented melange of 'madcap' zany japes and fantasy reminiscent of Beatles movies. Images of war merge with clips of Monkees concerts, the band trying to make a film, Micky Dolenz attacking a Coke machine in the desert. In a deeply disparaging review, *Newsweek* (2 December 1968) slammed the film as 'a wretched imitation of *Help*'.

Columbia bankrolled the film hoping that the Monkees' name would guarantee audiences, a faith not reflected in the box-office returns. But the film did have its fans among some critics; reviewing *Head* for the *Los Angeles Times* in November 1968, Kevin Thomas called it 'one of the year's most imaginative movies'. There is no drug use in the film at all, but reviewers clearly felt that with its lack of structure and linear development, crosscuts, jump cuts and dissolves, the film was geared to the 'turned-on generation' who would get most out of it by viewing *Head* when their heads were somewhere else. After a generally critical review, Renata Adler in the *New York Times* (6 November 1968) wrote:

'the movie is, nevertheless, of a certain fascination in its joining of two styles: pot and advertising. The special effects . . . are most accessible to marijuana; the use of pre-packaged stars gives the movie a kind of brand name respectability.' This did not sit easy with Stanley Kauffman of the *New Republic* (7 December), who bristled: 'I've been hearing that to enjoy *Head* you have to be high on pot. I enjoyed it while smoking a cigar.'

Another mainstream drug film of the year was not so successful – all the more surprising since it was directed by *Golden Arm* auteur Otto Preminger. *Skidoo* was supposed to be an LSD musical comedy, such an unlikely combination that you almost feel it was set up to be a tax scam like 'Springtime for Hitler' in *The Producers* (1968). If that was the subtext of *Skidoo* then it worked because the film bombed – even with a 'name' cast list of Groucho Marx, Jackie Gleason and Burgess Meredith. The scene where Jackie Gleason takes LSD in prison and hallucinates dancing rubbish bins in the yard was probably one of the more comprehensible scenes in a montage of absurdities and non-sequitur imagery that must have left the few who went to see it wondering 'What the hell was that all about?'

Ultimately, the majors really couldn't shoot from the hip when it came to counterculture movie-making. They simply couldn't bring themselves to get too enthusiastic about the requirements of the new generation of movie-goers coming up – like writer Stephen King, whose local first-run house just showed, 'Disney pictures, Bible epics and musicals in which wide-screen ensembles of well-scrubbed folks danced and sang'. Trouble was they were boring and predictable: 'During *The Parent Trap* I kept hoping Hayley Mills would run into Vic Morrow from *The Blackboard Jungle*.' The 13-year-old King wanted 'monsters that ate whole cities, radioactive corpses that came out of the ocean and ate surfers and girls in black bras who looked like trailer trash . . . Horror movies, science fiction movies, movies about teen gangs on the prowl, movies about losers on motorcycles – this was the stuff that turned my dials up to ten.'[3] A new breed of independent film companies like American International Pictures (AIP) and its star director Roger Corman duly obliged.

*

Jack Nicholson had roles in early Corman movies like *Cry Baby Killer* (1957) and *The Raven* (1963), one of a series of successful low-budget horror movies based on the stories of Edgar Allan Poe. Corman then turned his attention to youth culture movies, especially those featuring bikes and drugs.

According to Hunter S. Thompson, after the war most GIs wanted to get back to the safety of marriages, jobs, colleges, children and the routines of life. Most – but not all. Some vets had no intention of going back to their pre-war existence – they wanted freedom and more action. By 1947 California, the last frontier of the pioneering spirit, the final staging post for freedom, was alive to the sound of powerful Harley-Davidson bikes tearing up and down the freeways. Some riders were just motorcyclists trying to sort out their head, on the privacy of the road – some became the founding fathers of the Hell's Angels. On 4 July 1947 around 3,000 cyclists gathered at the town of Hollister, a farming community south of Oakland, for the Hollister hill climb. The fights, drunkenness and general mayhem that ensued inspired director Stanley Kramer to enshrine the legend of the bad boy bikers in *The Wild One* (1954). But in a sense this film created the legend before the public were really aware of biker gangs and Hell's Angels. They only became a cause for public concern in the early 1960s and so inevitably a subject for the exploitation movie.

But Corman had a different take on the bikers; prompted by a picture of the Angels in *Life* magazine attending the funeral of one of their number, he saw them not as hooligans and psychopaths but misfits and outlaws. And this was how he had begun to see himself. By the mid-1960s he was nearly 40 with a track record of over 50 films as either director or producer. But his attempts to work with the majors, as he said in his autobiography, 'led to disillusionment, some bitterness and anger. It was apparent I was not about to emerge as a "star" director in the Hollywood Establishment. Perhaps that is why the photograph of those outrageous and defiant bikers, living as outlaws on the fringe ... so intrigued me. I wanted to make a realistic, possibly even sympathetic, film about them.'[4] His ideas came together in *The Wild Angels* (1966), spawning dozens of sub-versions until the early 1970s when the genre rode itself out. The first script was rewritten by a young journalist and movie wannabe, Peter Bogdanovitch, one of many of the Hollywood alumni given their early break by Corman, including Martin Scorsese, Francis Ford Coppola, Jonathan Demme and John Sayles.

Corman wanted *West Side Story* star George Chakiris for the gang leader, Joe Black, but he couldn't ride a bike and didn't want to learn. Corman had a young actor, Peter Fonda, down to play Black's sidekick, Loser, but decided to promote Fonda to gang leader and give the Loser role to Bruce Dern. Fonda had a couple of films under his belt, including *Lillith* (1964) with Warren Beatty, Jean Seberg and Gene Hackman. Fonda says he told Corman he would play the part but only if the name was changed from Joe Black to Heavenly Blues, 'a morning glory that grows wild all around the place and if you take three or four hundred of their seeds, grind them up and drink with water, you'll have yourself quite a hallucination'.[5]

Corman says the film was the most gruelling he ever undertook because real Angels were involved and their behaviour was always unpredictable whatever agreements had been reached. There was fighting, theft, Nancy Sinatra (who played Fonda's girlfriend) tracked by bodyguards and Bruce Dern punched out for sporting Angel colours he wasn't entitled to wear. But from all the mayhem came the best biker movie of the 1960s, AIP's biggest box-office success, and it even won critical acclaim at the Venice Film Festival.[6]

Since the 1930s science fiction writers had turned their attention to both personal explorations of inner space and (with post-war fears of fascist or Communist totalitarianism) state control of the mind. Back in 1929, a short story by Fletcher Pratt published in *Amazing Stories* told of the use of madragora to induce 'transportation of the mind' which sent the experimenter off to Venus – while Huxley's *Brave New World* (1932) portrayed society somatised into happy compliance.

AIP's *Wild in the Streets* (1968) had teenagers taking over the country with the help of LSD, after the voting age is reduced to 14. Max, the world's top rock star, becomes President whose first act is to send everybody over 35 to retirement camps, where they are fed on a diet of LSD. You would have expected a film such as this either to be ignored or at least universally slammed by the critics. But one called it 'By far the best American film of the year so far . . . a brutally witty and intelligent film', while another praised *Wild on the Streets* as 'one of the most provocative and interesting movies to have come out of the Hollywood factories in a long time'.

The Trip (1968)

In the same year, AIP bankrolled another Corman production, *The Trip*. It became one of the most controversial drug movies ever made – only granted a certificate in the UK at the end of 2002, after several refusals.

After the success of *The Wild Angels*, Corman was looking for another topical youth subject – drugs was the obvious choice. As he explained in his autobiography: 'LSD, grass, hash, speed, the drug and hippie movement, dropping out, tuning in, free love – it was all part of a pervasive "outlaw" anti-Establishment consciousness in the country during the Vietnam era. More and more "straight" people were dropping out and "doing their own thing". I wanted to tell that story as an odyssey on acid.'[7]

Corman knew from the start what sort of film he wanted – less emphasis on plot, just an impressionistic free-form trip. Peter Fonda was chosen to play Paul Groves, the straight advertising executive going through a divorce and unhappy with his shallow life, feeling he has sold out creatively. His drug guru friend John (a bearded Bruce Dern replete with academically inclined turtleneck sweater and corduroy jacket) suggests an LSD trip of self-discovery. John introduces Paul to the counterculture represented by Dennis Hopper as the hippie high priest Max (who in one scene says 'man' 36 times) and one of Max's girlfriends, Glenn.

Peter Fonda, Dennis Hopper (who also directed the second unit for the desert scenes) and scriptwriter Jack Nicholson (who wanted Dern's part) had all tried LSD.[8] But as a conscientious director Corman felt he ought to try some as well:

I approached acid much the way I approached Freud and analysis. I did research. I read Timothy Leary, who believed you should trip with somebody you knew and be in a beautiful place. I got together a group of friends and decided to take a trip up north around Big Sur . . . We got this caravan together and went up to a grove of redwoods near a water-fall in Pfeiffer Big Sur State Park.

Corman took his acid on a sugar cube and for a while nothing happened. Then he lay face down on the floor and off he went:

I spent the next seven hours face down in the ground beneath a tree, not moving and absorbed in the most wonderful trip imaginable. Among other things, I am sure I invented an utterly new art form. This new art form was the very act of thinking and creating and you didn't need books or film or music to communicate it; anyone who wanted to experience. They would simply lie face down on the ground anywhere in the world at that moment and the work of art would be transmitted through the earth from the mind of its creator directly into the mind of the audience. To this day, I'd like to think that could work and it would be wonderful. I think of all the costs you could cut in production and distribution alone.

Corman spent seven hours in ecstasy dreaming of women and jewel-encrusted sailing ships coming out of the sun: 'my trip was so good, in fact, I decided when I shot the movie it would have to show some bummer scenes or else the film would seem totally pro-LSD. So I consciously went back to some of the imagery of horror from my Poe films to represent the bad end of acid tripping. When I came down, I thought there is no reason to exist in the real world.'

Groves's trip is a pretty accurate portrayal of the passage of a typical LSD experience. He starts off by seeing some of the archetypal geometric shapes so often seen by users. Sometimes we see what he sees, sometimes we step out of the trip to hear what he says as he is relaying the experience to John. Groves is overawed at what he perceives as the wonder and clarity of life. Everything is 'beautiful, man'. But as the trip continues, blackness descends. He is chased by hooded horsemen, imagines John is dead and experiences his own death by hanging played out against the medieval horror movie sets of previous Corman films. Towards the end of the trip, he goes to bed with Glenn and wakes up the following day refreshed.

As Corman shot the film, we are left with no real sense of whether this trip has made any difference to the executive's life. The hooded horsemen who persistently chase him are revealed as Glenn and his ex-wife – so perhaps this suggests that he cannot run away from relationships. Beyond that, he just walks off with a beatific smile on his face and the audience is none the wiser, although you feel it is unlikely that Groves will go back to the world of advertising. There is certainly no suggestion that he has suffered mental trauma as a result of the trip, particularly as he had the benefit of a 'spirit guide' (John) to calm him down when things got too hairy. However, much to Corman's disgust, his bosses at AIP added a crazy-paving cracked-screen image across Groves's face as the final shot, suggesting his life had been shattered by taking LSD.

But not even crude post-production devices or Groves's acid nightmares saved the movie from the more outraged of the critics. Because the film looked so good and because nobody actually died, went mad or got busted, one critic called *The Trip* 'an hour and a half commercial for LSD' and the film was banned outright in the UK.

In the late 1960s the British Board of Film Censors (BBFC) had to face the reality that drugs were increasingly likely to be the subject of films. For *The Trip* the BBFC wheeled in three psychiatrists who condemned the film as 'meretricious, inaccurate in its representation and therefore dangerous'.[9] Writer and barrister John Mortimer took a different view: 'LSD is a fact of life . . . an important contemporary problem. We are allowed to speak about it or write books or articles describing its effects. The book or article will not be censored merely because it is biased or inaccurate: most books and articles are. If a book is allowed, why not a good film; and if a good film – why in the name of adult sanity, not a bad film. The process of censorship proceeds on the continued assumption that we are incapable of making up our own minds.'[10]

Corman says he never took acid again. 'It wasn't reality . . . it was a chemically induced nirvana.' Years later, the *New York Times* called Corman up to ask for his reactions to an anti-drugs speech by Ronald Reagan. 'Why are you asking me?' said Corman. 'Because you're one of the spokesmen for the drug movement,' said the reporter.

*

In September 1967, Dennis Hopper took a call from Peter Fonda in the early hours of the morning pitching him a new idea for a film. 'Let's do a biker movie man', said Fonda. 'So what?' thought Hopper. They'd already done biker movies. But as Fonda gushed his idea, it was clear to Hopper that Fonda was on to something. Of *Wild Angels* and *The Trip* Corman said: 'No two films in my career reflect more vividly my natural attraction for stories about the outsider or the misfit.'[11] It was during Fonda's promotional tour for *The Trip* sitting in a Montreal hotel bedroom, that the idea for *Easy Rider* was born, combining the sensibilities of both his previous films for Roger Corman.

Easy Rider (1969)

This would not be the usual rape and pillage movie, but more of a modern Western with two 'buddies' as outlaws. They would make a pile of money from a drug deal and ride into retirement travelling west to east from LA to Florida. In the light of this idea's subsequent unprecedented commercial success, what happened next has been the subject of many claims and counter claims, some of which ended up in court and all of which left the key players grappling with much bitterness.[12] The story idea that developed into *Easy Rider* was an amalgam of scripting and editing input from Peter Fonda, Dennis Hopper and Terry Southern, directed by Hopper, co-produced by Bob Rafelson and Bert Scheider and photographed by Laszlo Kovacs.

With all the connections through Roger Corman, *Easy Rider* was first offered to AIP, but they dragged their feet and would not commit. The story goes that Nicholson got into the film by promising to get Columbia to back it because of his connections with their movie *Head*. Eventually, the film, originally called *The Loners*, was bankrolled by *Head* director Bob Rafelson and his business partner Bert Scheider with Columbia as the distributor.

Easy Rider operates on at least three levels and reflected the divided opinions and conflicting motivations of its creators – especially Peter Fonda and Dennis Hopper, who were never exactly kindred spirits even during the making of the film. Hopper says that Peter was never a hippie and never signed up to the whole counter culture schtick, while he was a total stoner and went on civil rights marches in the south led by Martin Luther King. Fonda said later: 'The amount of drugs I took is greatly exaggerated by the press . . . I tried lots of things – except with needles – and I didn't find it as interesting as the life I was having on my own. So I never got hooked on anything, unlike my friend Hopper who got really crazed . . . While everyone was burning their noses out with cocaine, I was out on the ocean.'[13]

At its most obvious, *Easy Rider* is a celebration of the 1960s youth revolt – bikes, drugs, free love, communes, rock music, freedom, long hair and fringed jackets. As Dennis Hopper said: 'Nobody had ever seen themselves portrayed in a movie. At every love-in across the country people were smoking grass and dropping LSD, while audiences were still watching Doris Day and Rock Hudson.' It was the nature of the drug taking that cemented *Easy Rider's* reputation as the quintessential drug movie. Drug use was not portrayed as an exotic vice. Nobody slips down the slope to a heroin oblivion; nobody skulks around looking for the furtive fix. Drug use is contextualised within the framework of how many young people thought and felt at the time – not the symptom of a warped and diseased personality.

The photography of Laszlo Kovacs showed all the brilliant light and richness of the landscape. Colours are acid-trip pin sharp – deserts, mountains, forests and the two-lane blacktop slicing through the land. Part of the appeal of the film for young audiences was simply watching two guys on cool bikes thunder through the country to the sound of great music.

And all the heroes die – the very antithesis of Hollywood. But this, too, was entirely acceptable to young audiences, who knew from the media and often through personal experience that mainstream American society felt very threatened by the new culture. As George Hanson, the Southern lawyer, superbly played by Jack Nicholson, says round the campfire in the film's key speech: 'They're not afraid of you; they're scared of what you represent.' Billy thinks it's the long hair, but it's deeper than that: 'What you represent to them is freedom. It's hard to be free when you are bought and sold in the market place'. Wyatt and Billy die because they represented a threat to straight society. But although most of the audience would have wanted them to win through, their deaths did help confirm the notion of a generational and ideological war going on through this period as students, anti-war protestors and civil rights demonstrators in America and in Europe fought it out with the police. This, you feel, is the Hopper/Billy (the Kid) perspective – the paranoid, hedonistic, restless, egocentric, free spirit.

Hopper was unsure whether Jack Nicholson was right for the part; Nicholson was then just another long-hair doper. But the actor cut his hair, donned a suit and modelled the role on a combination of Lyndon Johnson's Texan accent and Nicholson's own alcoholic grandfather. The resulting character, George Hanson, sits at the heart of *Easy Rider* as the bridge between the straights and the heads. Here was a white Southern lawyer who represented black people. He was a pillar of the community liked by the redneck law officers who still manages to secure Billy and Wyatt's release, calling them 'good ol boys' to their jailers – and an alcoholic who is wary of trying his first spliff in case he gets addicted. George tells Billy and Wyatt exactly what to expect for being different, but like them he is murdered by a community fearful of that difference and anybody associated with it.

With Fonda/Wyatt (Earp), another sensibility kicks in. Not so much New Age as Old Age. Wyatt Earp was not an outlaw – he was on the side of law and order. In the film, Wyatt's take on freedom is much more the old pioneering spirit of being your own boss and carving out your niche in the world, keeping your head down – patriotic, but at the same time resentful of any government interference. The conspiracy-driven survivalist movement in America would be an extreme version of this. Wyatt is aka Captain America with the Stars and Stripes on his jacket, helmet and gas tank. When they have to change a tyre on Wyatt's bike, we see them in the background in the farmer's barn doing the job, while in the foreground the farmer is reshoeing his horse. The juxta-position is crude, but serves to tie the freedom-living bikers in with their spiritual ancestors. Despite being wary of long-haired strangers, the farmer compliments Wyatt on his bike as he might compliment a fellow farmer's horse: 'mighty fine machine you got there.' Later, as they sit around the farmer's table, Wyatt returns the compliment: 'Well, you sure have a nice spread here. I mean it. You gotta nice place. Not every man can live off the land.' For his part, the farmer doesn't even know that LA stands for Los Angeles. He says that when he was younger he intended to head west, 'but you know how it is'.

Later, at the commune, Wyatt is impressed that they are trying to grow their own food in what is clearly a very inhospitable desert climate. Billy is realistic and says they haven't got a hope in hell. But Wyatt, in the most cringe-making line of the whole movie, says with a soppy smile on his face, 'They're gonna make it', just as so many of the old frontier families did in the face of enormous odds. And just to underscore the point that what is going on here is not *that* revolutionary, the whole community joins together to bless their food, using the same Christian vocabulary as the farmer saying grace at table.

Even the choice of music represents ambivalence about the trendy 1960s. Dennis Hopper chose the music, rejecting an idea that Crosby, Stills & Nash should do the whole score. As the *ne plus ultra* of 1960s chic, the music of Jimi Hendrix was an obvious choice – perhaps 'Purple Haze' or 'Are You Experienced?' – but instead Hopper chose 'If Six Was Nine', containing the line 'If all the hippies cut off all their hair, I don't care'. Only a few weeks after the film was released in July 1969, Hendrix also used the American flag to make a statement. His performance of the 'Star-Spangled Banner' at Woodstock stands as one of the defining moments of the era. It has been interpreted as the ultimate finger to the American state at war in Vietnam and fighting the civilian population at home. Yet only a year previously Hendrix justified Vietnam to the press in Europe as necessary in the war against Communism.

The third level of *Easy Rider* positions Billy and Wyatt simply as grubby exploitative businessmen. The film starts with them scoring a pile of cocaine in Mexico. At the end of the runway at LA airport, they sell on to a dealer (played by legendary music producer Phil Spector). This is their paydirt, their seed money for the good life that Wyatt stashes in his Stars and Stripes gas tank. America – land of opportunity, whatever the nature of the business. And then the first music that strikes up is Steppenwolf's 'The Pusher'. Singer John Kay's message is that grass and uppers and downers are OK, but the pusher's wares are damned because Kay says the pusher doesn't care whether people live or die and sends them out on to the streets with 'tombstones in their eyes'. It is true that cocaine was just coming back into vogue in the late 1960s and for the next 15 years would be regarded as a benign drug. And our heroes don't sell the coke themselves. Even so, the song is played out to the sight of Billy and Wyatt riding off with the cash. Scenes cut from the film include a chase with the Mexican police which would have sharpened their outlaw credibility. As it is, they appear compromised by the drug money. Eventually, they ship up in New Orleans for Mardi Gras, and they act like any out-of-town businessmen. They buy a meal in a posh restaurant and pay for two hookers. The very phrase '*Easy Rider*' means a man who lives off the earnings of his prostitute wife or girlfriend. Ultimately, Wyatt seems to know they have compromised at least *his* ideals. The strap-line for the film is 'A man went looking for America and couldn't find it anywhere'. Yet two of them are out there. Billy thinks everything is just dandy: they pulled off the drug deal and despite all the trouble on the road – run-in with rednecks, prison and the death of George – they still have the money. But Wyatt knows different: 'We blew it,' he says. They take the two hookers (played by Toni Basil and Karen Black) to a cemetery, drop acid given to them at the commune and, appropriately enough given the location, trip into a near-death experience. As director, Hopper badgered Fonda into reliving the experience of his mother's suicide, and this accentuates the feeling that for Wyatt, no less than for Heavenly Blues, ultimately, there is nowhere to run, nowhere to hide.

The film itself certainly did not blow it. It became that rare beast, a commercially successful cult film racking up $60 million worldwide. Corman's protégés had very different subsequent careers – Fonda's the least notable, Nicholson's the most. But Hopper's was a real rollercoaster. After *Easy Rider*, Hopper was the hot director on the block and copped $1 million to direct his own experimental and narratively complex film *The Last Movie*. And it very nearly was. Behind the camera was a chaos of drugs and sex: on camera, *The Last Movie* paid rather too much homage to Jean-Luc Godard's contention that a film should have a beginning, a middle and an end, 'but not necessarily in that order'. Hopper's sprawling 'film within a film' was a box-office flop, sending him into a drug-crazed wilderness for most of the 1970s. He stayed in Taos, New Mexico, living in a house once owned by D.H. Lawrence and putting away half a gallon of rum, 27 beers and three grammes of coke a day.[14]

8

Altered states II: highways to hell

Without LSD and cannabis there would have been no phenomenon known as 'the sixties'. The musicians, writers, painters and fashion designers who took LSD transmuted their visions in the creative artefacts of a generation and turned post-war grey into a riot of colour and artistic possibility. Drugs whose pharmacology promoted new ways of looking at the world helped frame a new aesthetic which challenged established views. But there was a dark side. Powerful drugs were unleashed on the world which could bend and warp vulnerable, unstable minds out of shape. There was collateral damage in the battle for hearts and minds, space cadets who took off for the planet acid and never quite found their way back.

Despite forests of books and academic papers about hallucinogenic drugs, we actually know very little about them. We know they act on the brain to produce altered states of consciousness. We know which bits of the brain they engage, but we have little idea about how these drugs work – why we are built to react to them in the way we do. Is it just through mixing with existing brain chemicals that these drugs open up the floodgates of all the thoughts, feelings, dreams, nightmares and emotions that rampage through our brains 24 hours a day, but which are normally suppressed in order for us to function? Or, as some think, are psychedelics the keys to alternative realities lurking just off station, beyond the white noise, awaiting visitations by the curious, the brave or the foolhardy?

The modern-day history of these drugs began in the laboratory of a chemist working for the Swiss-based Sandoz Pharmaceutical Company. Albert Hofmann started the whole chemical carousel in motion by accidentally discovering the hallucinogenic properties of LSD. He had been working with the compound as part of a general research programme into ergotamine for use in childbirth. He absorbed some through his fingers, felt funny, rode his bike home and the world was never quite the same again. Hofmann was no shaman, wizard or medicine man. Here was a rational scientist working for a respectable pharmaceutical company watching a neighbour turn into a witch, furniture change shape, colours explode with incredible intensity. Not surprisingly, he was totally overwhelmed by the experience, feeling he was seeing everything for the first time, 'as if newly created'.

Once the walls stopped moving, Hofmann's immediate thoughts were that LSD could help enormously with brain research, because the visions he and subsequently other colleagues experienced under LSD were similar to those described by schizophrenics. But as the effects of these drugs can be malevolent and destructive as well as benign and life-enhancing, so the early history of psychedelics had its dark side. Over at the military establishments, Cold War research was looking for a truth drug for use on enemy agents. LSD was added to the list of experimental drugs after all else had failed. The scientists soon discovered that LSD didn't work either, but the Americans were now so scared that the Russians and the Chinese would get hold of LSD that they switched research to finding ways for their own agents to resist the effects. A whole army dosed on LSD would be rendered incapable of fighting, while all their equipment and weaponry would be undamaged. The CIA began dosing volunteer and unsuspecting colleagues, army personnel, prisoners and psychiatric patients in a series of secret operations code-named Bluebird, Artichoke and finally MK-ULTRA.

The most notorious casualty of these unethical experiments was an army biochemist named Frank Olson. In November 1953 a group of CIA and army technicians gathered for a three-day work retreat at a remote hunting lodge in Maryland. On the second day, the MK-ULTRA programme director, Sidney Gottlieb, spiked their after-dinner drinks with LSD. They were only told when the drug started working. Everybody was laughing and joking except Olson, who went home and slid into a deep depression with paranoid delusions. Olson was kept under watch by several CIA doctors, but they could not prevent him nose-diving out of a New York hotel bedroom window. It took until 1977 for the US government to issue a formal apology to Olson's family and pay out $750,000 in compensation. The world of spooks and shrinks became ever more enmeshed. British patients undergoing LSD therapy at a mental hospital in the Midlands later recalled the presence of military personnel during the sessions.

During the 1950s, some 1,000 clinical papers were written on around 40,000 patients who underwent LSD psychotherapy, including a number of Hollywood stars, most notably Cary Grant, who claimed that LSD therapy enabled him to become a parent. Interest in psychedelic drugs, both natural and synthetic, was high among the creative community. Aldous Huxley wrote his highly influential book *The Doors of Perception* in 1954, describing his positive experiences with mescaline (from the peyote cactus). By contrast, William Burroughs published *The Yage Letters* (1963) based on his less positive experiences under the influence of the South American yage plant, twitching and vomiting as a drug tourist in Colombia. Around 1957 a substantial amount of LSD leaked out of the Sandoz New Jersey factory and found its way to Manhattan's East Village. But Uncle Sam was also responsible for turning on some of the counterculture leaders-to-be. Many of those who came to be regarded as enemies of the state for their dangerous and unorthodox views had their world perceptions shaken up by participating in spook-funded drug experiments. Allen Ginsberg first tried LSD in 1959 at the Mental Research Institute in Palo Alto, California. And there was Timothy Leary, the self-styled travelling salesman for LSD. His over-optimistic and over-loud championing of hallucinogenics influenced a generation but caused the whole LSD research programme to be terminated when the US government took fright, banning the drug while tagging Leary as the most dangerous man in the world.

The effects of drugs like LSD challenge all our assumptions of normality, with the potential to fashion heaven and hell even for the same person during the same trip. But for the media and the authorities during the 1960s there was only the dark side – the young people who dived off buildings or simply set off into inner space and never came back. There were the scare stories paraded as science later revealed to be hoaxes or just wrong. Stories circulated of those who supposedly went blind looking at the sun. Headlines declared that LSD caused damaged chromosomes, condemning the offspring of the flower children to a life of deformity and madness – until it was pointed out that a whole range of drugs break chromosomes, including aspirin, with no obvious side-effects.

Influenced by this kind of newspaper coverage, wary of accusations of being pro-drug and for the obvious dramatic potential of drug-induced psychosis, Hollywood took a predictably negative view on LSD. Creative rock bottom was reached with sexploitation 'hump and madness' films such as *Alice in Acidland* (1969) and the SF-based 'LSD user as basket case' genre of which *Blue Sunshine* (1977) was an especially grim example. This *tour de force* centred on 256 doses of Blue Sunshine LSD in circulation in 1967 which ten years later caused the users to go bald, mad and homicidal.

Cinema picked up on the visual possibilities of LSD from early on. Back in 1956, when LSD was found only in clinics and labs, the avant-garde film-maker Jordan Belson made a six-minute film, *LSD*, which some sources say was abandoned and reworked into a 1970 film, *Cosmos*, all of which is fairly academic because through Belson's own instructions it is virtually impossible to see any of his work.

The first 'overground' acid movie was reckoned to be from the stable of exploitation film-maker William Castle. In 1959 he released *The Tingler*, a 'mad scientist' movie starring Vincent Price trying to capture a creature, the tingler, formed of nervous energy located on the spine of frightened people which can only be repulsed by screams. Part of Price's plan is to inject himself with a special solution – 'not a drug; it's an acid' – which spirals him into waking nightmares as the room tilts from side to side. In the colour sequence, the water runs red from the tap. He manages to isolate the creature, but inevitably it kills him. In this era, when film-makers were desperately trying new tricks to win audiences away from television, Castle had the cinema seats wired up to give the audience a mild shock or 'tingle'.

The Man with X-Ray Eyes (1962)

Roger Corman produced and directed an altogether more intelligent look at the perils of wanting to tamper with nature, to see what shouldn't be seen in the world beyond the range of normal limits. The film started life as a title in search of a movie; Corman threw some ideas around with his AIP boss, Jim Nicholson: 'a jazz musician on weird drugs, a criminal who uses X-ray vision for robberies. They seemed like dead-end stories.'[1] The story developed into one of those SF movies based on the obsessive scientist who thinks his creation will be of great benefit to mankind, but then it all goes horribly wrong. Ray Milland plays James Xavier, a doctor who develops a serum which allows for dramatic improvements in human eyesight. In classic Dr Jekyll/psycho-naut mode, Xavier experiments on himself. He feels the world has fragmented and light floods his vision.

At first, his new-found skill enables him to see through clothes and women appear naked to his naked eye, but the effects are cumulative and soon he can see inside his patients and know what is wrong with them. Xavier becomes obsessed with seeing more and more into the make-up of the universe. He is gripped by the God-like possibilities. Although Xavier denies his serum is a drug, his friends think differently and believe the doctor is now hooked on his new discovery. During a struggle, his friend, Dr Brant, who is trying to stop Xavier from taking yet more doses, falls to his death and Xavier goes on the run. He hides away as a sideshow healer but is soon discovered and has to flee again. As he drives wildly, hardly able to see normally any more, the mystical, religious experience of seeing into the centre of the universe becomes a living hell. He sees 'a city unborn, flesh dissolved in an acid of light, a city of the dead'. Finally, with the police in hot pursuit and the car wrecked, he stumbles into a religious revivalist tent show and chal-lenges the preacher with what he can see. He reveals that he has been to the centre of everything and all he could find was an empty nothing-ness – which describes the beginning of all creation. The preacher quotes back the Gospel of Matthew: 'If thine right eye offends thee, pluck it out.' Craving darkness, Xavier goes one better and the film ends. At one level, the moral spins back to the Greek myth of Icarus, who flew too close to the sun, in the tradition of other 'mad scientists' undone by their inventions. At another, it served as a prescient warning to those who thought that the visions of psychedelic drugs were an answer to the problems of the world. Reviews for the film, full of interesting visual effects created on no money, were encouraging, and it rightly won a science fiction film award.

Awakening of the Beast (1969)

Although foreign-language films do not feature much in this book, no look at the dark side of LSD would be complete without a mention of one of the strangest acid horror movies ever produced by one of the strangest film-makers of all time. His name is José Mojica Marins, known to his friends as Mojica and to horror film fans the world over as Coffin Joe. Mojica was born and raised in São Paulo, Brazil, and from an early age decided he wanted to make films. His father managed a cinema, but may have been less enthusiastic about his son's chosen path when Mojica sold his parents' house to finance his first film, a Western called *Adventurers' Tale* (1958), without telling them. During a bout of depression, he dreamed of a black-clad gravedigger called Coffin Joe and decided to switch to horror movies. Starting with *At Midnight I'll Take Your Soul* (1963), the films of Coffin Joe, played by Mojica himself, propelled him to national fame and notoriety. The films, drenched in violence, sex and blasphemous imagery, thrilled audiences and shocked the authorities in equal measure. Mojica's battles with the censor were endless, culminating in his *pièce de résistance*, the acid nightmare *Awakening of the Beast*. As with previous Mojica films, he couldn't afford full colour so the film was divided into black and white and colour sequences. The black and white sections depicted a group of academics bemoaning the moral corruption of the country. To demonstrate this, we see a woman injecting herself, stripping and urinating in front of an audience of seated men – then a college girl, enticed away by a group of men, given marijuana to smoke and raped to death.

Colour is reserved for the descent into hell of four drug users who are the subject of a scientific experiment. The doctor tells them that the focus of their trip will be the world of Coffin Joe before injecting them with LSD. They tumble straight into a Bosch-like hell, with scenes of surreal violence and sadism mainly directed against women, while Joe drones on about the submissive role of women in world history. This highly distasteful movie nevertheless has an interesting denouement. The doctor is confronted by his peers, who accuse him of conducting unethical experiments ('even if they were addicts,' says one enlightened medic). But it turns out that they were only injected with distilled water. All they witnessed were products of their own undrugged minds, and Mojica concludes that while drug use needs to be moderated, you cannot lay all the ills of the world at the door of drugs.[2]

Brazil's military rulers were not impressed with Mojica's commentary on the moral and social dilemmas facing the largest Catholic country in the world and banned the film. After that, Mojica found it impossible to raise money for his work, and he sank into depression and drinking – at one time hiring himself out for parties dressed as Coffin Joe. But his fortunes have picked up of late with a film biography receiving accolades both in Brazil and at the Sundance Festival 2000.

Some films, while not directly about drugs, have been warmly recommended as perfect films to watch when stoned; Disney's *Fantasia* (1940) is one, ironic when one considers Disney's vision of himself as leader of the shock troops of wholesome family values. But like the poppies and the snow in *The Wizard of Oz*, perhaps there is more going on here. The film was promoted as 'see the music, hear the pictures'. This is synaesthesia, a classic phenomenon of senses being switched around often reported by users of psychedelic drugs. And Walt Disney's right-hand man on the project was a mescaline experimental subject of Kurt Beninger (an associate of Jung and Hermann Hesse) who in 1927 published *The Mescaline Intoxication*.

2001 (1969) is another of those 'see it while on another planet' films. One Internet film critic suggested that setting *2001* in outer space was the biggest movie McGuffin of all time when the film actually dealt with inner space. The spectacular star gate sequence is the most obvious link to the psychedelic experience. But wrapped up in that warp factor dash is a journey to the centre of creation, of astronaut Bowman's LSD-type ego death and rebirth as the star child. Film critic and Kubrick biographer Alexander Walker observed: 'Kubrick dissolves the astronaut's perception into a fabulous light show of the universe until Bowman's physical being is subsumed into a transcendental experience . . . He becomes part of all he has known.'[3] *American Cinematographer* in June 1968 noted: 'The sequence borrows imagery from every pattern the mind's eye is capable of registering . . . Constellations swell and burst. Optical effects put one in mind of such phenomena as phosphene flashes after the blinking of an eyelid or the swimming patterns of anaesthesia experienced by patients losing consciousness, and even the hallucinogenic light show induced by LSD.' This chimes with Dr Xavier's visit to the centre of nothingness and even more with the discovery of that ultimate horror made by William Hurt in Ken Russell's *Altered States* (1980) discussed below.

There is no evidence that Kubrick himself experimented with psychedelic drugs, but like any creative force working in the late 1960s he was aware of their cultural significance: 'There's no doubt that mind-enhancing drugs are going to be part of man's future. The brain is constructed the way it is today in order to filter out experience that doesn't have survival value in order to produce man the worker. As soon as man the worker loses some of his responsibilities, which he's rapidly doing in an automated society, the evolutionary development of the brain will no longer be particularly relevant. So I think that what may seem today like irresponsible action, at some point will seem completely valid and socially useful.' But he did realise some of the limitations, especially for the artist. Having spoken to friends who had tried LSD, he said he was 'particularly struck by . . . their sense of everything being interesting and everything being beautiful, which does not seem an ideal state of mind for the artist'. Or as a member of the band Daft Punk said on his decision to stop taking ecstasy in the studio: 'trouble was *all* the music sounded great.'

Kubrick then offered us a very different view of the drug-enhanced future with *A Clockwork Orange* (1971), which liberal writer Fred Hechinger of the *New York Times* (13 February 1972) took great exception to, calling Kubrick's vision 'the voice of fascism'. Hechinger identified a number of anti-liberal films that played up to whatever national paranoia was abroad at the time, including *The Manchurian Candidate* (1962) and *Easy Rider*, condemned by Hechinger for the casual death of the liberal lawyer: 'too bad about the fuzzy-minded fellow, but what can you expect . . . ' He concluded that the writers of *Easy Rider* were 'accurately picking up the vibrations of a deeply anti-liberal totalitarianism emanating from beneath the surface of the counterculture'.

A Clockwork Orange was slated as fascist because Kubrick viewed humans as 'ignoble savages', the phrase used by the director in an earlier interview about the film. Hechinger brings both *The French Con-*

nection (1971) and *Straw Dogs* (1972) into the argument as examples of how other film-makers had similarly given up on the human race – Neanderthal rapists and evil drug barons. Hechinger felt that the message of the current crop of Hollywood movies was that society needed a tough regime to keep a check on the ignoble savages – and so the accusation of fascism.

Kubrick fought back. Rather than a call to fascist arms (a reading of the film Kubrick called 'irrelevant . . . insensitive and inverted'), the director said his film 'warns against the new psychedelic fascism – the eye-popping, multimedia, quadrasonic, drug-oriented conditioning of human beings by other beings – which many believe will usher in the forfeiture of human citizenship and the beginnings of zombiedom'. The contrasting messages of *2001* with *A Clockwork Orange* and, say, Huxley's *Brave New World* with *The Doors of Perception* seemed to be that, for the individual, certain drugs can assist in opening up new ways of thinking and change outlooks and perceptions on life. But for society subjected to state-sponsored narcosis, the only outcome is to close down options, quieten the troublesome and make slaves of us all.

Performance (1971)

The same year saw the UK release of Donald Cammell's *Performance*, offering another glimpse of the dark side of the moon. Marianne Faithful said *Performance* 'preserves a whole era under glass' – London at the end of the 1960s – sexual freedoms, drug hedonism, decadence, baronial rock stars, louche aristos entranced by the wild side, the sense of corruption and decay and the seedy glamour of psychotic violence perpetrated by the Krays and the Richardsons. Warner Brothers thought they were getting a bouncy 'Swinging London' movie and were so put out by what they saw that it took two years of cutting and re-editing before they would release the film. On its UK release in January 1971, the film was arguably even more of its time. Manson had murdered, Brian Jones was gone, the Stones had presided over Altamont and the death of Meredith Hunter (stabbed by Hell's Angels), Jimi Hendrix and Janis Joplin had overdosed and Jim Morrison would die later that year.

Mick Jagger was the perfect choice as the disillusioned rock star

Turner because the Stones carried with them an aura of drug-driven destruction that destroyed or damaged many of those who became sucked into their orbit. The following year the Stones toured America, where record executives eager to say they went on the road with the Stones hardly lasted the first week.

And like 'Life with the Stones', the film left its mark on those who took part. James Fox, who plays the gangster Chas Devlin, was allegedly so disturbed by the events of the film that he gave up acting to become a Christian, while both Brian Jones's former girlfriend Anita Pallenberg (Pherber) and Michele Breton (Lucy) fell into the world of heroin addiction. Breton was, by her own account, very young and emotionally disturbed at the time, and perpetually stoned throughout what was to be her one and only film. The director Donald Cammell, too, had a troubled life after *Performance*. Apart from *Demon Seed* (1977) and *White of the Eye* (1988), he survived from writing scripts and treatments that were never filmed and swung between bouts of progressively more debilitating mental illness. When he shot himself in 1996, he had produced what was generally agreed was his best script for years: *33*, a film about the heroin trade.

On the run from both his fellow gangsters and the police, Chas Devlin overhears that the basement flat of Turner's house is available to rent and cons his way in posing as an entertainer. Neither Turner nor his girlfriend Pherber believe Devlin's story, but he tells them he needs a passport photo, so they help him alter his physical appearance and then they alter his mind, 'dissolving his identity – his performance – in a crucible of hallucinogenic drugs and sex'.[4]

As Mick Brown says in his analysis of *Performance*, it 'uniquely addressed the Sixties drug culture on its own terms: a film about drugs made for people for whom drugs were a part of everyday life. More than that, it was the first film properly to examine the use of drugs as an assault on the values of straight society and as an instrument of personal transformation and change.'[5] *The Trip* probably takes the plaudits on the second count, but certainly no other film had drawn the outside world into the drug culture. Devlin comes from the hard-edged gangster world of betting shops, boozers, brutality, being on time and wearing a suit. Once he steps into Turner's world, life goes soft at the edges like a Dali watch, wrapped up in the swirling mists of hashish (as the studio itself was during the making of the film).

When Pherber offers him some fly agaric hallucinogenic mushrooms, Devlin, not having a clue what they really are and reflecting on all the greasy spoon breakfasts he's ever eaten, says he prefers them fried. Devlin's trip starts out in standard fashion as he admires the beauty in objects he would normally ignore, but as his character begins to disintegrate he seeks reassurance that he isn't going mad. Pherber helpfully informs him: 'We've dismantled you a bit. That's all.' To which Turner adds: 'Then we can put you together, see? Your new image.' Like Paul Groves, the strait-laced advertising executive in *The Trip*, Chas Devlin is changed by the experience. The Devlin who has violent, sadistic sex with a woman at the start of the film seems to have been transformed into a Devlin who might actually be able to care for somebody.

But Devlin's escape plan fails and he is tracked down by the gang. He knows he is going to die and, when Turner says he wants to come with him, Devlin shoots him. But as Devlin is driven away to his fate, we see the face of Turner. Their identities have merged. As Turner says in the film while Devlin is tripping, 'The only performance that makes it, that really makes it, that makes it all the way, is the one that achieves madness'. The words are a homage to Donald Cammell's hero, the French writer Artaud, who spent his life smoking opium on the edges of sanity and proposed the idea of the theatre of cruelty, where the audience would be shaken out of their passivity and shocked into wakefulness by a sensory onslaught from the stage. When the film was released, both *Rolling Stone* and the British underground paper *International Times* warned their readers not to watch the film stoned on LSD.

Altered States (1980)

The scientist, like Dr Xavier, who overreaches himself with a face-off against Mother Nature, was picked up again by Ken Russell with a film partly based on the life of John Lilly, who conducted pioneering work into dolphin intelligence but was also fascinated about altered states as experienced both through the use of drugs and through sensory deprivation using a flotation tank.

William Hurt is the physiologist Eddie Jessup. The film is set in 1967, the summer of love, but Jessup is no hippie academic. After his first five-hour flotation tank experience, during which he hallucinates 'like a son of a bitch', he tells his colleague Arthur of the paucity of research into altered states, a few good people in the field 'but most of it radical, hip stuff, drug culture apologias'. The next scene takes us to Arthur's house, a party in progress, people smoking dope, drug culture apologists to a person – and the music of the Doors in the background. Because of his 'straight' views, Jessup is described by one of the guests as 'a bit flaky', someone whose interest in altered states has taken everybody by surprise.

His funded research is to examine the cause of schizophrenia. But as he tells Emily, the anthropologist he meets at the party who becomes his wife, 'I think we are chasing our tails'. Not only is he unconvinced that the disease has a single root cause but he takes a Laingian view in that 'I'm not even sure it is a disease'. One of his schizophrenic patients is given DMT to precipitate hallucinations. Asked how she feels, she replies, 'Like my heart is being touched by Christ', which confirms why Jessup says he is working in schizophrenia – because of the links to his real interest, which is the religious experiences of those hallucinating or dreaming as schizophrenics. The flotation tank is an ethical way to draw those experiences out in non-schizophrenic individuals.

During their first intense lovemaking session, Jessup tells Emily that as a child he had visions of saints and angels. When Jessup was 16, his father died of cancer, whispering the single word 'terrible' with his last breath. Jessup believed that under heavy sedation his father had seen beyond death and realised that there was nothing there. After that Jessup turned his back on religion and never had another vision. Eddie Jessup is an obsessive soul; even making love becomes a deep and frantic mystical experience and, as his wife points out, he would sell his soul to find a great truth.

Eddie and Emily have two kids, move to Boston, both teach at Harvard, but the marriage is not working out and divorce looms. Jessup is restless and unfulfilled and wants to return to his tank studies. Having turned away from God, he is looking to locate the original self in the individual, as a source of energy that could be tapped into – to find the physiological pathway to earlier levels of consciousness. Somewhere deep inside us, locked away in our memory going back six million years, believes Jessup, is our true self, the fulfilment of middle-class Americans everywhere – 'to find myself'.

He travels to Mexico and experiences the *Amanita muscari* (fly agaric) mushroom ceremony because he has heard that the mushrooms invoke all memories, even the ancient ones, 'the first flower' Jessup's Mexican guide Eduado tells him. Eduado asks the shaman or *brujo* in the tribal language what Jessup can expect. The shaman says: 'Your soul will return to the first soul.' 'What will this soul look like?' asks Jessup. 'Your unborn self,' says the shaman, walking away as if the answer was blindingly obvious. 'Then,' says the shaman as an afterthought, 'you will be propelled into the void. You will see a spot. It will become a crack. This is the crack between the nothing, and out of this nothing will come your unborn soul.' The shaman's knowledge is supported by the real-life work of Charles Tart in his 1969 book *Altered States of Consciousness*, in which he examined the phenomenon of directed or lucid dreaming.

They enter the cave for the ceremony framed in light very similar to the emergence of the aliens from the spaceship in *Close Encounters of the Third Kind* (1977). The soundtrack, too, bears a strong resemblance to the discordant brass we hear in Spielberg's movie as attempts are made to communicate with the visitors.

The sacred mushrooms are boiled into a bitter liquid and passed around the tribal elders, who are caked in white body paint. Jessup drinks. His mind is turned inside out with flashing lights, fireworks, visions of his wife, tribal dancing. A snake coils itself around his neck, nearly choking him. The scene calms. Emily appears naked in the sand lying in a sphinx-like pose. They lay facing each other until they both turn to sand and are gradually eroded away in the desert winds. The visions end. A lizard lies dead and the shaman says that Jessup killed it in his trance state. Jessup is angry and thinks he has just been made to look like a stupid gringo. Even so, he takes back some of the brew for analysis.

Jessup resumes his studies with the mushroom potion, giving Ken

Russell unfettered opportunity for his famous visual pyrotechnics. Eddie's boss, Mason, played by *Hill Street Blues* star Charles Haid (Renko), is not happy with Eddie using a strange Mexican drug on himself and demands that the work stops. Arthur, too, is concerned that the tests are getting out of hand, echoing the worries of Dr Xavier's friends and colleagues. But Jessup wants to try out the flotation tank again even though his boss ridicules the idea much as Jessup himself had done: 'I thought that went out in the 1960s with Timothy Leary and all those other gurus.'

Jessup tells the others that under the influence of the drug he feels he is being catapulted back millions of years, but in a blackout where he cannot see the hallucinations he feels are there. He wants to break through that darkness and see what there is to see. He doesn't want to increase the dose, so the only way to intensify the experience is to combine drug with tank.

As we enter the third act, Jessup achieves his breakthrough, back in the time of the first proto-humans. But with success at the edges of science and man playing God comes the payback: 'I'm no longer observing. I'm one of them.' And that's where Ken Russell blows it, sucked into a standard Jekyll and Hyde scenario where Jessup temporarily regresses into an apeman and goes on the rampage.

The experiment spirals out of control, massive energy destroys the tank and everything around it. He regresses to a form way back beyond human, a protean nothing, spiralling and howling through the atomic and subatomic world back to cellular beginnings. He finds himself 'in that ultimate moment of terror that is the beginning of life. It is nothing. A simple hideous nothing. The final truth of all things is that there is no final truth. Truth is what is transitory. It's human life that is real. What I am trying to tell you is that moment of terror is a real and living horror living and growing within me now.' He wants to get back to the garden but cannot, and you sense, like Xavier, that the pain of living outstrips the pain of dying. In his dreams, Jessup is isolated and feels the horror within every bit as much as Conrad's *Heart of Darkness*: 'We live as we dream – alone' and like Kurtz who at the end knows only 'The horror, the horror'.

*

The way drugs work in the body, especially hallucinogens like LSD, is more than just simple biochemical cause and effect. How people react to drugs is also governed by the mood they are in when they take them, their expectations of what will happen and by their surroundings. Powerful mind-altering drugs taken in extreme circumstances promise fireworks and nightmares.

British, American and Japanese soldiers had gone to war on officially sanctioned amphetamines as a way to psych up and fight battle fatigue. But Vietnam was probably the first war of modern times where thousands of troops were shooting heroin and smoking dope just to anaesthetise themselves from the fear and the terror of fighting an enemy they hardly ever saw in a hostile jungle environment. For much of the time, the army of the world's strongest superpower hardly knew what it was doing. In his seminal account of the war, *Dispatches*, a major influence on *Apocalypse Now*, Michael Herr reported that 'Entire divisions would function in a bad dream state, acting out a weird set of moves without any connection to their source'.[6]

By 1971 the Pentagon had estimated that nearly 30 per cent of US troops had tried heroin or opium. A helicopter pilot, Fred Hickey, later claimed that most of the troops were constantly stoned: 'For ten dollars, you could get a vial of pure heroin the size of a cigarette butt, and you could get liquid opium, speed, acid, anything you wanted. You could trade a box of Tide for a carton of pre-packed, pre-rolled marijuana cigarettes soaked in opium.'[7]

Apocalypse Now (1979)

Drugs had featured in war films, but usually as the rationale for the hero to have a drug habit – the result of morphine given for battle wounds. Drugs as an escape from one reality into another appears in Oliver Stone's *Platoon* (1986), among others, but *Apocalypse Now* is drug drenched. From the moment the film opens, when archstoner Jim Morrison ironically intones 'The End' as the choppers clatter across the jungle canopy, marijuana and napalm smoke intermingle. Joints are lit with as much regularity as the jungle ignites, and in common with other films we have covered, the fog drifted behind camera as crew and actors dropped acid and smoked dope together. The director, Francis

Coppola, was tolerant, although not with the helicopter pilots caught sniffing heroin. The writer, Karl French, says he knew somebody who went into isolation in order to kick heroin but allowed himself the luxury of a video of *Apocalypse* which he watched over and over again.[8]

Drugs frame the film at different levels and are an important motif throughout a film about a conflict dubbed by Michael Herr as 'the first rock'n'roll war'. 'Out on the street,' he wrote of Saigon, 'I couldn't tell the Vietnam veterans from the rock'n'roll veterans. The Sixties had made so many casualties, its war and its music had run off the same circuit for so long they didn't even have to fuse. The war primed you for lame years while rock and roll turned more lurid and dangerous than bullfighting, rock stars started falling like second lieutenants; ecstasy and death and (of course and for sure) life, but it didn't seem so then.'

Visually, the film is bathed in a hallucinatory glow from the mists and smoke blowing from the battles across the Nu River, to the rock show vibe of the Playboy Bunny visit at Hau Phat and the dreamy reverie of the old French plantation.

On board the PBR (patrol boat river) as it sails up the Nung River into off-limits Cambodia and towards the waiting Kurtz, the young crewman Lance represents an aberrant evolution of white 1960s American youth culture. He starts off as the surfing champion Californian beach bum, usually stoned on dope, who at one point water-skis behind the boat. As the boat approaches the Du Lung Bridge, Lance drops acid and describes the scene as 'beautiful' and Vietnam generally as 'better than Disneyland'.[9] The only member of Captain Willard's crew to survive, Lance ends up as a zonked-out member of Kurtz's cult – an echo of Charlie Manson (Chef reads the newspaper headline as they proceed up river), the Reverend Jim Jones and other cult leaders (including some running drug rehabilitation programmes) who preyed on the emotionally and spiritually dispossessed. Clean, played by a teenage Lawrence Fishburne, is the jive-talking Bronx ghetto kid listening to rock on his radio. Dope-smoking, pill-popping Clean was the other side of the youth culture coin – black street-smart cannon fodder for the US army, worshipping James Brown and the Stones in equal measure.

At the stores depot, Chef asks the supplies sergeant for Panama Red dope, and as Willard and Lance trek through the murderous chaos of the trenches near the Du Lung Bridge they pass abandoned black GIs firing aimlessly into the night, smoking dope and listening to Hendrix. In perhaps the most telling line of the whole film, Willard asks a solider 'Who is in charge here?', to which the bemused and terrified reply comes, 'Ain't choo?'

For these besieged soldiers, this really would be The End, but some, like the significantly named Roach – probably like Clean when he first joined up – don't give in. Among the screaming and the panic, he is psychotically calm, sporting a tooth necklace and war paint. He takes his M-79 grenade launcher and with great deliberation accurately shoots zen-like into the darkness, killing a manic, screaming sniper simply by sheer instinct.

Willard refuses all offers of drugs (regarding his fellow crew members as 'rock and rollers with one foot in their graves') until he reaches the French plantation[10] and lays down with the French woman, Roxanne. She prepares an opium pipe, as she did for her late husband, although Willard takes only one draw. And who better to greet Willard at the end of his journey in the arsehole of the world at Kurtz's HQ but that stoned apocalypse incarnate, Dennis Hopper, as the Tim Page-type photojournalist. Totally besotted and in awe of the mad colonel, he gabbles away on a manic stream of speeding consciousness.

'Oh, he's out there. He's really out there. Do you hear what the man's saying? Do you? This is dialectics. It's very simple dialectics. One through nine. No maybes, no supposes, no fractions. You can't travel in space, you can't go into space, you know, without, er, you know, with fractions. What are you going to land on? One quarter? Three-eighths? What are you going to do when you go from here to Venus or something? That's dialectic physics. Dialectic logic is there's only love and hate. You either love someone or you hate 'em.'

In *2001* Kubrick sent Bowman on a mission of outer/inner space discovery, a journey towards death but also rebirth. From the pre-monolith days of primitive ignorance, the journey moves towards self-enlightenment. For Captain Willard, the journey is very different; rather than the 'ultimate trip', as *2001* was sold, the journey upriver into the heart of darkness is a trip back from the technical sophistication of the US war machine to primordial savagery, the ultimate bad trip of nightmares and horrors. Bowman is reborn, while Willard, in his attempt to find reason amid unreason, simply unravels, as Kurtz had done. Willard does not plummet into degradation because of drugs, but through the destructive nature of the mind games he and the CIA play in order to understand Kurtz and his motivations in the search for truth.

Jacob's Ladder (1997)

Which takes us to the covert world of CIA-sponsored chemical warfare during the Vietnam War. *Jacob's Ladder* was an unlikely directorial outing for Adrian Lyne, whose oeuvre is the tale of sexual passion (*Lolita, Fatal Attraction, Nine and a Half Weeks, Indecent Proposal*) rather than the world of surreal horror. Ex-Vietnam vet Jacob Singer (Tim Robbins) slips out of reality and into a psychotic world of nightmare visions and hallucinations caused by MK-ULTRA-type army drug experiments. A mental hospital where the seriously disturbed wander confined but uncared for becomes a charnel house where dismembered human limbs clutter the hallway and heads spin furiously on bodies.

Both his psychiatrist and a buddy from the same troop, suffering the same mental anguish as Jacob, die when their cars explode. He is snatched off the street by spooks who tell him to forget all about it. But a chemist seeks him out and tells him that his suspicions are well founded. The chemist says he was busted for manufacturing LSD and faced a long prison sentence, but offered a deal to go to Vietnam and work for the military. There he was employed producing a drug that would unleash a soldier's basic violent animal instincts. The hippie chemist tells Singer: 'Most powerful thing I ever saw. Even a bad trip, and believe me I've had my share, do not compare to the fury of the ladder. That's what they called it. A fast trip straight down the ladder, right to the base anger.' Except they succeeded all too well, and on one fateful night Singer's troop start killing each other.

A note at the end of the film states: 'It was reported that the hallucinogenic drug BZ was used in experiments during the Vietnam War. The Pentagon denied the story.' But a CNN documentary investigating the alleged use of chemical weapons by the Americans identified BZ as one of four chemicals 'weaponised' at the time, although this does not mean it was actually used. Official US army papers found on the Internet state that the Americans did have stockpiles of BZ, but claim they were never used in a combat situation and stocks were destroyed by 1988 and specifically deny the validity of *Jacob's Ladder*. BZ was invented by the Army Chemical Corps with effects including 'maniacal behaviour' lasting on average three days, but anything up to six weeks of disorientation and hallucinations had been recorded.

Out of the Blue (1983)

As the last chapter ended with Dennis Hopper as a segue into drug dystopia, so we see out this chapter with our renegade auteur in a film that, like *Apocalypse Now*, explores the terrain of post-1960s despair and disillusionment.

Hopper was hired only to act in the film, but when an opportunity came up to direct he readily accepted on condition that he could ditch the original script by *Rebel without a Cause* writer Stewart Stern and recast most of the parts.

Out of the Blue tells the story of CeeBee, a 15-year-old tomboy fixated on Elvis Presley and punk and desperate to become a rock star. She lives with her drug addict mother awaiting the release of her father Donny (Dennis Hopper), serving five years for manslaughter after ploughing his truck into a school bus.

The whole family's life is a complete mess. CeeBee's mother Kathy is smashed out of her head much of the time and sleeping with her husband's best friend Charlie who is also supplying the drugs. CeeBee, who has recurrent nightmares about the crash, truants from school, runs away and is nearly raped. They both believe things will be much better when Donny gets out. They are wrong. He is an alcoholic who quickly loses his job at the local garbage dump as part of the vendetta waged against him by the father of one of the dead children. But not before he steals some dynamite which he hopes to sell. He dreams of getting his 'rig' together again which lies covered with weeds in the front yard – and taking CeeBee with him. The film comes to a climax when in a drunken state Donny suggests to an equally drunk Charlie that he should have sex with CeeBee to 'make sure she doesn't become a dyke'. CeeBee fends him off, but dark secrets are revealed and the end of the film is truly shocking.

The theme running through the film is Neil Young's homage to Johnny Rotten and punk, 'My, My, Hey, Hey', with the line 'Out of the blue/Into the black'. Young had been Hopper's drinking buddy as they scouted locations for a Dean Stockwell film, *Human Highway* (1982), produced by and starring Young. The singer offered to write an original song for *Out of the Blue* but eventually a song from his *Rust Never Sleeps* album was chosen which meshes perfectly with the theme of youthful nihilism captured in the line 'Better to burn out than to fade away'. But this was every bit the fate of 1960s heroes like Hendrix, Joplin and Jim Morrison, as it was Sid Vicious and Kurt Cobain. And although the focus of the film is disaffected youth of the 1980s as encapsulated by the figure of CeeBee, it could equally have been the story of *Easy Rider*'s Billy if he'd lived. He hooks up with a 'hippie chick', living out his hedonistic dream on the road under the wide blue skies, with some liquid blue LSD in his back pocket, but then slips out of the blue and into the decay and madness of the black. Which is where we go for our next trip – trekking in the wake of the pale riders.

9

The pale riders: heroin films from *Trash* to *Requiem for a Dream*

. . . he still talks about kicking, and at the same time he denies that he is hooked, and yet he has agreed with me again and again that if you simply put heroin down you are avoiding the issue. It isn't the horse, for all the melodramatic talk about withdrawal symptoms. It is the pale rider.

Cain's Book, Alexander Trocchi, 1963

Heroin provides a tremendous sense of wellbeing, even when all is clearly not well; it opens up the door that leads back to that happy childhood state where 'all's right with the world' . . . Once they have glimpsed it, junkies want to stay in this 'never never land' forever.

The Heroin Users, Tam Stewart, 1987

By the early 1970s the US government was fighting a phoney drugs war on two fronts. Classroom teachers were trying to shock young people out of trying marijuana and LSD by showing them scare movies specially made for schools, although research has consistently demonstrated that these have no impact on the general levels of drug use by young people.[1] Much more sinister was the deliberate falsification of the number of heroin users in order to generate a nationwide panic about heroin.

Under the cloak of a 'war against drugs', Richard Nixon wanted to create national security forces that would ride roughshod over civil rights and the constitution. And if any official statistics can be bent to fit the need, they were (and still are) the numbers about drug use. Like they say about Hollywood when it comes to picking which films will soar or flop, 'nobody knows anything'. In order to demonstrate what a good job it was doing, the Bureau of Narcotic Drugs (forerunner of the Drug Enforcement Administration) decided that the heroin-using population had stabilised at 69,000 in 1969 – until the need to appropriate more funds from Congress dictated that this figure should jump to 560,000 in 1971.[2] This sleight of hand was achieved by a simple reworking of the 1969 data. Instead of assuming that most heroin users would eventually come to the attention of the authorities, the new spin assumed that very few would and so the addict population suddenly leaped eight-fold.

The truth, of course, often lies in between. Young whites, both working and middle class, had discovered heroin. 'Heroin Hits the Young' was a *Time* magazine cover story in March 1970. 'The heroin plague: what can be done?' asked *Newsweek* in July 1971. Some commentators blamed government anti-drug propaganda for the escalating problem. A report for the Consumers Union suggested that lumping all drugs together as equally evil made it impossible to get across credible messages about heroin because of all the nonsense promulgated about marijuana, which shared the same legal status with heroin and cocaine as 'narcotics'. More seriously, the report believed that with marijuana illegal (as it had been since 1937), but now so widespread, this was driving young people towards the same underground and criminal networks that might deal in heroin. Supply, of course, was a key factor. More heroin was coming into the country than ever before from many countries, including Afghanistan, Burma, Laos, Thailand, Pakistan, Turkey, Iran and, much closer to home, Mexico.

Why did heroin become so popular? Easy to explain for those living in urban squalor with no proper home or job – especially if they were black as well. But what about middle-class white kids? Ann Marlowe, an ex-user, wrote recently in her insightful account, *How to Stop Time: Heroin from A to Z*: 'opiate addiction only became a social problem when it became a social solution.'[3] The drift towards heroin expressed a widespread longing and need among those who, despite having all their material and even most emotional needs catered for, nevertheless felt detached from the world of work and traditional family life. For those feeling bored and unmotivated, heroin replaced those central features of the 'straight world'.

A new wave of heroin movies gave starring roles to sympathetic characters, gallows humour, snappy streetwise dialogue and the gritty realism of documentary-style film-making. Contained within all of them are windows into a world few can understand but which most have a view on. Certainly, the idea of the junkie as the victim of this disease called addiction, which played front-of-house in the 1950s, is under-mined by characters who are addicted to the lifestyle at least as much as the drug and have made choices in their life. The black and the white of heroin mythology now fades to grey.

Those who first studied the impact of the media back in the 1930s developed a theory that visualised the media as a giant syringe injecting its ideologies into a passive body politic. Mass propaganda from a mass media to the mass of an undifferentiated population. We know now that this was too simplistic an analysis; we refract the media through the prism of our own belief systems. Those who would call themselves left of centre are unlikely to be avid readers of newspapers that propound a more conservative world view. But the media are still the primary source of information for most people. Our knowledge of the everyday world is still largely shaped by what the media report on and – equally important – what they don't report on. When it comes to an issue like drugs, our liberal media consumer might be more sympathetic to the plight of those with serious problems than the conservative consumer, but not necessarily better informed.

This is especially true with what is regarded as the most extreme form of drug use – injecting heroin. Even though it does nowhere near as much physical damage to the body as alcohol, in the pantheon of evil drugs heroin remains the satanic lord and master. Although some young people do not regard it as such, especially since the 1980s vogue for smoking heroin (dispensing with the need for needles), the drug retains its demonic image.

And as for getting the drug into the body, nothing causes more revulsion than the idea of willingly sticking a needle in your arm. Such behaviour seems so beyond the pale to most people: few of us know anybody who actually does this. We only get to hear and see about it through what the media serves up – mainly tabloid newspaper and TV documentary 'shock horror' stories of wasted young lives, cruel drug barons and distraught parents. And in that respect the old injecting metaphor holds true.

The popular perception of a 'typical' heroin addict goes something like this. A male under 30, unemployed and homeless, becomes a heroin user because he is weak and easily led. A chronic underachiever with low self-esteem and a poverty-ridden background where he suffered emotional neglect and physical abuse, he falls in with a 'bad lot' who are using a variety of drugs, which leads to experimentation with heroin. Not wanting to be left out of his new-found peer group, our hapless lad goes with the flow and quickly becomes addicted. With no income, he turns to petty crime, stealing, lying and cheating his way from one desperate fix to another. So deep is his self-loathing and need for money that he is keen to get others involved both to drag them down to his level and to provide him with a ready source of income as purchasers of his surplus heroin. Treatment is a waste of time because 'once an addict, always an addict'. At base, this is an evil, amoral person with no redeeming features who would slit his grandmother's throat for a £5 bag of heroin.

This is not a social type but a *stereotype* and as such represents more than just who the user is. He represents somebody who has gone several steps over the line, a benchmark against which we can judge ourselves. Stereotypes clear the muddy water; they filter the grey into the black and the white.

But as the films in this chapter show, anybody can become addicted to heroin. Some will fit our profile of poverty and deprivation. But not all poor and homeless people become heroin addicts. Not all people from emotionally deprived or abusive backgrounds become heroin addicts. You will find heroin addicts in the ranks of white-collar workers, the professional classes and the aristocracy. So does that mean there is a special type of 'addictive personality'? There is no clinical evidence for this either – but in any case use of heroin has risen so dramatically over the past 30 years as to be impossible to explain by a sudden rash of people with the 'addictive gene'. And they will fit any personality type you like, from gentle and unassuming to downright nasty.[4]

The main character(s) in these films has a destructive relationship with a needle, a syringe and an opiate drug, usually heroin. Beyond that, as a body of cinema they pretty much express the full range of what we might call 'the heroin experience' – reasons why people become addicted, social types, heroin lifestyle, personal relationships, the role of treatment, and denouement. Those films that play to a stereotypical view of heroin addiction are more likely to be structured like the classic Western morality tale – seduction, fall from grace and redemption – while others are more ambiguous and non-judgemental. So while films like *The Man with the Golden Arm* or *Trainspotting* may be regarded as classic drug movies, by no means can they be said to represent all sides of addiction.

Drug films (or any other films, come to that) do not reproduce reality. They frame reality to fit ideological or distorted images of real social relationships. 'The statement that a film makes bears the stamp of the cultural, social and economic contexts that surround the film-maker's work. The film is also the product of the teamwork, and of the political economics of production, distribution and consumption. Any film, in turn, builds upon patterns of meanings and action that exist in society at large. In so doing, it modifies those patterns of meaning and creates new experiences for viewers. In this way, film creates the realities it produces on the screen.'[5] But whether banal or subtle, all the films manage to convey some of the truths of heroin addiction as well as reinforcing some of the mythologies.

What this means is that in the protean complexities of the addiction film, there is no single frame of analysis. But there is a common theme – addiction to heroin – and therein lies a problem with the whole genre. There is much in addiction to do with nostalgia and security. This might be the safety and security associated with childhood (or at least the mythology of childhood). It might be the attempt to recapture that very first heroin rush – the one that's supposed to be better than sex. And it might be the security that comes from knowing exactly what you are going to be doing at any given point in the day. But from a dramatic point of view, for 'safety' read 'boring'. Watching people shoot up and fall asleep is not tremendously exciting, and the variations on a theme are limited. Remember that as far back as 1916, *Variety* was saying that the drug movie was dead and buried.

Jonathan Rosenbaum's review of *Panic in Needle Park* in the *Financial Times* (4 July 1975) looked at the issue of dramatic interest from another perspective. He wrote that the film 'has to contend with a handicap which faces virtually all films dealing with heroin addiction: how to keep its doomed characters dramatically interesting'. His take on the predictable nature of addiction was not so much the lifestyle as the outcome. '*The Man with the Golden Arm* offered studio expressionism, jazz and the star presences of Frank Sinatra and Kim Novak. More interestingly, *The Connection* confronted the audience with its own voyeurism regarding addicts, while Ivan Passer's *Born to Win* – made the same year as *Panic* and regrettably unseen in this country – brought up the subversive possibility that its addict hero – George Segal – really liked what he was doing because it simplified all of life's problems' – a point we will return to later.

Other film-makers have dealt with the monotony of addiction through the use of music, camera techniques, narrative style, injections of humour, settings and locations. And so we have films on the same subject but as different in look and feel as the deadpan, fly-on-the-wall home-movie approach of *Trash* (1970) and the stylised, high-tech, visceral impact of a near-drug horror film like *Requiem for a Dream* (2001).

A point about terminology. Because of the stigma attached to words like 'addiction' and 'addict', some of those working in the drugs field use phrases like 'problem drug use', 'heroin users' etc. Understandable though this is, the shorthand phrases are more convenient for the following narrative. But also words like 'addict' and even 'junkie' or the more archaic 'dope fiend' have actual resonance for some drug users themselves, which comes up time and again in the movies. These words are double-edged. Undoubtedly, they serve to marginalise and stigmatise people who are already fragile and damaged. Thus labelled, they are written off by society as weavers of their own destiny and so bottom of the heap for any kind of assistance. The problem is compounded immeasurably by having to live their daily lives outside the law in order to obtain their drugs.

But, curiously, these labels also give users an identity. For the person who has gone down the heroin route through a sense of alienation and lack of self-worth, being able to call yourself something instead of nothing can be 'life-affirming'. Instead of being a failed something or an ex-something you are now 'An Addict' with all the attention that can attract, welcome or otherwise. How the user sees himself or herself and how those around the main character(s) react can be very significant in the context of a study of drug films, a genre that particularly lends itself to the depiction of intense and dramatic relationships.[6]

Trash (1970)

Directed by Warhol protégé Paul Morrissey, *Trash* was part of the *Flesh, Trash, Heat* trilogy of street films made between 1970 and 1972. It tells the story of Joe, played by real-life user Joe Dellasandro, as he drifts around the city trying to earn cash for dope. He lives with Holly (transvestite Harold Danhaki), but the main problem he has is not so much the dope as the inability to have an erection – much to the chagrin of all the women he comes into contact with. Holly, meanwhile, is trying to better their lives by doing up their apartment with items she finds dumped in the street. Her sister gets pregnant, and Holly sees a way to welfare (and some security) by pretending to a social worker that she, too, is pregnant. The social worker is sympathetic but says that 'Mr Smith' (Joe) has to be on a methadone programme to get welfare. For Holly, the problem is that she is living with a common-law husband who is on drugs. So she can't get welfare either. Bizarrely, the social worker says he will get them some money if Holly gives him her silver shoes so he can make lamps out of them. Holly won't give them up and demands their right to welfare. A row ensues, during which she stands up and a pillow falls out. The film ends with Holly asking Joe if she can suck his cock. They are going nowhere and doing nothing.

Originally, the film was *Drug Trash*, targeting the rock fans who hung out at what the director called 'the Swillmore Vomitorium [the Fillmore Auditorium]'. Morrissey was determined to make an unashamedly anti-drug film to counteract what he saw as glamorisation in films like *Easy Rider* and *2001*. He wanted to dispel the myth that 'drugs are supposed to free people from inhibitions'. He went for the junkie jugular – 'the basic idea for the movie is that drug people are trash. There's no difference between a person using drugs and a piece of refuse.'[7] This is the insult screamed at Joe and Holly by the social worker as he leaves their apartment.

But within the film, the concept of 'trash' takes on a wider meaning. Holly kits out the apartment with old furniture she finds abandoned in the street. At one point Joe tries to burgle a house and is confronted by a young woman (with the most irritating voice in the history of cinema), who, far from calling the police, suggests Joe rapes her. Her husband arrives and the couple watch fascinated as Joe shoots up – but when he almost overdoses, they kick him out in the alley where they put their garbage. In *The Connection*, the users berate the cameraman (and by association the audience) for wanting a freak show. In *Trash* this voyeuristic scene of the 'straights' watching the junkie with a mixture of glee and repulsion mirrors the tabloid press, which both condemns and exploits drug users in the same breath. But with Jane the wife wanting to be raped and her husband Bruce egging her on to watch Joe injecting – who is the real trash? Later, when Holly catches Joe with her sister, she says she feels like a piece of garbage. But if the puritanical director wanted to hold up society's drug addled to ridicule, Holly Woodlawn created sympathy for a character trying to salvage ruined lives.

Holly breaks many of the junkie stereotypes, not least the views held by Paul Morrissey, who uses the character of the social worker to express his contempt for drug users. But she has values. From where she currently sits, receiving welfare is the passport to domesticity and stability. But she won't be exploited by the creepy pseudo-liberal (spouting 'groovy' and wearing a peace badge), who wants her shoes in exchange for a favourable welfare report.

Joe Dellasandro's performance was particularly significant because he was an injecting heroin user. His presentation was unexpressive, passive, drug-dazed, the sort of person to whom things *happen*, a person who is *done* to rather than doing. He might appear as a victim, but he was one of the first screen addicts to appear comfortable in his skin. Towards the end of the film he says to Holly that he will try to clean up, not for himself as he is 'perfectly happy', but because she wants him to.

Before he finds out he is being conned, the social worker tries to bond with the two lovers, calling them 'hippies' and 'flower children', but they aren't. The Hollys and Joes of New York were the edgy and the paranoid – speed and heroin rather than psychedelics, Velvet Underground rather than Grateful Dead.

Panic in Needle Park (1971)

Admitted to hospital after a botched abortion, Helen is befriended by Bobby (Al Pacino), a user and dealer from the 'Needle Park' area of New York's West Side. She goes to live with him and meets his user friends, including Hank, Bobby's brother, a professional burglar. There is a shortage of heroin in New York, producing a panic in the city's users. Helen slowly realises that Bobby has a worsening habit. He asks her to go and score for him and she is caught by Hotchner, the local narcotics officer. Meanwhile, Helen starts using as well, and Bobby says he wants to marry her. He agrees to go with Hank on a job to get some money to clean up and start over, but he misses the job when he ODs and on the next job he gets caught. While he is inside, Helen sells herself to pay for drugs and sleeps with Hank. On his release, Bobby becomes a distributor for Santo, who controls the West Side heroin trade. Helen's drug problem is getting worse; she is caught robbing clients and caught again selling pills. Hotchner seizes his chance and bullies Helen into betraying Bobby, so they can get to Santo. Eventually, she agrees. Bobby is arrested but for helping nail Santo gets only six months. On release, he and Helen carry on their unrewarding life.

In sifting through what was to be his first major screen role, Pacino turned down a number of offers, including *Catch 22*, because it meant signing a contract with Paramount for more than just the one film. Katherine 'Kitty' Winn was chosen to play Helen after being named 'discovery of the season' for her performance in the American Conservative Theater production of *St Joan* in San Francisco. And for her role as Helen she won Best Actress Prize at the 1971 Cannes Film Festival.[8]

There were a few tense moments during the shooting of the film, when a group of users thought the actors were undercover drugs officers. On another occasion, when Pacino was being filmed selling drugs, a real dealer thought he was trying to muscle in on his patch.

Pacino met a number of users at the Phoenix House and Reality House treatment centres trying to pin down exactly what a heroin addict 'was'. But every time he thought he had the nature and progress of addiction nailed, he'd talk to somebody with an entirely different story to tell. One user told him it was impossible to make love on heroin, another that it was absolutely the best sex when you're stoned.[9] *Trash* sided with one view on sex and heroin, *Panic* took the other view, except when Bobby was actually stoned.

Probably because of its subject matter, the film was not a huge success but it won many plaudits from the critics, who praised its realistic documentary feel, the screenplay (by Joan Didion and John Gregory Dunne from James Mills's novel) and the quality of the lead perform-ances. Incredibly, the film was banned in Britain until 1975, by which time Pacino had become an international star for his performance in *The Godfather* (1972). *Panic* was the first of the modern mainstream non-judgemental, morally neutral, 'tell it like it is' heroin movies.

Bobby is a street user and dealer very different from Joe in *Trash*. We see none of Joe's listless meanderings in Bobby. When Bobby goes down the street, he walks with fast, purposeful strides like a man with places to be and people to meet. His behaviour is anything but an escape from life – a typical view of what street heroin use is all about. He engages in meaningful activities and relationships seven days a week. The actual amount of time spent under the influence of heroin is very small. From his point of view the rest of his day is spent 'pursuing a career that is exacting, challenging, adventurous and rewarding'. He is always on the move and must be alert, flexible and resourceful.[10]

He is also instantly likeable. From the outset, he is wisecracking, swaggering, gum-chewing, funny, considerate of Helen and pretty much sweeps her off the sidewalk. After she comes out of hospital, she stays the night and next morning offers him the chance to make love. But Bobby, mindful of her operation, says no: 'it's too soon.'

He tells her all about his life as a petty criminal since the age of nine. He's proud of the number of times he's been inside. When the film opens, he is only a 'chipper' – injecting into the muscle rather than mainlining – so he has not become a criminal in order to support his habit. So why is he using? No answers are given; the question isn't even asked – but Bobby is clearly a risk taker and a chancer, and maybe a heroin user for the same reasons. Ann Marlowe wrote about a friend who drove very fast, wanted to fight in the Gulf War and took heroin instead. Bobby belongs to a subset of heavy drug users who spin out to the edge just to see if they can come back again. This is another group entirely from those looking for security and comfort among the predictability of addiction where they cannot find it in the straight world.

Marlowe offers us this insight: 'Addiction relies on the tension of enough/not enough, now/not now, to organise life and ward off chaos.' She asks: 'Why are junkies always running out of dope?'[11] The answer for many is obvious – no money – but for those with money, the only answer can be self-punishment and the pretence that you don't need any more because you are giving up tomorrow. But you are always worrying about running out – bits of dope get stashed all over the place like a squirrel collecting nuts for the winter. Later, in *Panic*, Bobby has (for once) got himself into a good position as a main dealer in the area. He's got as much access to drugs as he wants. Yet he still hides little bits of dope just for security reasons, just in case, just in case – and when his stash is stolen from a hole in a wall outside, he's beside himself with anger.

When Bobby asks Helen about her background, we get a taste of the early 1970s new breed of heroin user. Even though she has just come through an abortion after living with a loft artist, she has the well-scrubbed, soft features of a middle-class girl just off the bus.

She tells him her life 'was all right . . . I went to school. I had a father, mother and a little brother and a lawn. I was always going to art classes, and my mother was always going to the doctor. It was all right.' 'Why did you leave, then?' asks Bobby, not unreasonably. 'You just don't go round leaving people for no reason'. 'I wouldn't,' she says. 'You shouldn't. It ain't right.' 'I won't.' But whatever the reason was, Helen didn't want to tell. Instead, she just looks into the middle distance, sad and a little scared – and the subject is never raised again.

As often happens in real-life relationships, when one is using and the other isn't, an almost impenetrable barrier is thrown up. Often the only way to tear it down is for the non-user – usually the female – to start using. Given some accounts of the heroin high as being better than sex – and the problems some using couples on dope have with sex – injecting becomes a substitute for sex – most obviously when the man penetrates his partner with the needle. Here the situation is different. Helen starts using on her own and it takes a while for Bobby to notice the pinned eyes. He is very accepting; his only reaction is 'when did that happen?' This does cement the relationship, but her addiction portends chemical infighting when the panic kicks in and there is less to go around.

But they are genuinely devoted to each other and, like Frank in *Golden Arm* and Holly in *Trash*, dream of a better life. Bobby wants to get married. They get a little dog and take a boat trip. But they get high on the way back and lose the dog overboard. The dream turns to dust. It is hard to imagine Bobby out of the drug life. In one telling scene, Bobby gets a glimpse of the higher echelons of the trade. He is ushered into a room where heroin is being cut. A young man with a mask over his face sits in front of a pile of powder and begins the precise process of measuring out the drug and the additive, then mixing, remixing, chopping and melding – part croupier, part chef, part magician. It is all done in silence, no dialogue, no soundtrack. Bobby shakes his head in admiration of the artistry. This is where he belongs. And when he comes out of jail, you know where he is going.

Addict (aka Born to Win) (1971)

In this uneasy mix of comedy and drama, George Segal plays JJ, an erstwhile hairdresser on the skids. His marriage to Paula Prentiss, also a user, has collapsed, and he takes up with Parm (Karen Black) after she catches him failing to steal her car. The subtitle *Born to Win* (tattooed on JJ's arm) is ironic because he is a down-the-line loser who fails with most of the crime he attempts and is invariably ripped off by other users and dealers – the source for most of the comedy. Eventually, he is trapped into helping the police (an early role for a very young Robert de Niro) catch a big time trafficker. The deal is made, but meanwhile his best friend, Billy Dynamite, dies after injecting a 'hotshot' meant for JJ after he tries to rip off a dealer. JJ has no problem being a user; at one point he tells Parm: 'Sometimes I feel I wanna turn my head around. I'm a very boring guy when I'm straight.' But, none the less, at the end he is left sitting on a city bench alone contemplating his future. As with *Panic*, the British censors banned the film because of its graphic illustration of heroin use.

It is often the secondary characters who get some of the most telling lines about the nature of addiction. I have mentioned earlier the attraction for some people of the predictable nature of drug addiction. You know that if you buy a bag of heroin at 10 p.m., you know when you'll be high, when you'll be down and when you have to go out and get some more. This may sound a pretty drastic way to get some routine into your life. But it can be a powerful motivation for those people who have come to drugs by way of a lifetime of betrayal and disappointment, of never being able to trust anybody or any situation, being left and let down. In *Addict*, JJ's running buddy Billy expresses this beautifully when he exclaims: 'I love this life. Love it. 'Cos when we get up in the morning we know exactly what we're gonna do next. Lookin' for another bag. I wouldn't give it up for nothing. 'Cos we got a purpose in life. Know what I mean? How many people can really say that?'

Christiane F (1981)

Ulrich Edsel's debut film, a box-office success in both Germany and France, follows the true story of the spiralling self-destruction of a 13-year-old girl caught up in the bleak urban nightmare of Berlin tower-block life. Christiane lives with her mother and sister in a high-rise. Early on, her sister goes to live with dad. Mum works and starts a new relationship, leaving little 'quality time' to spend with her daughter. Christiane goes to Sounds, a local nightclub. On her first visit, she takes some LSD offered by somebody who then gropes her. She is approached by another teenager, Detlef, who looks after her and tells her that taking pills is stupid. What she doesn't know is that Detlef is already using heroin and earning money as a male prostitute. Soon Christiane is running with Detlef and his crew, committing petty crimes in and around the subway stations and dodging the police. When she finds out about the heroin, she asks him to choose between her and heroin. She loses. Seeing Detlef with another girl, Christiane demands from Detlef's flatmate, Atze, also a user, that she be allowed to use heroin as well, but backs away from injecting and snorts instead. Detlef is furious when he finds out she has been using, but she says she only did it to get nearer to him.

Then begins the slide into injecting, then regular use, then half-hearted attempts at prostitution to earn some money for heroin, all intercut with the classic lovers' dope rows about 'who is holding out on whom' common in these films. After Christiane collapses at home, the two young lovers decide to go cold turkey in the hope of breaking their habit. Afterwards, they try to convince themselves that they could use now and again without becoming hooked, but this never works for them. They both go back to prostitution, three friends die in 1977, but in the end Christiane survives to tell her story, originally serialised in *Stern* magazine.

The film is set in the late 1970s, but continued to have resonance during the period in which it was shown because of the changing nature of the drug scene in the UK and the rest of Europe. Up until this time, heroin had remained on the fringes of the drug scene, confined to a group of older users who had no fear of needles. But in 1979 the Shah of Iran was deposed and many wealthy Iranians fled the new regime of fundamentalist Islam, taking their wealth out of the country in any way they could. One way was to convert it into heroin, but in a form new to the UK and Europe. It was smokable, and it changed the face of the drug scene for ever. Young people could now use heroin without needles and in some cases without even realising it was heroin. All they saw was a brown powder whose fumes they inhaled from a piece of tinfoil, a practice known as 'chasing the dragon'. However, with most of the drug literally going up in smoke, this was never a cost-effective way of using, and those in for the long haul switched to injecting. This new form of escape tragically coincided with economic depression, especially in areas of heavy manufacturing. Millions of jobs were lost, and a feeling of despair and hopelessness gripped many young people. This was the 'blank generation' brought up on the nihilism and anarchy of punk who drifted through life feeling that they had nothing to aim for and no prospects. For them the question was not 'why take heroin?' but 'why not?'

Critics were divided about the film. They acknowledged the desire to detail all the horror and degradation of teenagers selling themselves on the streets, injecting heroin and dying. Was this honest and non-patronising – or did it play to the worst voyeuristic passions of the audience? Why did two million Germans see this film? Concern for the social condition of their country or to witness the downfall of an attractive teenage girl? Derek Malcolm of the *Guardian* (3 December 1981) thought that, although the story was true, the unremitting squalor of the tale, where we are asked to believe that Christiane had no options at all, would make 'those who take drugs sneer and terrify those who anyway wouldn't'.

Christiane narrates the story, so we are made aware that this is a story to be told from her point of view. This is important when trying to analyse why she makes the choices she does. For example, viewed objectively, one cannot really blame Christiane's mother for what happens. She is a single parent, needing both to work and rebuild her life. The flat is clean, there is food to eat, she worries about Christiane, gets her tickets to see her favourite rock star, David Bowie, and ultimately gets her out of danger and into the country. That she did not realise her daughter was using heroin until faced with the undeniable truth is not uncommon. Yet from Christiane's point of view, she is unloved and uncared for. A key moment, early on in the film, is when she comes home from school to find her sister Sabine packing her bags to go to live with their father. She begs Sabine to stay, but to no avail. Her father has left, her mother has a boyfriend and now her sister is leaving. Who is there for Christiane? It is at the point where she thinks she might lose Detlef as well, as he chooses heroin over her, that she decides she must join him to keep him. It works. One of the most poignant moments in the film is when, during the throes of withdrawal, she tears off the wallpaper in her bedroom to reveal an earlier nursery pattern underneath from a time when everything was warm, safe and certain.

Lack of self-esteem is often cited as a root cause of drug use among young people. Yet it is Christiane's friend Kessi who gets her into the disco underage and introduces her to boys and drugs. Kessi is 'top of my class and everyone [i.e., parents and teachers] approves of her'. But she loses Kessi as well when Kessi's mother catches them hanging out at the station early one morning, when Kessi was supposed to be on a sleepover with Christiane. From the point of view of the young people in the film, families are a non-starter: Detlef lives in a squat, while Christiane's friend Babsi looks around for places to stay because she can't stand being at home. When her mother's boyfriend Klaus is there, Christiane feels the same.

When she arrives at Sounds for the first time, she is assailed by the sounds of David Bowie, whose music is the central motif running through the film. Later, she and her friends commit petty crimes to Bowie's 'Heroes', and she happily gobbles pills in front of Bowie at the concert while he eulogises about cocaine in 'Station to Station'. Bowie is as much the soundtrack to the lives of Christiane and her friends as Charlie Parker was for a particular group of young people growing up in the 1950s. Bowie himself was living in Berlin during the mid-to-late 1970s, and the combination of his depressive themes and the new nihilistic shriek of punk mirrored perfectly the adolescent sensibilities of Christiane and her friends. In his deeply critical review of Bowie's album *Low*, Charles Shaar Murray condemned Bowie for producing music that glorified 'futility and death wish . . . an elaborate embalming job for a suicide's grave . . . an act of pure hatred and destructiveness'. No wonder those like Christiane, Babsi, Detlef and his friend Atze, who hang around the Banhof Zoo Station selling themselves for drugs, hang on to Bowie's every word. *Christiane F* is a trenchant anti-drug movie, harshly lit to emphasise the ghostly drug pallor and backed by a mini-malist industrial synthesiser soundtrack punctuating the downfall of the new children of the night. But the heroine (no pun intended) survives: 'Mum took me to my gran and auntie in a village near Hamburg. I've been clean for 18 months. It frightens me to think of Detlef. I often think of him. I'd like to give him some of my strength and help him. But first I need the strength myself.'

Drugstore Cowboy (1989)

Gus Van Sant's wry, non-judgemental tale of Matt Dillon as Bob Hughes leading a bunch of users whose income derives mainly from robbing drugstore pharmacies elaborated hugely on the guilt-free drug-driven lifestyle of Bobby and his Needle Park friends. This was America's first heroin movie for 18 years: during the interregnum, the middle class had fallen in love with drugs (especially cocaine) and they really didn't want to hear (or see) the bad news. Yet by the time the film was released, America had been subjected to several years of Ronald Reagan's revitalised 'War on Drugs' and Nancy's 'Just Say No' cam-paign. This probably explains why the film was set in the early 1970s, both for political reasons and as a touch of nostalgia for a more inno-cent time before AIDS and crack.

America's best-ever film about the heroin lifestyle takes place in Port-land, Oregon, and kicks off with Bob being taken to hospital after being shot. The rest trips back to Bob leading his band – girlfriend Dianne, dim-witted protégé Rick and his jailbait hanger-on Nadine. They steal, deal, shoot up and crash out. Bob plays mind games with the local narcs led by Gentry, leading one of them to be shot by an irate neighbour. The turning point in the film occurs when Nadine ODs while the gang is on a botched hospital pharmacy raid. Bob buries Nadine in the countryside (because their motel is about to be taken over for a police conference). He vows that if he gets out of this jam, he'll give up drugs. He asks Dianne to come with him and give up the life, but she refuses. At the clinic, he meets the defrocked junkie priest, played by William Burroughs, who introduced him to drugs when he was an altar boy. Now clean, away from his friends and with a flat and a job, Hughes is warned by Gentry that the officer injured because of Hughes's antics is out for blood. Dianne (now with Rick) comes to visit and leaves some drugs as a present. Bob gives the stash to the priest but is beaten up and shot by an old junkie acquaintance who thinks Bob is still holding. Gentry wants to know who shot him, but Bob won't tell.

Like *Christiane F,* the world is seen through the eyes of the user narrating the story, but that is where the similarity ends. There is no redemption, remorse or retribution. Even though Bob gets shot in the end, he is going to survive and he is quite happy to be in hospital because of the limitless supply of drugs. We never find out why Bob got into heavy drug use and he doesn't care, revelling instead in the 'dope fiend' tag. He turns up at his mum's house, she hugs him and then shuts the door in his face while she hides her handbag. Once the door is opened, mum says to Dianne, whom Bob has known since childhood: 'You are grown up now. And yet you still act as children who want to run around and play. You cannot run and play all your life.'

Like Billy Dynamite in *Addict,* Bob revels in the routine of addiction. 'Most people don't know how they're gonna feel from one minute to the next. But a dope fiend has a pretty good idea. All you gotta do is look at the labels on the little bottles.' Gus Van Sant eschews the *de rigueur* cold turkey scenes for avant-garde and surreal episodes of Bob being stoned, reminiscent of Anthony Balch's early-1960s movie *Towers of Fire* featuring our resident cinematic junkie, Bill Burroughs.

It is Burroughs who lays out one of the central themes of the film. Bob is a natural rebel, and it was always going to be us against them:

anarchy versus control, state versus the individual. 'In the future,' says the priest, 'the right-wingers will use drug hysteria as a pretext to set up a national police apparatus. I'm an old man, and I probably won't live to see the Final Solution to the drug problem.' Burroughs's presence as an elderly Catholic cleric with a lifelong drug problem is a neat black-humoured twist on the idea of the priest as a source of redemption. He also reminds us that chronic drug users come in all shapes and sizes, including those eligible for bus passes and Saga holidays.

Bob takes the risks because he enjoys outgunning the police. He takes the drugs because he enjoys them. But after the trauma of having to dispose of Nadine's body, something snaps. He tells Dianne that he is tired, he wants to go home, 'maybe get into a 21-day methadone programme, clean up my act'. Ironically, it is Dianne who can't believe what she's hearing – she wants to carry on in the life and doesn't want to withdraw. Not that either of them ever appears to be hooked – no hunted features, chalky pallor or runny noses. These are catwalk junkies – good-looking, unhurried and self-assured.

Once in the clinic, he rails against the nurse trying to do a clinical history: 'I'm a junkie. I like drugs. I like the whole lifestyle. It just didn't pay off. You don't see my kind of people. My kind of people don't come down here and beg dope. They go out and get it and if they miss they go to jail and they kick along with nothing in some holding tank.' Nor does he have much time for therapy. He doesn't believe that a junkie can ever leave drugs alone if they are under pressure – 'nobody, and I mean nobody, can talk a junkie out of using. You can talk to them for years, but sooner or later they'll get hold of something . . . anything will do to relieve the pressures of their everyday life, like havin' to tie their shoes . . . even a gunshot in the head.'

This is a key statement in the film. With stunning simplicity, he is saying that there are people who find living in the world such a painful experience that they sincerely believe obliterating drugs like heroin are their only option. That or death. As Gus Van Sant said about Bob trying to give up drugs, 'it's not as if he sees the light. It's just that he's afraid of the darkness.'

The Basketball Diaries (1994)

For his first starring role, Leonardo DiCaprio, like Al Pacino, chose to play a drug user. This classic morality tale details the gradual drift into the delinquent then junkie lifestyle of promising school basketball player and would-be writer Jim Carroll, devastated by the death from cancer of his best friend. After a spell in Riker's Island juvenile reformatory, his determination to escape the sewer using his literary skills sets him on the road to recovery and redemption.[12]

Jim is no Bobby or Bob – he is full of self-hate, self-pity and guilt. He wakes every morning to the sound of a mad woman opposite cursing the Virgin Mary. A large crucifix hangs over his bed and the teachings of the Church are regularly beaten into him at school by a sadistic Catholic priest.

His descent into degradation and humiliation is remorseless. He turns away from all offers of help but eventually comes crawling back to his mother in a pitiful state, begging for money outside the door while she weeps inside. Although well played by DiCaprio, as the young, artistic but deeply tortured soul, there are no great insights into addiction and, at the end telling his tale to an audience, the rather beatific smile on his face is all a little too good to be true. There is, however, one insightful moment worth a special mention – another important point made by a secondary character.

At his lowest ebb, Jim is sleeping rough in a derelict building. He sits talking to another user who says that his mother has been nagging him to go to church and 'put yourself in Christ's hands'. 'I go, man, High Mass, the choir and everything, and the first thing I see on the right, the side altar, are those little candles in the glass, in the red glass that we used to use when it was windy to cook up in. And then, man, this altar boy he's comin' down the aisle with this six-foot candle and I had this vision of this huge spoon with shopping bags full of dope inside of it. Then the priest starts doing the thing with the incense and it's wafting out and I'm in the back and it finally hits me – where do I know that smell from? It's the smell exactly of really primo dope cookin' up. Exactly the same.' He starts to prepare some heroin by heating the drug in a spoon over a candle. 'At that point, I split. I went home, went into my closet, got my stash out of the inside pocket of my sharkskin Easter suit and I got stoned. I love the ritual.'

As many drug users do. We have spoken of the incessant nostalgic search for the first buzz, the comfort and security of the predictable experience and the pull of the lifestyle. And there is also the love of the ritual. Some users just revel in the whole procedure. There's all the paraphernalia, the stash, the spoon, the lemon juice to break down the heroin, the lighter, the cotton wool to filter out some of the impurities, and the tourniquet. You set it all out, cook up the heroin, find the vein, tie off and prepare the syringe for shooting up. Some enjoy the experience of shooting up so much they'll shoot warm water if there's no heroin to hand.

At one point in New York in the early 1980s, the purity of heroin was down to less than five per cent, a level at which it would be very difficult to become seriously addicted. Yet the users were all out there taking care of business just like Bobby in *Needle Park*. One who was interviewed for British TV said that with the drugs so weak, it was all about being in the life, of having a sense of purpose and then going through the whole thing of shooting up.

Trainspotting (1995)

This is *the* seminal British film about heroin addiction, which has grown in importance way beyond its conception and is now written about as a major landmark in British cinema history.[13]

If *Trainspotting* had been a standard social realism film about addiction, it would have caused only a minor stir. Instead, it became one of the most controversial British movies since *A Clockwork Orange*. Specifically, the film provoked accusations of glamorising heroin use because of its playful style, pace and dark humour – 'opium doesn't grow on trees, you know'; 'for all the good they've done me [opium suppositories] I might as well have stuck them up my arse'.

Set in the underbelly of 1980's Edinburgh, the film chronicles the adventures of Mark Renton (Ewan McGregor) and the motley crew he shares a flat with – the dapper Sick Boy and the manic speed-freak Spud. Sharing a flat with them is Alison, who has a baby, Dawn, by one of the other three. Also numbered in the crew is Tommy, who at the start is healthy and drug-free and who lives with his girlfriend Lizzie and the drinking psycho Begbie.

The film takes us through episodes in the lives of this group both collectively and individually. Spud goes for jobs and makes sure he doesn't get them. Mark pulls a woman and ends up back at her house only to find she is a 14-year-old schoolgirl. Tommy loses the video of him and Lizzie making love. There's a dealer called Mother Superior on account of the length of his habit, and Renton dives headlong into the toilet in search of opium suppositories. All this is wrapped up with the plethora of scams and wheezes of the addict life on the streets and the quiet moments with Renton flat on his back stoned.

Then *Trainspotting* takes a darker turn. Dawn's baby dies in her cot, Spud is jailed for shoplifting and Renton first ODs and then undergoes cold turkey under lock and key at home. Realising he must get away, Renton heads for London and a job as an estate agent. But Begbie and Sick Boy both turn up on his doorstep. All three are called back to Scotland for the funeral of the once-clean Tommy, who has died of AIDS, and while there Begbie scores £4,000-worth of heroin. With Spud now out of jail, the gang sell the stash for £16,000, which Renton (finally seeing a way out of the life) steals, leaving Spud's share in a left-luggage locker.

All the most telling comments about addiction, touching on many of the points we have already raised, are done as voice-overs by Renton – statements aimed directly at the audience. With films like *Addict, Drugstore Cowboy* and *Basketball Diaries*, observations about the positive side of heroin use from the user's viewpoint are part of the internal dialogue of the film. But in *Trainspotting*, they are in your face, which (apart from the lovingly shot scenes of using) are central to the shock value of the film and subsequent condemnations.

Right from the start, as he runs from shop security guards, Renton mocks the values of straight society. He wants to acquire the same material goods as we all do, but only to sell them on to buy drugs. Accompanied by Iggy Pop's 'Lust for Life', Renton sneers: 'Choose life. Choose a job. Choose a career. Choose a family. Choose a fucking big television. Choose washing machines, cars, compact disc players and electrical tin openers.'

'Choose good health, low cholesterol and dental insurance. Choose fixed-interest mortgage repayments. Choose a starter home. Choose your friends.'

'Choose leisurewear and matching luggage. Choose a three-piece suite on hire purchase in a range of fucking fabrics. Choose DIY and wondering who the fuck you are on a Sunday morning. Choose sitting on that couch watching mind-numbing, spirit-crushing game shows, stuffing fucking junk food into your mouth. Choose rotting away at the end of it all, pissing your last in a miserable home, nothing more than an embarrassment to the selfish fucked-up brats you have spawned to replace yourself. Choose your future. Choose your life.'

Renton challenges full-on some of the primary stereotypes of heroin use: 'People think it's all about misery and desperation and death and all that shite, which is not to be ignored, but what they forget is the pleasure of it. Otherwise we wouldn't do it. After all, we're not fucking stupid. At least not that fucking stupid. Take the best orgasm you ever had, multiply it by a thousand and you're still nowhere near it. When you're on junk you have only one worry: scoring. When you're off it you are suddenly obliged to worry about all other sorts of shite. Got no money: can't get pished. Got money: drinking too much. Can't get a bird: no chance of a ride. You have to worry about bills, about food, about some football team that never fucking wins, about human relationships and all the things that really don't matter when you've got a sincere and truthful junk habit.'

He goes straight to the heart of the appeal of drugs for many young people. Having listed all the drugs they have taken, Renton says: 'Fuck it, we would have injected vitamin C if only they'd made it illegal.'

Finally, he makes explicit what we know from *Needle Park, Addict* and *Drugstore Cowboy*: 'It looks easy, this, but it's not. It looks like a doss, like a soft option, but living like this, it's a full-time business.'

At the end, he goes through the whole materialistic, consumer-focused list again, only instead of dissing normality he's embracing it – with a little help from £16,000 of drug money, of course.

Gridlocked (1996)

The first drug buddy movie brilliantly played out by Tim Roth (Stretch) and the late rap star Tupac Shakur (Spoon) and the first and only movie to attack the bureaucratic hoops that users have to jump through in order to get treatment. The two friends are desperate to get on to a methadone programme by the end of the day while on the run from dealers they have ripped off and the police who want them for a murder investigation.

Stretch, Spoon and a woman, Cookie, arrive back at their flat after a successful gig for their jazz/poetry group. Cookie tries heroin for the first time and slips into a coma. They get her to hospital and then resolve to kick the habit. Cookie's coma sobers up her man Spoon to the Russian roulette they are playing with their lives. He says to Stretch: 'We don't even get high on this shit no more. This shit ain't no fun no more.'

But first Stretch rips off the area's main dealer, D-Reper (played by the film's director and writer, Curtis Hall), with a fake video camera and takes the money to their own connection for one last hit before the detox.

However, they can't get into the programme unless they have a Medicaid card. If they agree to take an HIV test, they can get in quicker, otherwise it's six weeks. They are given a yellow card, which gets them on an HIV-tested waiting list and then it's a week to ten days to get into detox, and that's when they need to have the Medicaid card. They go off to a local rehab centre to try there. They are ninety-first and ninety-second in line, with more forms to fill out. They fall asleep and miss their turn. When they get to the desk, they are told that the centre is now only for alcoholics, not drug users. Next step – temporary Medicaid. They go to Welfare to tell them it's an emergency and they need to get into detox. But they can't get temporary Medicaid cards unless they are already on Welfare. And they can't get the cards anyway unless it is a medical necessity. Stretch loses his rag. The Welfare man is not sympathetic and sends them to the Medicaid office. When they get there, they find that the office moved out three weeks previously and they get sent back to where they have just come from. Yet more forms to fill in back at Social Security. By the time they get to the desk, it's almost five o'clock and the clerk tells them they are not giving out any more appointments and to come back tomorrow. But even if they had got the appointment, they would still have had to come back in a week to ten days to see an interviewer to get emergency Medicaid. The interviewer reviews the case, then they notify by mail, which can take another month. There was never any chance they could have got Medicaid in a day. Then they find out that the only way to get on is if they are HIV positive. But then you need a letter of proof from a doctor. And they need the test results that they can't get until tomorrow. Then Stretch announces that he is HIV positive. Spoon didn't know.

The frustrations of Spoon and Stretch make for good comedy, but this is the reality for many drug users trying to get into treatment, both in the US and in the UK. A British drugs worker once developed a role-play game for use in training to demonstrate the frustrations of the system. The game was a great success – those who played became very angry that they couldn't make progress towards securing a treatment appointment.

One major difference between the American and British approach to drugs was the willingness back in the 1980s for the UK to supply users with free needles and syringes to help prevent the spread of HIV. For most Americans, this smacked of the worst excesses of liberalism. Stretch turns on the TV in time to catch a phone-in programme on the subject: 'Addicts – do we really want to give them free needles?' And this is in the mid-1990s.

As Kim Newman said in his review for *Sight and Sound* (June 1997), Roth and Shakur are 'sweet-natured holy fools rather than horrifying exemplars of dead-end American nihilism'. For Spoon read straight man Oliver Hardy; for Stretch read a goofy, bemused and semi-suicidal version of Stan Laurel prepared to call a black dealer 'Nigger' to his face and then stare unflinchingly down the barrel of the automatic levelled at him – one of several fine messes for Spoon to sort out.

Spoon's account of his first taste of heroin is another epiphany of childlike innocence. He was at a rich white boy's house – a college friend who often invited black kids to his big house to hang out when his parents were away. They were smoking a bit of weed and drinking rum. And then somebody turns up with some white powder – nobody knew what it was, but they tried some anyway. Everybody was sick as a dog. But for Spoon – and he struggles to find the words – 'that shit was like going back to the womb . . . I never felt such peace. I was home. I was 16 fuckin' years old. First I'd just get fucked up at the weekend . . . Somehow I don't think this was what my parents dreamed for me.' Ann

Marlowe expressed similar sentiments: 'Dope was home, a psychic space that filled the essential functions of the physical construct, providing a predictable comfort and security. Heroin becomes the place where, when you showed up, they had to let you in.'[14] But eventually he faces a new reality: 'If gettin' high's turnin' into a job – what's the point? Getting high is supposed to be fun.'

Permanent Midnight (1998)

Comedian Ben Stiller plays the screenwriter Jerry Stahl in this biopic of his life as a heroin addict.

The film opens with Stiller working in a fast-food outlet. He goes off with a customer, Kitty, to a motel and they have sex . . . almost. 'I'm sorry I've never done this straight before. Trust me, on smack I was a real stud.' Kitty's been off drugs for seven years, he for ninety-two days. Having come through rehab, he is on his way back to LA, to try to pick up his career as a writer for kids' TV programmes. He says in all seriousness that he moved to LA from New York 'to get away from drugs . . . I miscalculated.'

He has a casual girlfriend, Sandra (Liz Hurley), who needs a green card to stay in the country and they get married in an all-night chapel. She works for the producer of a kids' puppet programme, Mr Chompers, and Stiller gets the gig writing for the show if he can turn a duff script into a good one, which he does under the influence of 'enough pot to blind an ox and whatever else was laying around.'

Instead of Jim Carroll's Catholic guilt, we have Stahl's Jewish guilt, which seems to tie in somehow to his father's suicide, his mother's increasing infirmity, but moreover that underlying sense of never being good enough to match up to everybody's expectations. Although these are never explicitly punted as reasons for Stahl's drug use, we see somebody whose self-esteem couldn't really be much lower. In trying to pump himself up to deal with the world, and come to terms with the fact that he is a writer of serious fiction selling his soul to Hollywood, he simply drugs himself into incoherence and out of work. The knife twists further when his mother, too, commits suicide.

Kitty deserts him, so he goes back to LA and moves in with Sandra to begin a bizarre life combining healthy eating and jogging with injecting

heroin – as he says, he *is* an LA junkie – and writing for Mr Chompers.
He is on self-destruct all through the film, losing jobs and messing up a
big literary agent who wants to help his career.

Stahl appears himself in the film as a very cynical drug-treatment
doctor. From the other side of the counter with his back to 'Jerry', he
goes through the standard health checklist then says: 'Think you can
kick?'

'Excuse me?'

'Methadone will get rid of the shakes, but basically you're trading
one habit for another and you wanna quit. It's up to you.'

'Well, that's very informative. Thank you.'

'How long you been using?'

'A couple of years.'

'You won't make it. It's a cycle. Probably be using again in a month
and back here etc. etc. I'll start you off on a 80-milligramme, 21-day
detox. Show up here once a week and piss in a cup.' 'Any questions?'

'Piss in a cup? You don't sound very optimistic.'

'You want optimistic? Some people make it, some people end up
dead. Good luck.'

Jesus' Son (2000)

Yet another modern addiction movie set in the early 1970s, this one is
based on the short stories of Denis Johnson (with the title from Lou
Reed's song 'Heroin'), who takes us to Idaho and the tales of the gentle,
disaster-prone Fuckhead (aka FH, played by Billy Crudup) and his
fable-like odyssey to redemption. At the start of the movie he is involved
in a car crash while hitchhiking. He returns to his apartment and is
visited by his ex-girlfriend, Michelle. FH reminisces as voiceover about
meeting Michelle (Samantha Morton) for the first time at a party. Both
heroin users, they move in together. FH agrees to help Wayne, whom he
meets in a bar, strip a house of its copper wiring. Wayne rationalises that
this cannot be theft because the house used to be his until it was
repossessed. With the money raised, they both buy heroin. Both go
home and both OD – Wayne dies, but FH is revived by Michelle. FH
gets a job in a hospital, where he and a workmate (Jack Black) rob the
hospital pharmacy. Eventually, after tripping out, FH returns home,

where Michelle tells him she is pregnant. But she has an abortion and leaves FH for another man.

After the car crash, FH and Michelle get back together, but after an argument Michelle dies of an overdose. Grief-stricken, FH tries to kill himself with heroin but is sent to a rehab. The film ends when, some months later, we find FH working at a hospice in Arizona. 'There's a price to be paid for dreaming,' says one deranged patient, who grabs FH as he walks past.

Like Joe in *Trash*, FH is one of those who bob and weave as the waves of life take them, generally good-hearted and wanting to do the right thing despite his transgressions along the way. And this is the mood of the whole film, a languid portrait of listless Americana where very ordinary people shoot heroin in very ordinary towns in very mundane circumstances. Some die, and nobody knows or cares.

Requiem for a Dream (2001)

A relentlessly morbid and very stylish *Reefer Madness* for the millennium played out as two parallel stories. The more arresting concerns Sara Goldfarb (played by Ellen Burstyn) as a middle-aged, overweight widow whose only comforts are the TV and eating. She receives a phone call telling her that she has been chosen to appear on her favourite show. Suddenly, she is a celebrity among the other women in her apartment block and she becomes obsessed with fitting into the red dress she has long outgrown. Ordinary diets fail, so she goes to a slimming clinic, which feeds her a steady stream of amphetamine-based tablets. The weight comes off, but so do her wheels as she rapidly descends into amphetamine psychosis – the TV game show stars come into her living room to mock her as a pathetic old woman; the fridge hunts her down. Now totally deranged, she goes to the TV studio, where the security guards call an ambulance and have her committed to a mental hospital, where she is subjected to force-feeding and ECT and ends up as a vegetable.

Sara's son Harry, his girlfriend Marion and best friend Tyrone feature in the parallel story. For drug money, Harry regularly hocks his mother's TV, which she patiently redeems. All three are users, but this does not appear to be out of control. At one point Harry tells his mother that he doesn't really know why he uses drugs; Tyrone lost his mother when he was eight, while Marion is in rebellion against her rich parents, who ignore her save for paying her rent and psychiatrist's bills.

They all have dreams. Sara wants to be on TV, Harry and Tyrone dream of saving up enough money to buy a pound of pure heroin, which they will cut and sell so they can retire from the streets. Harry in turn wants to use his share to set up Marion, a talented clothes designer, in her own store.

Things go well at first. They buy small bags of heroin to sell on and the money begins to pile up. Then a war breaks out between Harry and Tyrone's black drug-dealing connection and the Mafia. Tyrone gets caught up in the trouble, is arrested and has all the money confiscated. This causes a shortage on the streets, and the three friends realise their heroin use has moved beyond 'take it or leave it'.

It is the last 20 minutes that took away the breath (and lunch) of both audience and critics – a wild, cross-cutting, free fall into hell as all the major protagonists pay for their addiction. In the other films discussed, the users are pulled back from the brink. In *Drugstore Cowboy*, Bob gets shot but survives; Bobby in *Panic* lives to fight many more days; Renton walks away with a bag of money; Christiane's mother spirits her away to safety. Here, the full horror of retribution is delivered in spades.

Director Daniel Aronofsky based his highly controversial film on the novel by Hubert Selby in the 12 weeks of Selby's recovery from life-threatening pneumonia. And what he wrote was more than just a tale of heroin addiction. It is really about the dangers of chasing the Great American Dream and A Better Life Through Chemistry.

As a lonely widow, Sara feels she can only recover her sense of self-worth through appearing on the TV. All the old Jewish yentas in her building sit outside during the day and just the promise of a TV appearance quite literally gets Sara her 15 minutes in the sun. She tells her son: 'You see who had the sun seat? You notice your mother in the special spot getting the sun? You know who everybody talks to? You know who's somebody now? Who's no longer just a widow in an apartment who lives alone? I'm somebody now, Harry. Everyone likes me. Soon millions of people will see me and like me. I'll tell them about you and your father. I'll tell them how your father liked the red dress and how good he was to us. Remember?'

Harry and Tyrone dream of being off the streets and Harry dreams of earning the money for Marion's store. One subtle measure of how badly awry these plans have gone is Tyrone sitting in the police station flicking through a copy of *Fortune* magazine, now as far away from his dream as he can get.

The central relationship in the film is not between Harry and Marion but between Harry and his mother. Interviewed by the *Guardian* (12 January 2001) Hubert Selby said: 'I wanted a strong relationship between Sara and Harry to emphasise the nature of the problem. Most addicts are people with families, hopes, dreams, the same as anyone else. Most addicts are not living on the streets, stealing for a fix. Most are middle-class people with love in their lives who go to their doctor or pharmacists for drugs. It could be said that Sara's love was suffocating, oppressive at times, but it was also grounded in wanting the very best for her son.'

Like Jerry Stahl, Harry is crushed by Jewish guilt. He loves his mother dearly, worries for her happiness. As he starts earning as a dealer, he buys her a new TV. He knows this is her drug of choice as much as heroin is his. He is also very concerned when he discovers that his mother is hooked on amphetamine. She knows he hocks her TV for money but doesn't know why and so she can't understand how he can challenge the wisdom of the nice doctor who is helping her lose weight.

How can we sum all this up? Every picture tells a story, but no picture can tell the whole story. At bottom, addiction is a deeply complex phenomenon and truly does involve the broadest categories of people and personality types in all possible personal, social and cultural situations who get into a chronic relationship with heroin and other drugs for every conceivable reason. As Neil Young wrote: 'I've seen the needle and the damage done/A little part of it in everyone.'

The films that most people can understand and accept are those like the 1950s films described earlier, *Basketball Diaries* and *Permanent Midnight*, where heroin users are portrayed as essentially weak characters who are tempted, fall from grace, suffer for their sins and are then redeemed. *Panic in Needle Park*, *Drugstore Cowboy*, *Trainspotting* and

Gridlocked present an altogether more dangerous, challenging and threatening scenario – a heroin-driven life outside the envelope as (for a while anyway) a positive career option bringing routine, ritual and a perverse security into otherwise aimless, drifting lives. Having struggled with the idea through the 1970s that heroin had come out of the ghetto and was now everybody's problem, by the mid-1980s America realised that the drug it fell in love with during the same period and which was thought harmless was anything but.

10

Snowblind friends: cocaine returns to Hollywood

The biggest moneymaker in Hollywood last year was Colombia. Not the studio – the country.

Johnny Carson, 1981 Academy Awards

Since its first appearance as the new wonder drug, cocaine had been a legal pick-me-up, praised by some doctors, vilified by others; a legal recreational drug of urban street urchins and an illicit status symbol for movie stars. *The Pace That Kills* (1928) and its talkie remake, *Cocaine Fiends* (1936), portrayed coke as the teenage gateway drug to morphine and heroin. With the Production Code tightening its grip, Chaplin as the convict in *Modern Times* (1936) who accidentally swallows some coke and saves the prison from a riot, was the last blush of drug humour for nearly 40 years. But as war approached, the single most remarkable fact about cocaine was that it had largely disappeared as an illicit street drug. The Mayor's Committee for New York City declared that 'cocaine as an addiction has ceased to be a problem'. The decline of cocaine use was the one thing that liberal sociologist Alfred Lindesmith and Bureau of Narcotics Chief Harry Anslinger could agree on. So what happened? During the 1930s, amphetamine made its appearance in the medical market, but it would not be until after the war that consumption would soar as new pill formulations were gobbled up by women desperate to lose weight and truck drivers desperate to stay awake. So what else?

The production of cocaine pre-war was very different from today. There were no processing laboratories in South America. Instead, coca was shipped to America, where it was processed into cocaine for the medical market by legitimate pharmaceutical companies like Parke, Davis. But cocaine had been gathering such a bad press that one by one the manufacturers pulled out. By the 1930s, Merck and Maywood (who processed coca leaves for Coca-Cola) were the only two pharmaceutical companies left in the legal cocaine market. With so few legitimate manufacturers to police, the enforcement agencies found it relatively easy to control supply as opposed to the unregulated market of today dominated by a complex network of violent gangsters and smugglers using underground laboratories in out-of-the-way places.

While cocaine was being outlawed in the States, US-backed 'scientific research' was undermining traditional use of the coca leaf in Peru. The US paid for coca studies that purported to show that coca, used by the indigenous population for thousands of years, had the same harmful effects as cocaine. A special United Nations Commission was set up to investigate the health effects of coca. Collared by a journalist, the Commission President, Howard Fonda, a close friend of Harry Anslinger, condemned the plant even before the study commenced. A further blow to the livelihood of Peruvian coca farmers was the breaking of their monopoly by the Dutch and the Japanese, who exported the plant to Indonesia, much as Brazilian rubber had been stolen by colonial robber barons to start the industry in Malaya.

With American cocaine production shut down, the coca plant attacked by the international diplomatic and scientific community and their growing monopoly lost overseas, the Peruvian coca farmers found no legitimate outlet for their product and threw in their lot with a new and ultimately highly lucrative customer.

Cuba was the key to the door that would eventually open the floodgates of cocaine into America. Less than an hour's flight from mainland America, Cuba had long been a bolt-hole for gangsters and bootleggers. In 1952 Fulgencio Batista took over the country and immediately struck deals with the Mafia's top brass, Bugsy Siegal and Meyer Lansky, who invested heavily in the island's tourist industry. But they had other business interests, including drugs. Lansky had been the brains behind the French Connection, running heroin through Cuba on its way to the States. But heroin was not a drug for the fun island of Cuba. With no need for needles and all the old Hollywood images of glamour, mystery and expense still in place, cocaine became the perfect party drug for rich Americans on holiday. Lansky knew the plant grew in Peru and Bolivia, but where to refine it for convenient transport to Cuba? The answer was Chile, where the government helpfully ordered the army to assist the Mafia transport cocaine to Cuba. Through the 1950s, the Mafia looked for other cocaine suppliers to spread the risk – Colombians and Mexicans – from countries steeped in smuggling traditions.

Batista and his mobster cronies were thrown out by Castro in 1959. The now-exiled anti-Communist Cubans living in Florida received CIA training to help them plot the overthrow of Castro, in return for the proverbial blind eye turned to increasing smuggling of all kinds, including cocaine. Much of US foreign policy has been based on the idea that being anti-Communist was way more important than being anti-drug. And if you needed a bit of help on the drugs front to strengthen your economy (or line your pockets) and increase the robustness of your anti-Communist stance – so be it. The breaking of the French Connection and economic depression in Colombia both gave added impetus to the growth of the cocaine trade that Hollywood was to embrace so enthusiastically.

When Peter Fonda came up with his idea of two friends earning a pile of money from a drug deal and heading for Florida into retirement, they had to decide what drug they would be selling. Marijuana was too bulky; heroin had too much of a bad image. It was Dennis Hopper who suggested cocaine: 'I had got it from Benny Shapiro, the music promoter, who had gotten it from Duke Ellington.'[1] When famous music producer Phil Spector in his cameo role in what became *Easy Rider* is seen sampling the wares in the movie, he is sniffing baking soda. Not because cocaine was illegal, but at over $1,000 an ounce the budget couldn't handle it. The film was important in the rehabilitation of cocaine as the drug of the rich and powerful, first the rock musicians, then once again, like the 1920s, the movie stars.

By the mid-1960s, the major Hollywood studios were in trouble. Audiences were falling as families stayed in to watch television. The average age of cinema audiences was also falling, and this new 1960s teenage audience did not want to see standard Hollywood fare. They wanted films they could relate to. The classic Hollywood studio system dominated by an autocratic studio head like Harry Cohn at Columbia or Louis Mayer at MGM was replaced by an industry that fêted young directors like Martin Scorsese, Francis Coppola, William Friedkin and Bob Rafelson and the next generation of stars like Dustin Hoffman, Robert Redford, Jack Nicholson and Robert de Niro. Those who made and went to see films like *Easy Rider, Five Easy Pieces* (1970), *The Godfather*

(1972) and *The Exorcist* (1973) were also part of the rock 'n' roll generation, and the new Hollywood elite were captivated by rock music. Actors hung out with musicians, and rock soundtracks now propelled many movies. A new era of Hollywood excess was under way driven by a blizzard of cocaine.

According to Jack Nicholson, cocaine was 'well suited to the driven megalomaniacal macho lifestyle of Hollywood – in your brain, you're bulletproof; you can write, you can act, you can direct.'[2] Director Paul Schrader, who wrote *Taxi Driver* (1976), was a major drug user in the 1970s who acknowledged the upside of using cocaine and drugs generally: 'Out of the drug taking came a lot of swampy ideas, but also a lot of creative thinking and, most importantly, breaking down of personal barriers and that ridiculousness of pride and holding one to oneself and a phoney social persona. If that hadn't been the case, none of us would have developed our talents.'[3] On the set of his 1978 film *Blue Collar*, a line producer put a vial of cocaine in front of Schrader telling him it would make him work better. Martin Scorsese was another who used cocaine to stimulate the creative juices: 'I kept pushing and shoving and twisting and turning myself in different ways and I started taking drugs to explore.'[4] When he first started using cocaine, producer Robert Evans felt he could 'make five films at once'.[5] Another coke-fuelled producer was Don Simpson, who (for better or worse) made millions for Hollywood with the so-called 'High-concept' movies like *Beverly Hills Cop* (1984) and *Top Gun* (1986). The idea was conceived and driven by cocaine, films which threw the audience into an adrenalin-stimulant ride, a vicarious coke experience. The hero rushes off at a lick, falls into a pit of despair (the coke crash) and ends on another high. Simpson would be up most of the night dictating memos that his secretaries would type up the next day. 'The memos themselves were rambling and unfocused, but within their manic maelstrom were always bits and pieces of true genius, the crystallised flakes of story and character that would ultimately turn into blockbuster movies.'[6]

As well as driving the creative spirit, cocaine was the perfect drug for dealing with the enormous pressures of the industry itself. The cocaine experience mirrored precisely the experience of working in the film industry as a star, a director or a studio executive – the short-lived soaring high of success and the crashing depression of failure anxiety and paranoia hovering over every studio.

In her autobiography, producer Julia Phillips, one of the most notorious Hollywood coke users of the 1970s, said of *Taxi Driver*. 'It's a cokey movie. Big pressure, short schedule and short money. New York in the summer. Night shooting. I have only visited the set once and they are all doing blow. I don't see it. I just know it.'[7]

One film producer commented about cocaine: 'It's the '70s drug. . . I think our generation is now more into productivity than creativity . . . It comes with growing up a little. To take psychedelics, it takes three days – one to prepare, one to drop and one to recover. Who has that kind of time in this town? Coke is really easy – a toot here, a toot there. Of course, you have the occasional lost weekend when you do maybe a gramme or two . . . But it's a neat drug – makes you feel good, you can function on it . . . It's getting bigger all the time.'

As the first woman producer to break through the Hollywood glass ceiling, Julia Phillips felt a special pressure to succeed: 'I take a little toot and I am ten feet tall. That is really all you need to do to be a good producer; you have to convince them that you are ten feet tall all the time. And that you can do something a little crazy. So they had better watch it.'[8] As a major-league appetite suppressant, cocaine had an additional appeal for women in the body-image-dominated world of entertainment and fashion. In that sense, it is more of an equal-opportunities drug than heroin. However, like sex, when men sleep around they are 'lads' while women are 'sluts': with coke the woman asking for coke is tagged a 'coke whore'. Julia Phillips said she always had to be careful on that score: 'It's always better in the power equation if you give rather than receive. Particularly if you are a woman. Particularly with coke.'[9]

Cocaine was the warp and weft of Hollywood's social fabric. As Robert Sabbag wrote: 'To snort cocaine is to make a statement. It's like flying to Paris for breakfast . . . It's what's happenin'. And at a thousand dollars an ounce it is probably not happenin' to you.'[10] No Hollywood party was complete without coke set out in bowls and dishes. At Jack Nicholson's place, there was the 'upstairs' top-drawer coke for VIPs and the 'downstairs' coke for the also-rans. Julia Phillips used so much she had her own supplies of Peruvian coke smuggled in by a gang of surfers. One non-using executive complained that at industry functions it was impossible to get to the lavatory for the lines of people queuing up to do their lines.

If you look back into the history of drugs, you find that any drug adopted by the upper echelons more readily finds acceptance lower down in society – tobacco and coffee being two good examples. And so it was with cocaine in the 1970s. Where the media aristocracy led, others followed: cocaine became a drug of its time to 'reinforce and boost what we recognise as the highest aspirations of American initiative, energy, frenetic achievement and ebullient optimism'.[11]

For an illegal drug, it had an incredibly clean image; it looked clean – white, sparkly, fluffy and pharmaceutical. *Esquire* put a gold coke spoon on its front cover. *Newsweek* in 1971 described cocaine as 'the status symbol of the American middle-class pothead'. The *New York Times* Magazine heralded 'Cocaine: the champagne of drugs'. Leisure Time Products advertised sterling-silver cocaine accessories in *High Times* magazine, and patrons of the Beverly Hills Head Shop could pay over $2000 for a coke spoon. The *Hi-Life* magazine cover for January 1979 announced: 'Hollywood Goes Better With Coke'.

The first modern writings on cocaine underpinned this unalloyed enthusiasm. In 1974 *Esquire* published extracts of a work in progress, a novel by Bruce Jay Friedman, *About Harry Towns*, describing the early 1970s coke scene as experienced by a successful screenwriter. Towns becomes a heavy user, but he doesn't fall apart, doesn't become an aggressive brutal coke fiend. Cocaine is an important part of Harry's life, but is still only a part.

The following year, journalist Richard Ashley published a history of cocaine which claimed that there was no medical basis in all the scare stories about cocaine prior to control in 1914 and that it was racism alone that drove the legislation.

Two eminent drug researchers, Lester Grinspoon and James Bakalar, published *Cocaine: A Drug and Its Social Evolution* in 1976. Like Ashley, they took the reader on a historical journey looking at traditional uses of coca and the modern history of cocaine, attempting to explain how cocaine acquired the fiendish image that resulted in control. What the book did reveal was the lack of current scientific evidence as to the dangers of the drug. There were no 'captive' groups of clinical patients for researchers to study. Few ordinary people were coming forward with cocaine problems, because to have a problem you had to be using a lot of cocaine for most of the time – and the only people who could afford to do that in the 1970s were very rich Hollywood types. Medical papers written during the early to mid 1970s largely relied on studies conducted several decades earlier. But these studies tended to be dismissed by contemporary commentators, both because it was assumed that their methodology would now not be clinically rigorous enough and because they were published in a climate of 1920s and 1930s scaremongering and panic.

Cocaine's benign image was further underscored by the observation that it was not physically addictive in the same way as heroin. Those who stop using do not go into sweats and convulsions like the classic heroin withdrawal. Nobody throws themselves around, banging off the walls like Gene Hackman in *The French Connection*. Because just about the worst thing you say about a drug is that it's addictive – even more than it can kill you. After all, any painkiller you can buy in the supermarket can kill you if you take enough. You can die crossing the road or walking down the stairs. But the word 'addiction' carries with it a whole baggage of slow decline, degradation, lies, deception, crime, misery, ill health and needles – all from the need to have that fix. None of that was associated with cocaine because most people could have the odd toot without coming to any obvious harm – there was no 'one hit and you're hooked' Armageddon awaiting the hapless experimenter.

Not only doctors gave coke the thumbs up. Irving Swank, deputy director of Chicago's Bureau of Narcotics told *Newsweek* (27 September 1971): 'So much publicity has gone out on heroin that people don't want to get started on it. But you get a good high on coke and you don't get hooked.' Given the American establishment view on drugs, this was an extraordinary statement for an American narcotics officer to make and shows the degree to which cocaine rapidly swam through the collective consciousness of the nation as a drug that was only illegal on a technicality. In 1977 the Carter Administration gave active consideration to reducing the penalties for cocaine possession, while a Massachusetts municipal court judge declared that classifying cocaine as a 'narcotic' (i.e. in US legal parlance a dangerous drug) was 'irrational', stemming from the mythology that had grown up about cocaine over the years.

The image of cocaine was unchanged from the 1920s: the drug was expensive and large consumption was associated with high living. But in the 1970s the use of the drug was increasing dramatically through the general population in America. This is best exemplified in film by the coke party scene in Paul Shrader's 1978 film *Blue Collar*, starring Richard Pryor and Harvey Keitel, about car assembly-line workers and their run-in with a corrupt union. People bought not so much a drug, but an image, the coke spoon, the rolled-up banknote, the symbol of what that drug meant, the personal statement its use made, the status, the gourmet trip. Relatively pure cocaine produces feelings of energy, mental alertness and power. But the effects are subtle and you might have to learn how you are feeling – even with high-quality coke because first-time users might not realise they are high. 'Cocaine has no edge. It is strictly a motor drug. It does not alter your perception; it will not even wire you up like amphetamines. No pictures, no time/space warping, no danger, no fun, no edge . . . Coke is to acid what jazz is to rock. You have to appreciate it. *It* does not come to *you*.'[12] By 1986 official figures showed that nearly ten per cent of the US population, that's 25 million people, were hip to the jive of the cocaine high.

And what were all these people buying? Why did cocaine take America by storm? How the drug works in the brain is the key to why people go on coke binges until the drug or the money runs out. Cocaine triggers all the pleasure centres in the brain at once – a bit like experiencing the pleasure of a great meal, a warm bath and top sex all at once. And it keeps on doing it – there isn't a tolerance with cocaine; you don't have to take increasing doses to get the same effect, you take more because you want more. With a drug like heroin, it's different. The chronic user has to keep upping the dose to get any effect at all and ends up using regularly not to get high but just to stave off the withdrawal and stop feeling sick.

But when you take coke, flight and fight brain chemicals are released into the brain, and then the coke prevents the brain from reabsorbing the chemicals for when they are needed for real flight or fight situations. This leaves the chemicals sloshing around all dressed up with nowhere to go. Because they have been released when they weren't really needed, the user is left feeling very tense, agitated, edgy and, with continued use, highly anxious and paranoid – in other words, your off-the-shelf standard-issue New York or LA rock musician, film star, studio executive or high financier. No wonder nobody noticed anything was wrong.

In October 1979 the US Congress Select Committee on Narcotics Abuse and Control held special hearings on the subject of 'cocaine – a major drug issue of the 1970s.' Representative Wolff told his congressional colleagues: 'I assure you that if many people in the entertainment industry knew the hazards that they are facing, they wouldn't be snorting the amount of cocaine they are.' Behind the scenes, some knew all too well.

Several leading lights of New Hollywood found themselves in trouble with cocaine and other drugs during the 1970s and early 1980s – actors and actresses including Richard Dreyfuss, Robin Williams, Richard Pryor, Steve McQueen, Judy Kahn, Louise Lasser, Stacey Keach; directors Martin Scorsese, Paul Schrader and Hal Ashby; producers Julia Phillips, Robert Evans and Don Simpson. On the set of *New York, New York* (1977), Scorsese was often sick and late on the set. The following year, weighing only just over seven stones, he almost died from internal haemorrhaging. Robert Evans wrote that hitting the coke hard sent him to bed four days a week 'because you were exhausted and your body couldn't take it . . . what started up as a fuck drug all but ruined my fucking life'. When Paul Schrader moved up to a gramme of coke a day 'then it wasn't fun any more. After writing all night and finding the next morning I only had a page and a half, I realised I wasn't producing. It got to the point where I couldn't hit the keys. I got paranoid, I couldn't focus.'[13] By the time he died of a heart attack aged 52, blockbuster producer Don Simpson was spending $60,000 a month on prescription drugs – the list of drugs takes up nearly a page in Charles Fleming's biography – on top of unknown thousands spent on coke.

Some of those who got into the worst problems were deeply troubled and driven spirits who were badly served by so-called friends and the industry itself. When comedian John Belushi, star of the TV show *Saturday Night Live* and *The Blues Brothers* (1980) died on 5 March 1982 at the Chateau Marmont Hotel on Sunset Strip, he became the first celebrity coke fatality.

Belushi got into coke in 1974–5 along with his fellow stars on *Saturday Night Live*, when cocaine was the logical drug for all of them. It provided a sense of clear-headedness, of intellectual power, and it kept them awake as they wrote, polished and rehearsed into the early hours. At one point they did four shows in a row with no break. Nearly everybody did coke to keep going. 'Mirrors and pictures in the staff offices were off the walls and on the desks and were littered with razor blades, makeshift straws and a fine white residue from the cocaine that had been chopped into powder on the hard glass surfaces.'[14]

But coke took its toll on the show. Candice Bergen, who hosted the show twice, noticed the difference when she came to do her second in December 1976. As Bob Woodward wrote, 'The warmth and openness had dissipated and in its place was a cool toughness . . . The pressure had squeezed something vital out of the show and out of the people. They seemed to resent both one another and her. It has become a coke show . . . There was a great deal of talent, but the humanity had been drained out. Drugs, cocaine, was the reason . . . The cast had come to resemble what they were parodying.'[15]

When it came to the shooting of *The Blues Brothers* in 1979 with all the rock musicians on the set, Belushi's use spiralled out of control: he was snorting an estimated four grammes of coke a day. He would never admit he had a problem, reluctantly went to see the occasional shrink and always thought he was in control. Belushi was hooked on the drug/rock lifestyle – he would often stay up for days on end. Sometimes he would refuse drug offers, but people persisted. He would take out a quarter of an ounce – worth $500 to $600 – and lay it out in a single line, several feet long, on an upturned mirror. Then he would challenge someone to start at the other end. Belushi normally won.

He would use drugs to deal with all the pressures of being funny, or recording records, touring, writing etc. – but he would wind himself up still further if he felt the work wasn't challenging. 'You put the heat on yourself,' he once said.

His wife told biographer Bob Woodward: 'Giving or selling drugs to John was a kind of game, like feeding popcorn to the seals at the zoo; give him a little and he would perform, be crazy and outrageous; a little more and he'd stay up all night, outdancing, outdoing, outlasting everyone around him.'[16] Like rock stars, film stars are surrounded by gaggles of hangers-on and gofers who ache to bathe in reflected glory, who make themselves indispensable by supplying drugs – their calling card into a world of power and glamour.

John Belushi had people who cared, who were worried about him – but either they were doing drugs as well or had no control over him whatsoever. There were minders who did their best, tried to keep track of him and keep the dealers away, but it was a forlorn hope. As long as Belushi delivered what was expected, nobody at the studio said a word. In fact, he seems to have been encouraged in his excess. All his bills were paid for by his accountants in New York – limos, credit cards, hotels – but he still got $2,500 a week in cash from the studio – most of which went on coke.

Actor Chevy Chase, who also battled with a cocaine problem, suggested that John Belushi's tragedy was that he was 'just coming to self-knowledge. Entertainers want to be famous and recognised, and there is a long period when that does not happen . . . So when we are successful, we want to go back, want to go home, which is when we were rejected – become a clown, a druggie, a fuck-up . . . Actors search for rejection. If they do not get it, they reject themselves.'

Julia Phillips fought a similar battle with the inner demons of anxiety and depression. Much of her drug use was a process of self-medication out of despair. When she went up to collect the Best Picture Oscar for *The Sting* in 1973, she had worked out her perfect cocktail for the night: 'a diet pill, a small amount of coke, two joints, six halves of valium . . . and a glass and a half of wine.' But that 'small amount of coke' escalated to the point where she couldn't function and she was removed from the making of *Close Encounters of the Third Kind* (1977). Eventually, she managed to come off cocaine, alcohol and all the other drugs she was taking but failed to rekindle her career. She burned her boats with a best-selling 'tell-all' autobiography, *You'll Never Eat Lunch in this Town Again* (1991), and a subsequent less successful novel. She wrote that she was more scared of growing old than dying – a fear she never had to face, succumbing to cancer aged 57 in January 2002.

But the coke problems of Hollywood in the 1970s only came from the revelations of the 1990s. How did Hollywood respond at the time? Did any of these behind-the-scenes problems hit the screen? The short answer is no. There was no longer a Production Code hanging over Hollywood; instead, an unwritten code dictated that you didn't show people having a good time on drugs whatever the payoff. As one producer said, 'if you don't follow the code, Church and civic leaders will be on your back. Gossip columnists will drop your name in bad company and pretty soon the corporation executives will be breathing down your neck.'[17]

There were some coded hints that all might not be well: perhaps in Nicol Williamson's portrayal of Sherlock Holmes's runaway cocaine paranoia in *The Seven Per Cent Solution* (1976). But this was contrasted by the famous scene in Woody Allen's *Annie Hall* (1977) where he sneezes $2,000-worth of top-quality Bolivian flake into the air. Allen pokes fun at the rituals of urban middle-class consumerism of which cocaine was an integral part.

In 1982 *China Syndrome* director James Bridges wrote and directed an underrated low-key movie, *Mike's Murder*, one of the first to lift the lid on Hollywood's coke scene. But apparently the first finished cut was too near the mark. Eventually, the film was re-edited and wasn't released until 1984. A young tennis player, Mike Chuhutsky, coaching at a local club, supplements his income with some small-time coke dealing. Already in trouble for poaching on another dealer's territory, he is tempted by a friend to rip off their supplier and both become targets for revenge. It was not possible to view an original cut of the film, but it might be relevant to the problems the film originally ran into that in the re-edit the Hollywood elite with gangster connections is represented not by a white film producer but by a gay, black rock manager. Mike is murdered, but we never find out exactly who killed him. The point is not so much the 'who' but the 'what'. Bridges is saying that while the image of coke might be upbeat and non-threatening, the reality of how coke reaches patrician noses is very different.

Nineteen eighty-four was also the year in which warning bells began to ring in the media about coke. The big novel of the year, Jay McInerney's *Bright Lights, Big City*, reflected growing unease about the drug among New York's young middle class. By now, Jimmy Carter was gone, and under the Reagan regime the war on drugs was in full swing, fronted by Nancy's 'Just Say No' campaign. Most of the states that had liberalised their cannabis laws returned to more punitive measures – not because cannabis use had shot up in those areas, simply because the political climate had changed. In 1986 Reagan declared that cocaine was the nation's number-one drug menace and Hollywood responded with four anti-coke movies in two years.

First up was a film version of Bret Easton Ellis's novel *Less Than Zero* (1987) in which Robert Downey Jnr starred as Julian, a college graduate with entertainment business aspirations. These resolutely fail to materialise, and in a foretaste of Downey's off-screen problems, Julian's soaring coke habit reduces him to a snivelling wreck, disowned by his family and having sex with men to pay off his dealer debts. The shallowness of Downey's wealthy hedonistic drug-using set is well captured: bored young people with absent parents living empty lives in palatial houses and fashionable clubs. There is tremendous poignancy in Downey's performance: despite Julian's self-destructive lifestyle, which he can never explain, you feel sorry for the character and want him to win through. But although reconciled with his father at the end, redemption comes too late. His body finally packs up as he rides in a car with the only two friends who stuck by him.

James Bridges had another go at a coke movie directing McInerney's novel with a screenplay written by the author. *Bright Lights, Big City* (1988) starred Michael J. Fox as a too-young-looking James Conway, who works as a fact-checker for a New York magazine. Egged on by a yuppie rake, Tad Allagash, played by Keifer Sutherland, James hits the booze and the coke to help him forget the death of his mother a year earlier, his failed marriage to the lovely Amanda and to compensate for literary pretensions never realised. The film covers a week in his chaotic life, but is really *Lost Weekend* for the 1980s – wasted days and misplaced nights in an east coast version of *Less Than Zero*'s drug and disco club scene. In a brilliant cameo as the magazine's drunken, resentful fiction editor, Jason Robards shows James just how far he could fall, and eventually, with blood pouring from his nose, James hits rock bottom. But in a rather contrived ending, he swaps the dark glasses and coke for a healthy loaf of early-morning bread and a possible relationship with Tad's beautiful and intelligent cousin – with no real notion of how he is actually going to make the transition out of the mire.

Released in the same year, *The Boost* featured James Woods as the ill-starred Lenny, the go-getting real estate salesman selling leveraged tax havens. He has it all – the big house, expensive car and suits and beautiful wife, Linda, who dotes on him. On a roll, with money coming out of his socks, he invests unwisely in a nightclub. Then Congress changes the tax laws and his business collapses. This is the wrong time to meet cocaine. The reality is that Lenny is on the skids. Coke reality puts him on top of the world. Linda joins Lenny on the slopes as their lives unravel. Linda gets pregnant but loses the baby in a fall while stoned. They end up in a crummy apartment where Linda leaves him for the doctor who nursed her back to health after a savage attack by her coke-crazed husband. Lenny becomes a dealer, and the film ends with him sitting alone, forlornly chopping lines of coke waiting for the next customer to call.

Yet another 1988 release was *Clean and Sober* with Michael Keaton as Darryl Poynter, another real estate agent living life on the edge. The film opens with a girl dying in his bed of a cocaine overdose. He drives a fast car, consumes vast quantities of booze and coke and speculates on Wall Street with $92,000 he borrows from a company escrow account. The gamble fails, and he is several thousand dollars in the hole. Like the friends in *Gridlocked*, he has people on his tail. The police want to investigate further the death of the girl, and his company has found out about the failed speculation. His answer, like Spoon and Stretch, is to get off the streets and into treatment. But unlike them he has no trouble with admission. He just walks into a detox unit and the treatment begins. But here the similarity with other drug movies ends because *Clean and Sober* is one of the very few to take the audience inside Alcoholics/Narcotics Anonymous, the most famous drug and alcohol treatment system in the world.

From a cinematic viewpoint, the introduction of the AA/NA concept gave Hollywood the chance to construct a heroic story about a man (usually) struggling against something that wasn't his fault. *Clean and Sober* proceeds through the next 30 days in Darryl's life as he gradually comes to terms with the fact that he might need help. But the word here is 'gradual'. He goes through the detox and then has to attend group therapy sessions run by the counsellor played with quiet, deter-mined authority by Morgan Freeman. Darryl really doesn't want to be there – he is only in treatment to get off the streets. There is no motivation to give up drugs and alcohol, so he doesn't. In fact, most of the time he is trying to use Freeman's phone to call up dealers, none of whom will extend him any more credit.[18]

At the first meeting he finds himself a 'sponsor' who will befriend him. But he is always on the make and eventually gets involved with a woman (perhaps deliberately named Charlie) who is addicted to drugs and alcohol – and to a low-life husband whom she just can't seem to ditch however badly he treats her. The action of the film splits between Darryl playing cat and mouse with his counsellor and getting kicked off the programme – and trying to persuade Charlie to leave her husband. Events send Darryl back to AA and a public admission that he has a problem. But even as he speaks, you feel that he is never convinced. At one point he says to Charlie: 'You really buy into this shit, don't you?'

For a decade, it all went quiet on the coke film front and then came another clutch – this time edging much closer to Hollywood's cocaine chaos.

Paul Thomas Anderson's excellent *Boogie Nights* (1997) takes us through a crucial period in the history of the LA adult film business from 1977 to 1984 when the industry came out of the cinema and on to video – killing off the last hope that anybody could make a porn movie that was any more than serial fucking. The film, populated with a slew of engagingly damaged characters, starts in an era when drug use was so prevalent in America that Jimmy Carter almost managed to push through some very far-reaching law changes which had the backing of the DEA and the National Institute on Drug Abuse. Already in 11 US states, the penalty for cannabis possession had been reduced from a felony offence to a misdemeanour – the equivalent of a parking ticket.

Eddie Adams washes dishes in a Hollywood nightclub until discovered by a big-time porn film producer, Jack Horner (Burt Reynolds). Renaming himself Dirk Diggler, Eddie's major asset sees him rise to the top. Coke is everywhere, which isn't a problem for Eddie (although a girl ODs early on in the film) until he realises he is no longer the 'new kid on the street'. Buoyed up by coke chutzpah and fearing his star is on the wane, he rows with Jack and is sacked. Now in need of cash, he gets mixed up with some LA lowlife and is almost killed when a coke deal goes wrong. Tail (and other bits) between his legs, he goes back to Jack and all is forgiven.

In the same year, director Abel Ferrara released *The Blackout*, another coke/booze movie played out against a porn background. Matthew Modine plays Matty, an A-list movie star whose suicidal drug use cuts a huge swath through his personal life. Although hobnobbing with Bruce Willis and Demi Moore, he roughs it on the side with Mickey Wayne (Dennis Hopper), a manic club owner who uses his club as the setting for shooting a video porn movie starring Annie, Matty's French girlfriend, and a host of club extras.

This was Ferrara's third examination of the nature of addiction following on from the stunning *Bad Lieutenant* (1992) with Harvey Keitel (see Chapter Twelve) and *Addiction* (1995) mentioned earlier. As the title suggests, Matty suffers from drug- and alcohol-induced blackouts during which he may or may not have murdered a young waitress who has the same name as his ex-girlfriend.

Director Anthony Drazan's *Hurly Burly* (1998), based on the 1984 off-Broadway play by David Rabe, is probably the closest movie yet to Hollywood's cocaine underbelly. This might explain why, despite starring Sean Penn, Kevin Spacey and Meg Ryan, financing the film proved difficult.

Films based on stage plays are often wordy and here the actors get to talk and talk and talk. But it works so well because the talk is spot-on Hollywood coke-talk, just reams and reams of crackling intense pretension, non sequiturs and Kentucky-fried ramblings. At just on two hours, the effect is both mesmerising and nearly impossible to watch.

Penn and Spacey play Eddie and Mickey, business partners in a casting agency and housemates who spend their time with a wannabe actor and full-time thug, Phil (Chazz Palminteri), and a writer, Artie (Gary Shandling). They drink, they do coke, they treat the women in the film like shit. Phil on his own beats his wife, head-butts a 16-year-old girl staying at the house (a 'care package' for Eddie and Phil from Artie) and pushes a hooker (Meg Ryan) out of his speeding car.

Mickey and Artie stand to one side in cynical, uncaring amusement while Eddie and Phil aggressively self-destruct in a miasma of whingeing self-obsession. Eddie agonises over his relationship with Darlene (who has a brief affair with Mickey) as his escalating coke habit sends him searching for something he cannot articulate and drowns him in paranoia. Phil does battle with his wife, who keeps throwing him out, and eventually his rage and self-loathing drive him literally over the edge. These guys come across as the scummiest barrel-scrapers of Hollywood culture. The fear is that they are not alone.

So what role does cocaine play in the lives of all these desperate characters? We have real estate salesmen, actors, writers and others involved in the entertainment business. These are the stereotypical cocaine customers because of the high-pressure nature of their job, the need to always appear on top and their ability to access large amounts of disposable income. But they are all different people.

Michael Keaton as Darryl convincingly plays a man very much out of control; manic, paranoid, edgy and very ruffled, yet still very sure of himself – a combination of natural cockiness and cocaine confidence. Lenny has the front, but deep down he is very insecure and often overplays the pitch. He can't even believe that Linda wanted to marry him. He always believed she would leave him and finally his behaviour leaves her no option. For Darryl and Lenny, coke lines trace their downfall. Darryl is clearly in big trouble right from the start of the film – urgently calling his dealer from all over town. We never find out exactly how he gets into such a mess with substances – but coke-fuelled over-confidence drove him to speculate with money that wasn't his to gamble with.

Lenny is introduced to coke at a party just at the moment when he is trying to pretend to the outside world that the closure of the very lucrative tax loophole, which has wiped him out, is actually no big deal and that he is about to bounce back with an even bigger deal – which, of course, never happens. He loses the prestige and possessions he craved, the trust of the man who made him rich, his baby, his wife and, through a cocaine seizure, nearly his life. The only constant companion is cocaine, and when he gives that up for a while with all the big money gone – his new friends were sedative Quaaludes (Mandrax).

Moreover, in *The Boost* and *Clean and Sober* you also feel the weight of moral justice bearing down on Darryl and Lenny, with cocaine as the snake, there to tempt those not content with the Garden of Earthly Delights which is already theirs. In *Less Than Zero*, Julian also battles with loss, not so much his business plans, but the love and affection of his family. Having graduated, he was never destined for the conventional lifestyle, but cocaine serves to underscore just how alienated he has become. Drugs are used to self-medicate the pain, the self-loathing and disappointments. And he pays the ultimate price.

In *The Blackout* Matty's professional and personal lives are imploding into a black hole. He says he is waiting for his girlfriend Annie to tell him that it's all over – 'a baby doesn't cut his own umbilical cord' – which speaks legions for the type of person Matty is. He admits he hasn't got the tools to take control of his life. Like some of the heroin characters from the previous chapter, Matty never grows up.

Other 'cocaine fiends' get off more lightly. Michael J. Fox as James Conway is just a sweet schmuck pining for lost relationships and opportunities. In the novel of *Bright Lights, Big City*, you don't get the sense that cocaine is really that much of a problem. Cocaine and heavy nights on the town are just a cover for James's own lack of self-confidence and frustrated ambition. Cocaine helps drive a life that was already chaotic and wayward. The end of the film is unconvincing because it indicates a far more serious cocaine problem than McInerney describes in the book, but still sticks to the book's ending where James looks as if he can take cocaine or leave it.

For Eddie/Dirk in *Boogie Nights*, cocaine angst drives him from his surrogate home under the protection of Jack Horner and his wife Amanda – and marks out the trail of his decline. But when he hits the bottom, he rises back to the top and at the end is booted and suited to restart his career. The other Eddie – Sean Penn in *Hurly Burly* – never even admits to a problem during the film – and nobody points this out to him either, apart from this little interchange when the ever-dry, laconic Mickey notices Eddie frantically snorting coke first thing in the morning. He makes some simple, understated observations.

'Edward. What are you doing?'

'Gotta wake up. How am I gonna wake up?'

'*Some* people have coffee.'

'Caffeine's fuckin' poison. Don't you know that?'

'Oh, right. So what's this? Bolivian health food?'

Moments later, with Mickey about to leave for their office, Eddie hits the dope: 'Eddie, do you now realise that you're tokin' up at 8.58 in the morning on top of the shit you have already put up your nose? You're gonna show up for work looking like you've got a radish for a face. You're gonna show up there . . . talkin' like a fish.'

Eddie says everything will be all right. Mickey is unconvinced, but leaves anyway. You sense Eddie will carry on until his nose falls out or his heart stops.

Nobody seems to gain much benefit from treatment. Apart from *Clean and Sober,* where we travel with Darryl into the world of AA, the idea of getting help is only fleetingly referred to. Matty does his bit at the meetings, only to relapse hard, while only the merest mention is made of Lenny's and Julian's unsuccessful trips to rehab. Neither James nor Eddie/Dirk appear to need any treatment, while Sean Penn's Eddie would surely ridicule the notion.

In some respects, the failure of treatment as depicted in these films is not altogether surprising. Because of the nature of the drug and the people most likely to get seriously hooked, admitting a problem is a major hurdle. Nor is there any drug substitute for cocaine, a chemical carrot to help stabilise people while they undergo therapy. Some American clinicians are getting excited about the idea of cocaine vaccinations. But then we get into the murky waters of determining who is most at risk.

Over two decades, from 1970 to 1990, the public image of cocaine changed dramatically from a non-addictive, almost semi-legal drug to one that could cause as many problems as heroin – if you had enough money to indulge. But despite more articles and documentaries warning of the dangers, having access to abundant supplies of the product remained a powerful statement of position and status in the film industry. The Hollywood letters overlooking Los Angeles were still etched in lines of coke.

In 2000 Mike Zymanski wrote for E-online: 'He's only one of dozens of dealers to the stars. In his black-tailored jacket, he saunters to the front of the line at the exclusive hotel bar. The bouncer nods him in. He doesn't need a reservation because there's an actor who once earned an Oscar nomination waiting for him by the pool . . . [The dealer] takes a small plastic bag from his pocket. The actor pulls out a roll of $20 bills. They make the exchange.' This same dealer then delivers drugs to a club and then up to a reclusive actor hidden in the Hollywood Hills. Going to Narcotics Anonymous and checking in and out of rehab may be the new rock 'n' roll, but nothing much has changed except the faces and the drugs.

After the excesses of the 1970s and early 1980s a new generation of bratpackers like Charlie Sheen, Drew Barrymore and Robert Lowe, along with Christian Slater, Melanie Griffiths, Jamie Lee Curtis and *Natural Born Killers* star Juliette Lewis, are among many who have temporarily lost themselves in a sea of substances. Comedian Chris Farley died in similar circumstances to John Belushi – the coke/heroin hotshot. For many, the biggest drug shock was the death of River Phoenix outside Johnny Depp's Viper Club. The star of *My Own Private Idaho* had gone on the record about his antipathy towards drugs. But the film star who wanted to be a musician took the well-trodden path of so many rock heroes. Phoenix consumed a cocktail of drugs and booze, including the new drug in town, GHB, or gammahydroxybutyrate. GHB is a sedative drug in liquid form, colourless, odourless and with a slightly salty taste formerly used as a pre-op sedative. Mike Hundahl of the Probe Club said he got tired of calling ambulances for those who had passed out on GHB in the alley behind his club and put a 'No GHB' flash on the club advertisements.

It didn't take long for drugs to be good for the rock business rather than bad. After the initial jolt of Paul McCartney admitting publicly in 1967 that he had tried LSD, rock musicians wore their drugs and their drug busts like shields of honour. 'Must hoover up all known substances and reduce hotel suites to matchwood' were written into the rock star job spec. The image of excess put bums on seats, T-shirts on backs and dollars in company wallets. Not so in Hollywood. This is essentially a family industry. The major studios go to great lengths to cover up scandal, especially if it involves those who have a wholesome screen image. The trials and tribulations of being a star in Hollywood are no different now than they were in the 1920s, when Tinseltown first acquired its sleazy reputation. Young people with good looks who happen to be in the right place at the right time are thrust into the public gaze and loaded with more money than they know what to do with. Every time they step outside the door, cameras go off in their face and the media pack eye their every move. You have no privacy. You live your life in a fishbowl. You are constantly performing for the crowd. And that's when things are going well. One minute you can be surrounded by admirers, well-wishers, agents, journalists and all the legions of the business; next, they are all crossing the street to avoid you. Nobody likes a loser – and in Hollywood failure is believed to be contagious. Add to that the notoriously fragile temperaments of many movie stars – living lives fraught with anxiety, slaves to the ego that got them to the top and paranoid about what happens when the offers dry up. Add to that the long, boring hours it takes to shoot a movie in the first place. And finally in the mix are the hordes of hangers-on waiting to push dope on you in the hope of gaining access to the hallowed halls, and it is no wonder that some film stars go right off the rails.

The studios are under pressure all the time to keep their stars on track. There is a scene in *Postcards from the Edge* (1990), based on the autobiography of actress Carrie Fisher, where she is asked to take a drug test at the beginning of a film shoot because she has just come out of rehab. This is now standard procedure. A studio insider told this author:

> With US production accounting for over three-quarters of the world's films and rising by three per cent a year, it has become very important to protect one's investment. Consequently, employment insurance clauses frequently require drug tests, and in-house PR machines damage-manage all outgoing information. Studios now employ minders to watch stars who may be stuck in a hotel on overseas location for months at a time. They are there to take care of the star's needs, but they are in effect wardens. You can't control it absolutely, but one can minimise the damage to a degree never before seen . . . [although] there are still a few serious coke-problem stars around.

Even if the cocaine problem is less public, the risk of celebrity addiction remains. This might explain the recent spate of revelations about addiction to painkillers. Matthew Perry of *Friends*, Diana Ross and Michael Jackson are just three stars revealed to have been treated for this problem. Less shame and blame attaches to a dependency on drugs which might have been prescribed by a doctor rather than purchased on your behalf from a low-rent dealer in a shadowy Sunset Boulevard night club.

Problems still accrue to those who work behind the scenes – the movers and shakers of the industry. A recent victim was Jay Moloney of Creative Arts Agency (CAA). A protégé of Michael Ovitz, Moloney's clients included Dustin Hoffman, Sean Connery and Bill Murray – and he poached directors Mike Nichols and Tim Burton from rival agencies. His drug use became well known around Hollywood in 1993, and he was fired by CAA in 1996. In November 1999, aged 35, he hanged himself.

The life and death of Moloney became the focus for Bernard Rose's well-received movie *Ivans XTC* (2002), based on *The Death of Ivan Illyich* by Leo Tolstoy with John Huston's son Danny in the starring role. Rose, another Moloney client, who directed *Candyman* (1992) and *Immortal Beloved* (1995), said that he had trouble financing the film and claimed that CAA tried to prevent the film from being made. With no studio backing, he eventually shot the film on video for $500,000 in the houses of all those involved and with the cast acting as the crew.

But say 'Hollywood drug use' and just one name comes to mind – Robert Downey Jnr. As he demonstrated in *Less Than Zero, Chaplin* (1992) and other films, he is an extremely gifted actor, but one who said that he has manifestly failed to cope with the fame that came too early. So much is he now associated with the Hollywood drug scene that one is led to think that he is carrying the can for everybody's chemical misdemeanours. And he has the misfortune to live in a state with the ferocious 'three strikes and you're out' law that has seen tens of thousands of people stashed away in prison for years – in one notorious case for doing nothing more than stealing a slice of pizza.

To say that the actor has been his own worst enemy would be putting it mildly. He has been given many chances to rehabilitate and invariably failed – once absconding by climbing out of a window in his hospital gown and hitchhiking back to Malibu. He has been found wandering the streets barefooted carrying a gun. He has spent time in some of the most horrendous jails where he barely escaped with his life. But his treatment at the hands of American justice leaves a nasty taste in the mouth.

Addiction is a chronic relapsing condition. Most users trying to get off go through this 'one step forward, two steps back' dance routine as they struggle to move towards a life without having to depend on drugs to get up in the morning. That Downey should have faced jail time for every backwards motion is an affront to human rights.

One also has to be highly suspicious of the circumstances of his repeated arrests. In London in the late 1960s there was a detective in the Metropolitan Police who made it his business to bust pop stars. They were the arrogant, rich and young face of the swinging city and so prime targets to be taken down a peg or two by jealous policemen out for some of their own glory. The police would tip off journalists of an impending arrest to be sure of front-page coverage when the hapless musician was hauled from his flat.

In a compassionate piece in the *Independent on Sunday* (6 May 2001), film critic David Thomson wonders how on earth Downey managed to get caught in an expensive hotel in the exclusive resort of Palm Springs. He wrote that ' . . . the whole area of Palm Springs is a series of walled compounds where the grass grows and the crème brûlée and the crab cakes are only ten minutes away by room service, while beyond the barred gates and the electronic security systems there is desert, snakes and the huddled poor. In other words, Palm Springs is a place made for the rich and famous to do their naughty stuff safely. Always has been. Getting arrested in Palm Springs smells. It is a sign of a kind of carelessness that is begging to be arrested or of a very hostile world ganging up on you.'

The question marks hanging over Downey's drug problems – Who is supposed to be looking after him? Why has he been *walking* LA at night by himself looking for drugs? Is he being set up to be busted? – highlight the battleground of conflicting tensions and interests at the intersection of drugs, the media and politics. Film-makers who want to show how the world is struggle for funds and tussle with regulators who are naturally cautious about what we see on our screens and sensitive to the unease drugs cause among the general public. Attacks rain down on film and TV companies for 'encouraging drug use' in the face of a complete lack of evidence that this actually happens. And Hollywood executives take government dollars to waste on anti-drug advertising campaigns while leaving it to Robert Downey Jnr to deflect attention away from what lies beneath.

11

Honey, I smoked the kids: crack and black film

Don't push me 'cos I'm close to the edge.
He was America's nightmare. Young, black and didn't give a fuck.

'The Message', Grandmaster Flash
Menace II Society

On 9 June 1980 Richard Pryor's maid heard screaming coming from the bedroom of his home in the suburbs of LA. Rushing in with his aunt Jenny, she found the actor engulfed in flames. The two women smothered Pryor in bedclothes but, shocked and suffering third-degree burns from the waist up, his shirtsleeves melted into his skin, he fled into the street. Pryor told the police that he'd been freebasing cocaine – igniting the drug with 151 per cent rum prior to smoking the drug in a pipe. Once the story hit the newspapers, it was the first time most people had heard the word 'freebase'.

Writing in the *Journal of Psychoactive Drugs* in 1982, Dr Ron Siegel, who helped Julia Phillips with her cocaine problem, suggested that the idea of smoking the drug probably arrived in America by accident. Smugglers doing business in South America in the early 1970s came across people smoking coca paste which they called basé (pronounced bah-say). Roughly speaking, coca paste is a halfway house in the cocaine process between the coca leaves and the finished product and is very powerful. Coca chewing had been part of everyday life in Peru and Bolivia for thousands of years without any detriment to the local people and some manifest benefits. But smoking any drug is almost as effective in transporting it to the brain as injecting – and many of those locals who began smoking coca paste found they couldn't stop. Back in America, the smugglers who had their heads blown off smoking basé tried to re-create the experience. But all their underground chemist friends had to work with was the finished product, cocaine hydrochloride powder. Their understanding of the word 'base' was entirely different – nothing like the product being smoked down south. They worked backwards, heating the cocaine powder with alcohol or (less dangerous) baking soda to 'free' the cocaine alkaloid from the hydrochloride salt 'base'. The resulting purified cocaine crystals were called 'freebase', an entirely new form of the drug.

Once freebase began to circulate among California's cocaine elite, a new paraphernalia industry quickly sprang up, supplying chemicals, pipes, screens, tools and torches for a whole new set of exciting, mysterious and seductive drug rituals. In 1975–6 Julia Phillips was spending $60,000 a month on freebase and kept a propane torch burning in her office, which had been specially constructed so she could use her drugs in private. In 1980, three years after she'd given up cocaine, she still dreamed of freebase: 'the shimmering white dust igniting and liquefying into amber, circling down the stem of the pipe to be collected and rewashed into another higher substance later . . . the smoke . . . the taste . . . the high . . . She would wake up sweaty, with her ears ringing, her heart and head and groin pounding with fear and excitement.'[1]

In *Less Than Zero*, Julian goes downhill fast when he hits the pipe, but at least for the Hollywood types who got in trouble with cocaine there was access to treatment and rehab (whatever the outcome), access to large amounts of disposable income, comfortable houses and a protective and secretive industry to hide behind, desperate to protect its reputation. When cocaine smoking hit the streets of south central Los Angeles, it was a very different story. Cocaine as the catalyst of the Great American Dream became a wake-up call for the Great American Nightmare.

When Warner Brothers released Mario van Peebles's *New Jack City* in the spring of 1991, it grossed $43.6m in 11 weeks, making it the only major picture for the period to break even just from domestic release alone. The summer opening of John Singleton's *Boyz N the Hood* was equally successful; the per screen average gross of $12,091 was higher than *Terminator 2*. It took $42 million in the first five weeks against Columbia's $6 million investment, $15 million of that in the first weekend, and eventually earned over $100 million across the US and overseas plus two Academy Award nominations. Two years later the Hughes Brothers'

Menace II Society grossed $27 million in domestic sales against a $3 million investment. Black faces on the screen were big business even if they were (or perhaps because they were) covered in blood. It wasn't always like that.

A hundred years ago, lurid tales of murderous, drug-crazed black men could only be had in the newspapers. Audiences would never have stood for seeing huge black faces on the screen, however evilly portrayed. To create a credible story line, the film would have to imbue black people[2] with human characteristics like feelings, emotions and motivations – very much at odds with the popular representation of the black community as an undifferentiated subhuman rabble. When black people did appear on screen, it had to be as happy, comical, naive and simple folk – the loyal servant, the jokey fool, the big-mamma figure. Early documentary film might show a group of black men taking part in a watermelon eating contest. In fact, in the very early days of cinema there was no technology for film editing so some portraits of black people were accurate and dignified. Thomas Edison made a film of the 9th and 10th Cavalry regiments returning from Cuba: 'when you saw those soldiers, they were black soldiers, there in their formations, on their horses. So . . . blacks were both exactly the way whites wanted them to be [content to eat watermelons], and also exactly as blacks would have proudly wished to be – as soldiers.'[3]

However, once film could be edited, any chance for dignified and accurate portrayals of black people was gone, especially with a fictional drama. D.W. Griffith's *Birth of a Nation* set the tone for many years to come. Everything was there, 'the black buck, the mammy, the coon . . . The film . . . showed blacks in such a poor light it glorified the formation of the Clan.'[4] But worse still, Griffith showed black raiders raping and pillaging and then, during Reconstruction, 'uppity niggers' from the North corrupting former slaves, goading them on to wreak their revenge on the white South. Griffith's central thesis was that the pre-Civil War south stood for order where black people knew their place. This was shattered by the war and chaos ensued. Through one film Griffith did as much damage to the public perception of black people as Hearst had done with sheaves of yellow journalism. From then on, black performers were largely restricted to parts as maids, servants, comics or musicians. The first black actor to shatter the stereotypes was

Sidney Poitier, starting with his debut in *No Way Out* (1950) but more famously with *The Defiant Ones* (1958) and *In the Heat of the Night* (1967).

There were even fewer opportunities for black people behind the camera, although as they migrated to the cities early in the twentieth century they were entertained by so-called race movies produced by black film-makers. The most famous of these was Oscar Micheaux, the first black film-maker to produce and direct a feature-length sound movie. But ironically, as the black community became more integrated, the audience for race movies evaporated. Community leaders felt that the best way to achieve equality was to be as much like the white majority as possible, and they turned their back on anything emphasising difference.

The next major period of black film-making came at the end of the 1960s. This was an era of renaissance in black culture and an affirmation of black pride born out of the civil rights movement, the political radicalism of the Black Panthers and the inspiration of individual black icons like Malcolm X, Martin Luther King and Mohammed Ali. Black athletes dominated the 1968 Olympic Games in Mexico where the sprinters gave the Panther salute from the podium. Old and new generations of black musicians dominated the charts and headlined at white rock festivals – Marvin Gaye, Otis Redding, Jimi Hendrix, Aretha Franklin, B.B. King and Muddy Waters to name but a few.

Life magazine photographer Gordon Parks became the first black director of a Hollywood movie, *The Learning Tree* (1969), about a 14-year-old black boy growing up in the 1920s South. Ossie Davis's *Cotton Comes to Harlem* (1970) was a successful mix of crime and comedy based on a Chester Himes novel. Important, too, was the 1971 release of Melvin Peebles's independently financed *Sweet Sweetback's Baadass Song*. The film tells the story of a black pimp who kills two policemen for beating up a black militant and ushered in a genre of movies known as blaxploitation. What these films exploited was the new black urban cinema audience now living in areas previously occupied by whites who had fled to the suburbs. This flight (and the rise of television) had caused great chasms to open up in the coffers of the film companies, and they needed to find niche areas to claw back some profits. The success of Melvin Peebles's film showed the way. It was followed by *Shaft*

(1971) and a host of lesser films featuring an orgy of killing, kung-fu, shooting and sex that outraged black community leaders, who felt these films played up to the worst white stereotypes of black people.

The most controversial of the blaxploitation movies, however, was *Superfly* (1972). The film, directed by Gordon Parks Jnr, whose father had gone on to direct *Shaft*, told the story of Priest, a cocaine dealer so named because he carried his samples of cocaine (superfly) in a crucifix around his neck. He decides to get out of the business by making one big score of 301 kilogrammes of cocaine and retiring on the proceeds. The corrupt police chief who has supplied the drugs tries to trap Priest into dealing for him long-term. But Priest gets the drop on him and walks free out of the dealing life to enjoy his money.

Producer Sig Shore struggled to raise the $300,000 budget. Everything was against him. *Superfly* was shot in the middle of winter with half the locations outdoors. The power came from nearby streetlights. The production was shut down twice because Shore couldn't afford the film stock. A local Lower East Side gang leader appears in the film as a junkie in exchange for letting the shoot take place. As this was Gordon Parks Jnr's first film, the distribution company wanted to see the daily rushes before handing over the completion money, which Parks refused to do. And it was screenwriter Phil Fenty's first script: much of it was improvised and later lip-synched in a studio.

Blacks against Narcotics and Genocide (BANG) was one of several black organisations who objected to the film, and they picketed outside cinemas in several cities. They didn't like the fact that nobody seems to suffer through drugs in the film and that Priest is shown enjoying his flashy and expensive lifestyle – the $18,000 Cadillac (owned by a real pimp), the sweeping calf-length coat, the wide-brim hat, colour TV in every room – and never suffers for his crimes. Black Panther Huey Newton generally condemned the whole genre (and *Superfly* in particular) as symptomatic of black self-hate and highly dangerous in its glorification of deviant and criminal activities. Black actor and director Ossie Davies bluntly stated 'We're paying for images of our degradation', while a black psychiatrist, Alvin Pouissant, wrote in *Psychology Today* (February 1974) about 'cheap thrills that degrade blacks'.

Sig Shore went on the defensive, saying that the film was about the dope dealer's life – not the dope. Actor Ron O'Neal, who played Priest, asked not unreasonably: why shouldn't the dealer win – it happens in real life all the time? He said the whole point of the film was that Priest was trying to get out of the life but, more significantly, 'movies have always emasculated black men. We don't do that in *Superfly*.'

But the real beef with *Superfly* was the notion of a drug dealer who does not get his comeuppance and who, because of the horrendous impact of drugs on the black community, is dealing death to his own people. The film was given a substantial boost in popularity by Curtis Mayfield's supercharged film score. The hit track from the movie was 'Freddie's Dead', the inclusion of which some claim gave the film an otherwise absent moral conscience. Freddie is one of Priest's dealers who owes him money. He is portrayed as basically an ordinary Joe who deals a bit of coke, has nothing to do with guns and violence, but becomes just another faceless casualty in the drug war when he gets knocked down and killed while running away from police custody. The film very much glosses over what happens to Freddie, but Curtis Mayfield picked up on this minor incident and turned it into a hit song. 'Remove Curtis from the equation,' said Ben Edmonds, writing for a *Mojo* magazine special on movie music (June 2002), 'and the criticisms levelled at *Superfly* become harder to deflect.' Although Mayfield's score is very much at odds with what appears to be a glorification of the drug dealer and his life, I'm less convinced that the character of Priest is so completely amoral.

Priest was actually based on a coke dealer acquaintance of the writer Phillip Fenty, who said the dealer had 'many celebrity clients'. This is important because most of those clients would have been white. In the film, neither Priest nor any of his dealers is seen dealing to poor black people. At one point the film takes us through a set of photographic stills – from Priest obtaining his big weight of coke, through cutting, packaging and selling – and the end users are all white. As Ron O'Neal said at the time in defence of the film, it was the heroin dealer who was the scourge of the black community – black people couldn't afford cocaine.[5] The evidence bears this out.

Cocaine had all but disappeared off the streets from the 1940s through to the late 1960s. Heroin use, on the other hand, had been growing rapidly since the end of the war and the resumption of the Mafia's heroin trade. There is a scene in *The Godfather* where the Dons of the five families have a meeting at which they discuss the drug trade. Vito Corleone opposes the trade on moral grounds. But the Kansas boss says they should sell drugs but only to 'the dark people' because, he adds, 'they're animals anyway, let them lose their souls'. Vietnam was another impetus to the heroin trade in black urban areas. Some soldiers did come home with habits picked up in the Far East, but nowhere near as many as was feared when the extent of drug use in the military overseas was first revealed. For the most part, even those who regularly used heroin or opium gave up when they got home away from the terrors of the war zone. However, as Nick Nolte showed in *Dog Soldiers* (aka *Who'll Stop The Rain?*) (1978), drugs were a good hedge against unemployment, and military smuggling accounted for an unknown increase in the amount of heroin available in American cities.

So while Priest might have been a big-time black drug dealer, his activities were not aimed at his own community – albeit because most of his own couldn't afford it. And in a genre full of gratuitous violence and deeply misogynous, Priest had a semblance of a moral code. He never kills anybody, even the guy he chases and grabs after being mugged in a hallway, and is relatively respectful of women. And as his clientele are mainly white middle class, you might argue that as a black man he is grabbing a far bigger piece of their American pie than any legitimate employment would allow.[6]

And black audiences loved these movies. They could enjoy the sight of handsome and beautiful black actors and actresses like Jim Brown, Fred Williamson, Pam Grier and Tamara Dobson taking on the Mafia, corrupt police and anybody else who threatened their community and whupping their ass to the sound of brilliant music. Every time whitey got whacked, the audience cheered. Writer Nelson George believes that the key to the appeal of these films was 'aggressive black heroism . . . Even the antisocial coke dealer Priest [has] a sly cinematic presence that only church ladies and the NAACP people could resist'. After the 'relative passive' Sidney Poitier marched through the 1960s in a white shirt and dark suit as the embodiment of noble striving, says George, the blaxploitation guys and girls 'were funky as multicolored bell-bottoms and two-toned platform shoes . . . these movies dressed their stars in state-of-the-art threads that allowed them to live as large and insolently as we all dreamed we could'.[7]

The genre of blaxploitation came to an end with the new-style block-buster movies like *Jaws* (1975). Hollywood discovered that black people were just as likely to go to see movies like these as white people, and so the need for special niche films evaporated. What sparked the next phase in the development of mainstream black film-making was Ronald Reagan and crack cocaine.

For the majority of working-class black people, the promise of the 1960s civil rights movement was not realised. As Nelson George observed, the non-violence philosophy of Martin Luther King and the radical activism of the Black Panthers receded into memory as 'heroin's vicious grip, the mercenary diligence of FBI informants and the philosophy of benign neglect replaced liberal guilt as the engine of our government's policy towards the poor'.[8]

The doors of opportunity did open for some – those who became black urban professionals, 'the products of tokenism, affirmative action and their own hard work'.[9] Like most 1970s middle-class Americans, they lived in middle-class suburbs where they dabbled in cocaine, 'seeking the slick rush and status its ingestion implied'.[10] Those further down the social and economic ladder, the bus drivers, the teachers and the bureaucrats, also found themselves with the freedom to live wherever they could afford to and not be confined to the ghetto areas of bleak inner cities. But once they had gone, only the poorest remained, and the neighbourhoods were wide open for crime and drugs which flooded into areas like the Bronx and Harlem in New York, South Side in Chicago and South Central and East Los Angeles. The Hughes Brothers' movie *Dead Presidents* (1995), set in 1968, tells of a black GI who leaves a tough but still hopeful neighbourhood for Vietnam and comes back to a heroin-soaked ghetto.

The long-standing problems of ghetto areas were compounded by the economic restructuring of America from the 1970s onwards and the rise of social conservatism founded on the philosophies of Reaganomics, the New Right and the Moral Majority. Together they forged a new political dialectic which said that those who are *in* trouble are those who *cause* trouble. The prominence of this discourse allowed the government to slash welfare programmes and all sorts of aid for the poorest in society, do nothing to improve inner-city life and then fill up the jails with the most disaffected groups in society – primarily young black males.

The arrival of crack cocaine in the mid-1980s 'was a godsend for the Right: they used it as an ideological figleaf to place over unsightly urban ills which had increased markedly under the Reagan Administration. They used it as a scapegoat on which to blame many economic and urban problems.'[11]

Until the early 1980s, smoking cocaine as freebase had been largely confined to the upper echelons of the entertainment business and other well-offs among white middle-class professionals. What brought cocaine within the reach of working-class black people was a huge drop in price – from $50,000 a kilogramme in 1980 to $35,000 in 1984 and then a further slump to $12,000 by 1992. Crack could be bought for as little as $2 a rock in vials with different-coloured caps to denote the wares of a certain dealer or his product.

As well as creating enormous profits for a handful of dealers, the crack explosion produced hitherto unavailable employment for around 150,000 in New York by the early 1990s, mainly teenagers packing vials and acting as gofers and lookouts. The ridiculous amount of money to be made out of crack created a new climate of violence and a new vocabulary of weapons – the Uzi, the Glock, the Desert Eagle.

As crack spread, the jails became full to bursting point. There was discriminatory sentencing for those in possession and dealing crack (mainly black people) over cocaine powder (mainly white people). The Washington-based charity Sentencing Project calculated that in 1990 one in four black males aged 20 to 29 were either in prison or on probation – that's 600,000 – compared with the 400,000 in higher education. Why so many black people in prison when in absolute terms the majority of drug users were and are white middle class? An assistant to William Bennett, America's first drug tsar, was asked this very question. He said it was much easier for the police to spot and apprehend black dealers operating in the poorest black areas than to infiltrate white clubs and social gatherings. So if you want to be seen to be doing something about drugs, you hit the black community.

This level of incarceration had a profoundly alienating effect on the mentality of black culture. Dealer-related street violence was made worse by the ebb and flow of young men in and out of prison, who through their prison experiences became increasingly blasé about death. They viewed jail not as a punishment but as a rite of passage and a critical training ground for life on the streets.

From this new crack-driven lifestyle, a rampantly macho world of bravado, violence and guns, came the most explosive offshoot of hip-hop, 'gangsta rap' – the sound which drove all the ghetto action movies of the 1990s. Unless you grab that connection between crack and gangsta rap, says Nelson George, 'nothing else that happened in hip-hop's journey to national scapegoat will make sense'.

Hip-hop speaks to a sector of the American population who exist in a world where they are not wanted. It's like 'trying to run through hell in gasoline drawers – the chance of getting burned increases substantially with every step.'[12]

Hip-hop has had no identifiable leaders and does not embrace any overt form of politics:

> Instead, this era is personified by several figures who possess similar characteristics and an open contempt for politics of any kind. The figure in question is the 'nigga' and his politics are those of the truly disadvantaged. Those who fall under this rubric have had the most impact on culture as well as the most destructive impact on themselves and their community . . . They occupy a world of chaos and nihilism that enriches at the same time as it destroys.[13]

The era began with NWA's 1988 release *Straight Outa Compton*, moved rapidly to the 1992 LA riots following the Rodney King verdict 'and has evolved to the status of a societal threat as several conservative politicians have targeted the themes it expresses as a fundamental threat to American morality'. This was best expressed by an extraordinary speech by Pat Buchanan at the 1992 Republican Party National Convention – a speech tailored to exploit the growing conservative shift. He said the country was involved in a 'cultural war for the soul of America' and discussed the LA riots in a way very similar to the late Enoch Powell's 'rivers of blood' immigration speech to his Midlands constituents in 1968. Buchanan declared that as the National Guard 'took back the streets of LA block by block, so we must take back our cities and take back our culture and take back our country'. He didn't mention any specific 'enemy', but everybody knew who he was talking about.[14]

Rap was the latest in a long line of black musical genres to capture the imagination of white kids, from swing and bebop jazz to blues and soul in the States – and, in the UK, reggae, ska and bluebeat. In America, rap took over from heavy metal as Music Most Likely to Infuriate My Parents, with Run DMC and Public Enemy as the first crossover bands. 'The term gangsta rap became a household term used widely by politicians, journalists and civic and religious leaders who were, in their own way, concerned about the intensification of sexual and violent imagery', which they saw as 'responsible for an erosion of traditional values and escalating youth crime and drug use'.[15]

The chaos of black urban life left hordes of poor young black males wandering around the housing projects with nothing to do. A dangerous and violent, yet also glamorous and lucrative drug economy, filled the employment vacuum while the government orchestrated a war against poor people (as opposed to poverty). The rappers gave voice to an alienation and sense of anger and hopelessness that cut right through a whole generation of young people.

This was the political, cultural and social context in which gangsta rap was able to give new young black cinema such a flying start with new young black audiences. The success of the films was due in no small part to the use of rap music and rap artists, already massive among both black and white audiences. Inevitably, the films discussed below would bring down all the expected criticisms from all the usual suspects of stereotyping the black community, glorifying violence and so on. The Coalition Against Media Racism in America was particularly critical. But such criticisms served only to gloss over the fact that just because the news is bad you shouldn't shoot the messenger. And nobody criticised *Trainspotting* for failing to address adequately issues of poverty and social exclusion.

Spike Lee's *Do the Right Thing* (1989) demonstrated that there existed a market among the black community for those who wanted to see themselves and their lives up there on the screen. But for the most part, until *Clockers* (1995), Lee kept out of the ghetto action or rites-of-passage movie and focused instead on issues of racism and xenophobia and how these impact on individuals and communities. Drugs are for the most part absent from his films. Annoyed at the reaction of some critics to his first movie, he told *Rolling Stone* (13 July 1989): 'This film is not about drugs. It's about people and racism. Drugs are at every level of society today in America. How many of you went to see *Working Girl* or *Rain Man* and asked, "Where are the drugs?" Nobody. But the minute we have a black film that takes place in the ghetto, people want to know where the drugs are . . . because that's the way you think of black people.'

Drugs do intrude into one Lee film: *Jungle Fever* (1991). The theme is very much in keeping with the Lee oeuvre – interracial love between Flipper (Wesley Snipes), a married black architect, and his white secretary. But Flipper has a crack addict brother, Gator, who 'symbolises the increasing class division that differentiates the everyday experiences of the black middle class from those of the black urban poor'.[16] Gator is a mess, an intrusion into the upwardly mobile black middle-class dream. The presence of Gator suggests that the success of the black middle class has come at a price – although it is hard to see what this group could have done to prevent the creation of a black underclass or halt the decline of the urban poor.

But the true ghetto action movies kicked off with *New Jack City* (1991), written and directed by Mario van Peebles and the only true gangsta/ gangster film of the genre – a black *Scarface* and a very different role for Wesley Snipes. He plays Nino Brown, a cocaine powder dealer who hits the big time when crack rides into town. At first he is not impressed when one of his henchmen waxes lyrical about how the punters keep coming back for more: 'You soundin' like this shit is the wheel or somethin'. Like it's gonna change the world.' 'I don't know about all that change the world shit, but what I do know is they be goin' crazy over this, man.' Nino is soon convinced.

He often watches Brian de Palma's 1983 remake of *Scarface* on video. He sees Al Pacino give a memorable performance as the Cuban refugee Tony Montana, who arrives in America with nothing, but through unremitting ruthlessness and cunning achieves spectacular wealth dealing cocaine and is able to grab all the trappings of the American Dream with both hands. But as he becomes more powerful, Tony transgresses the golden rule – 'never get high on your own supply' – and goes down in a hail of bullets, mountains of cocaine and rampant psychosis.

Nino regards Tony as a role model for the new gangsters on the block who are taking over from the old-style Italian Mafia. American popular culture has always had a soft spot for the gangster – both for providing much-needed public services like alcohol during Prohibition and for showing the finger to the federal authorities. The huge success of *The Godfather* trilogy and *The Sopranos* are testament to the long-standing and still current fascination and sneaking admiration for those who are essentially violent criminals and murderers, but who are invariably portrayed as men of honour and dignity with a passionate commitment to the family.[17] No such admiration has been extended to the new crime families who are simply regarded as marauding alien outsiders and soulless killers, whether they are Colombians, Jamaican Yardies or Blacks.

The film flies its political colours from the top of the pole. Set in 1986, the year in which Ronald Reagan declared cocaine to be the nation's number-one drug problem, it was also the height of the conservative movement's profit-uber alles era.[18] As Brown tells his gang: 'You gotta rob in the Reagan era to get rich.' Brown and his crew take over a whole apartment block to make and sell crack, with an area set aside in the courtyard for people to use what they have bought. They wander zombie-like around Nino's fortress compound like the tribal acolytes of Kurtz in *Apocalypse Now,* equally damaged by the ravages of a different war.

Nino Brown has Cosa Nostra and a black detective rapper, Ice T, on his back. The police need somebody on the inside: Scotty chooses Pookie (Chris Rock), an ex-crack user whom he pushes through rehab. Trouble is that once Pookie is surrounded by the product, his restraint goes and so does his cover. Pookie becomes a victim twice over. We first see him as a hopeless addict, living rough, desperate for food. Despite the subtext of most of New Black Cinema, this is one of the few films where black people are shown smoking crack, probably because, as Spike Lee pointed out, that's what audiences expect to see. Nor, because the black community has suffered most from inner-city drug use, do black writers tend to glamorise drug use or even try to elicit sympathy for those caught up. In the mainstream Hollywood white middle-class cocaine movies, the plots centre on the user as victim, somebody who needs help. In films like *NJC,* the user is seen not as a structural victim of economic genocide but just weak and pathetic. Hip-hop culture is as 'traditional' in its views about drug users as it is about women and gays.

The other major genre film dealing directly with drugs in the black community was Spike Lee's *Clockers* (1995), written by Richard Price from his own novel. Price had previously written *The Wanderers*, which had been made into a successful 1979 film about an Italian gang growing up in the Bronx in the early 1960s – and he wrote *The Colour of Money* (1986) directed by Martin Scorsese.

Clockers, too, was originally to be directed by Scorsese, but he chose instead *Casino* (1995), retaining his interest as the film's producer. Bringing in Spike Lee completely changed the focus of the film, although the main plot line remained the same: who killed Darryl Adams, the cocaine dealer who ran a fast-food outlet? Price had made Rocco Klein, an Italian-Jewish detective played by Harvey Keitel, the main protagonist. With Lee co-writing, the focus switched to Strike, a young black clocker dealing around the clock from the park benches – and the whole film takes on a more political tone: 'drugs exist in *Clockers* as a form of generic white-powder Moby Dick. They don't just make you crazy, but everyone else as well. In a society where only the cops have real jobs, you are what you choose to stick in your face. The American Dream for the likes of Strike and Darryl is to deal drugs and burgers at the same time.'[19]

Strike operates under the watchful eye of Rodney Little, the local drug boss who uses his grocery store as a front. Rodney wraps Strike up in a pretence that he is the father Strike never had and lays on him the mythological seduction of crack:

If God created anything better than crack cocaine, he kept that shit for himself. That shit is like truth serum. It will truly expose who you are. I mean, you happen to be a lowlife rat bastard mutherfucka who would sell off his newborn for a suck off that glass dick. Crack'll bring it right on in the light. I don't care if you black, white, Chinese, rich, poor, you take that first hit – you're on a mission and that mission'll never end, even when the house, the money, the loved ones are gone, they send you to the joint, you're gonna try and cop. Only time it ends that mission, when you six feet under. And that's why I don't ever want to hear about you usin' this shit. You understand me? . . . 'Cos it's also the reason why I ain't ever goin' outta business . . . I got me the world's greatest product.

But the real heart of the movie is the character of Strike, under pressure from all sides – from Rodney, from Rocco trying to find the killer, from a local policeman constantly hassling him and from his life as a clocker. Although he is dealing drugs to his own, Strike is portrayed as both human and vulnerable. The life that crowds in on him ulcerates his stomach and he lives mostly on chocolate milk drinks. And however streetwise he might be, he is a child at heart. He is obsessed with trains; the proceeds from dealing have bought him a train set. He shows the trains to Tyrone, a 12-year-old kid who lives in Strike's block and who idolises the young dealer and his gangsta life. There is one scene that sums up the deep tragedy of the lives of so many young black males in America. Strike invites Tyrone to his flat to play with the trains. But he also shows him how to cut cocaine – 'Anything you want costs money. And this [pointing to the pile of powder] is how you get it. The profit's in the cut. Don't ever forget that.'

The film is all about pressure, the pressure felt within the black community, whether you are doing good or doing bad, and it's a theme replayed through the other films in this genre. They don't deal directly with drugs in the way of *NJC* or *Clockers*, but like the music, would probably not have happened but for the reinvention by media and politicians of the black man crazed by drugs and the celebration of the gangsta life that followed. *Boyz N the Hood* (1991), *Straight out of Brooklyn* (1991), *Juice* (1992) and *Menace II Society* (1993) owe a small debt to another movie about growing up in the ghetto from the 1960s. This was Shirley Clarke's *Cool World* (1963). Based on a 1959 novel and a 1960 Broadway play and shot entirely in Harlem with a Mal Waldron jazz score played by Dizzy Gillespie, this was the desperate odyssey of 15-year-old Duke and his struggle to attain manhood by gaining power as a gang leader. *Variety* called it the least patronising film ever made about Negro life in New York.

Duke lives with his mother and grandmother. Like so many of these films to come, there is no father figure at home. Instead (like Tyrone) he looks up to Priest, who has become a full-time hood. Duke is a member of the Royal Pythons and wants to buy a gun. He takes over the leadership when the incumbent gets hooked on heroin. Priest is killed by white mafiosi; Duke goes to prison after a fight with local rivals, the Wolves, as his mother steps out with another new boyfriend. Carl Lee played Priest in this film and later appeared in *Superfly* as Priest's partner Eddie.

If *Cool World* was a 'positive' antecedent behind the ghetto movies, then Dennis Hopper's *Colors* (1988) was the negative. The film starts with the cold statistics that there are over 600 street gangs in LA with a combined membership of over 70,000, with hundreds of gang-related killings every year. Hopper takes a vivid and paranoid look at the LAPD's siege mentality as they try to keep the lid on Los Angeles gang violence. *Colors* is a white cop buddy movie starring Robert Duvall as the elder statesman on the verge of retirement, trying to broker peaceful relations and reasonable behaviour between black and Chicano gangs[20] while having to control trigger-and fist-happy rookie Sean Penn. It is tempting to view the series of films beginning with John Singleton's *Boyz N the Hood* as a rejoinder to Hopper – showing that individual and family lives are played out in the black community just like anywhere else. There is more to the black community than standoffs and shoot-outs between the Bloods and the Crips.

The hood movies have much in common. The ghetto is portrayed as a war zone, with its inhabitants under siege. We get aerial shots of the projects and, in another nod to *Apocalypse Now*, the wup, wup, wup of police helicopter rotor blades are as much a part of the soundtrack of the films as rap songs.

The idea of getting out of the projects weighs heavily on the minds of many of the characters. Tre in *Boyz*, supported by his father Furious (Lawrence Fishburne) – the only positive male role model in this whole sequence of movies – makes it to college. In *M2S*, Caine learns to survive from early on; his mother overdoses on heroin, his father dies in a drug deal. Caine goes to school but also sells drugs. With his 'homeys' going down like flies, it is only a matter of time. The good, like potential star footballer Ricky, die young; the bad, like 'don't give a fuck' O-Dog, might yet survive.

Others don't want to escape; they just want to be the top of whatever pile they can scale – like Tupac Shakur as the deadly Bishop in *Juice*, who just gets tired of running and decides to fight back, with murderous results. He knows that his only escape is death, in a blaze of glory if possible, like James Cagney in *Angels with Dirty Faces* (1938).

In *Straight out of Brooklyn*, Dennis's escape plan is a 'doomed to fail' theft of money from a local drug dealer. Dennis is desperate; his father is deeply embittered by the way he is treated in society and takes it out on Dennis's long-suffering mother. The writer, producer, director Matty Rich was only 19 when he raised the $100,000 to make this bleak and despairing movie.

Dennis tries to convey to his girlfriend that if they are going to get out of the projects, then rules will have to be broken. They look out over the business district of New York City. 'This is what it's all about,' says Dennis. 'Yeah, this is what we fought for. It's the American Dream, Shirley. That's what my mother and father worked like dogs all their life for . . . There's no wrong way outta here. You look over there. You see that? You know how they did that? You think they did that the right way? No, you know how they did that? By steppin' on the black man. I'm not gonna let that happen to me. And I'm not gonna let that happen to my family.' He is pointing straight at the Twin Towers.

12

Clear and present dangers: the war on drugs

That's the whole game, baby – nobody's got control.

Rush (1991)

Travel writer Bill Bryson wrote a column for the *Mail on Sunday* entitled 'Notes from a Big Country', later collected into a book. For his column on Sunday 11 May 1997, he wrote that an old friend had told him about how the drug laws were enacted in his home state of Iowa: ' . . . if you are caught in possession of a single dose of LSD . . . you face a mandatory sentence of seven years in prison without the possibility of parole.'
Bryson was outraged:

> Never mind that you are, say, 18 years old and of previous good character, that this will ruin your life, that it will cost the state $25,000 a year to keep you incarcerated. Never mind that, perhaps, you didn't know you had the LSD – that a friend put it in the glove box of your car without your knowledge . . . Never mind any extenuating circumstances whatever. This is America in 1997 and there are no exceptions where drugs are concerned. Sorry but that's the way it is. Next.

As he said later in the article, 'it is not remotely my intention here to speak in favour of drugs'. Like many of us, he knows what drugs can do, the trouble that they can cause for individuals, families and society. But also like an increasing number of people, he was aghast at the assault on civil liberties and natural justice perpetrated in the name of 'fighting the war against drugs'. He quoted other facts. In 15 American states, possession of a single cannabis plant can get you life in prison. You are more likely to spend time in prison as a first-time drug offender than if you committed acts of violence. Those serving mandatory sentences for drug offences with no chance of parole are filling up US jails so fast that murderers and rapists are serving less jail time to make way for the druggies. An elderly couple had their house seized as an asset of drug trafficking because unknown to them, their grandson was selling cannabis out of his bedroom. Going through Congress in 1997 was a bill which if passed would have meant the death penalty for importing as little as two ounces of cannabis. 'Call me soft,' said Bryson, 'but that seems to me a trifle disproportionate'. And if you care to log on to the website of a drug reform organisation called DrugSense, the list of such bizarre and extreme law enforcement fills screen after screen. America has the highest prison population in the world per 100,000 people; more than half of them are in there for drug offences, and most of the inmates are black and Hispanic even though far more drug users are white. New York's so-called Rockefeller Laws, named after the governor who enacted them in 1973, require mandatory minimum sentences of 15 years to life for possessing four ounces or selling two ounces of heroin or cocaine – even for first offenders. In the eight years of Bill 'I didn't inhale' Clinton's Administration, over four million cannabis users were arrested in the States and so on.

But, observed Bryson, many of his fellow Americans would like to see every single drug user behind bars 'and they are prepared to pay almost any price to achieve this'. One look at the figures reveals they are paying a huge price for an arm of government activity that isn't working. In 1985 the federal drug budget was $2.7 billion; by 1999 it was up 600 per cent to $17 billion and that does not include the money spent by the individual states. There is clearly more at stake here than simply the health of the nation; the alcohol, tobacco and fast-food conglomerates are hardly acting in the best interests of the wider community albeit their products are legal. Even without descending into the murky depths of conspiracy theory, it is self-evident that there is substantial vested interest in the 'drugs war'. This interest runs from bottom to top – from local police forces who top up stretched budgets through highly dubious 'asset' seizures, through to the wider geopolitical aims of US foreign policy, which has turned a blind eye to (or even assisted in) drug trafficking in return for local anti-Communist support or traded aid for crop eradication.

Stories of brave policemen, private dicks and secret service agents hunting down evil drug barons are as old as the film industry itself. For most of the first 30 years of its history, the movies reflected a monolithic view of trafficking – America was the prime target for inscrutable Chinese traffickers and white slavers. Up to the point where the Production Code forbade any mention of drug trafficking, there were nearly 40 American silent films with an opium-smuggling theme. Many involved smuggling across the Pacific from China into San Francisco. In the days before specially assigned drug-enforcement agencies, it was the job of the intelligence services to chase traffickers and their consignments across borders. So a number of films had as their twist the baddie who turns out to be an undercover secret agent and brings down the slitty-eyed villain.

These films played up to the anti-Chinese sentiments displayed in the American media, but also reflected the fascination with the mystic Orient and the vicarious thrill of opium dens and the fate of abducted white girls. The tie-in between drugs and prostitution began with the Danish film *The White Slave Traffic* (1910) and carried on into the 1920s with the Fu Manchu movies.

Yet the implication that China was flooding America with opium was greatly exaggerated. It is true that once the US banned opium imports in 1910, the owners of opium dens had to acquire their stocks through smuggling. But most of the addiction suffered by Americans was due to medically prescribed drugs, patent medicines, drugs sold on to the streets through thefts from drugstores and factories or direct sales by unscrupulous pharmacists. In fact, if anybody had a beef, it was the Chinese government; 90 per cent of the world's opium production was consumed in China.

But little or nothing of drug trade realities reached the big screen. Despite newspapers full of stories of evil drug peddlers, the self-censors of the film industry decided that simply acknowledging the existence of an illegal drug trade could lay the business open to criticism and damaging boycotts. So in 1930 it was declared that the 'Illegal drug traffic must never be presented. Because of its evil consequences, the drug traffic should never be presented in any form. The existence of the trade should not be brought to the attention of the audience.'

Not that the censors needed to worry. It is most unlikely that the major studios would have wanted to turn the stones on the traffic in drugs as it really was in America in the 1930s. There were no more cocaine- and morphine-laced patent medicines, and doctors could no longer prescribe drugs to their addict patients. Learning during Prohibition about the techniques of organisation and how much people will pay for intoxicants denied them, the new wave of Italian and Jewish gangsters led by 'Lucky' Luciano and Meyer Lansky gained control of the illegal traffic in controlled drugs. This new source of income was partly bankrolled by another new and highly lucrative income stream – Hollywood.

Once America's crime bosses realised how popular the movies had become, they began to carve up the territory and battle was joined between Al Capone's Chicago mob and New York's Five Families dominated by Luciano. Between them, Luciano and Capone controlled the unions to which the film projectionists and film extras belonged. That power alone could bring the industry to a standstill if the extortion payments were not made. Studios found themselves paying gangsters to act as agents for the purchase of film stock and for a whole range of other essential film lot services. Some of Hollywood's biggest names, including Jean Harlow, Clark Gable, Cary Grant, George Raft, Frank Sinatra and later Marilyn Monroe, were 'protégés' of leading crime figures. Bugsy Siegal, who ran Luciano's LA drugs, gambling, prostitution and extortion rackets, was secretly married to actress Virginia Hill. Siegel's payment of $50,000 for the re-election campaign of the Los Angeles District Attorney did him no harm in securing his acquittal on a murder charge defended on his behalf by Jerry Geisler, who acted for Charlie Chaplin, Errol Flynn and Robert Mitchum. It is often thought that the singer who gets a helping hand in his Hollywood film career from Don Corleone in *The Godfather* was based on Sinatra.

Wartime saw imported drug supplies severely reduced and Luciano in prison convicted on a prostitution racket charge and sentenced to a staggering 30 to 50 years. Luciano's imprisonment was a final victory for New York Governor Thomas Dewey, who'd spent years trying to find any charge that would stick to his personal nemesis. Yet it was Dewey who agreed to Luciano's deportation to Italy after serving ten years. This led to speculation at the time that Dewey had accepted a bribe. But since then it has been revealed that Luciano did a deal with US Naval Intelligence, giving some assistance, through his contacts, to the Allied landings in Sicily in exchange for his release. How much assistance is not known or how important his help was. One thing for sure: a major international trafficker was released from prison and given free rein to re-establish the heroin supply chain back into New York first from Italy and then from Cuba, a key drugs transit point, to where he later moved. Lucky Luciano died of a heart attack at Naples airport in January 1962.

Straight after the war, the Production Code was amended slightly to allow a degree of latitude for those who wanted to make films about drug trafficking. Hollywood offered up three in quick succession, all made with the help of Anslinger's Federal Bureau of Narcotics and majoring on the brave fight of heroic individuals to keep drugs out of the USA.

To the Ends of the Earth (1948) starred Dick Powell following shipments of opium to the ends of the earth in the 1930s, hopping between Shanghai, Egypt and Cuba. The film conveniently harked back to the period when the Japanese, recently nuked into surrender, were major smugglers of opium into China.[1]

In exchange for help on *Johnny Stool Pigeon* (1949), with Shelley Winters and Tony Curtis, Universal agreed to FBI script approval and there was a special pre-release screening for officials from the Treasury, Customs and Narcotics Bureau. The only point of interest in *Port of New York* (1949) was a film debut for Yul Bryner as the leader of a dope gang. Essentially, these and other plots were the same: heroic law-enforcement official wins out over unscrupulous drug smugglers. Slightly different was *Slattery's Hurricane* (1949), based on a story by Herman Wouk, starring Richard Widmark as an ex-navy flier who shuns the chance to be a dope smuggler while flying into a hurricane to warn Miami about the impending storm. It was important for the flow of FBN funds to keep up the pressure on Congress – especially as Anslinger's own men, seconded to what became the CIA, had a role in the release of Luciano. In the days before mass-audience television, cinema was regarded as an important propaganda tool.

Johnny Stool Pigeon was one of the first films to feature Mexico as a source of US opiates, filling the void caused by the disruption of wartime supplies from overseas. Mexico was also the setting for Orson Welles's *Touch of Evil* (1958), an early example of a corrupt police chief taking advantage of draconian drug laws to frame the 'Mexican' police hero, a deeply tanned Charlton Heston.

But once the Production Code began to lose credibility and television mounted a serious attack on cinema audiences, drugs as the plot device or backdrop for poorly produced, badly directed, dreary low-budget melodramas became commonplace. Glenn Ford and Joseph Cotton appeared as corrupt cops in *Money Trap* (1966), and Mexico again featured in other B-movies like *Sol Madrid* (1968) and *The Candyman* (1969).[2] The major studios, however, were still fighting shy of the subject. Fourteen years elapsed from the release of *The Man with the Golden Arm* to the most famous drug war action movie ever made.

The French Connection (1970) was named after the production chain which started in the growing fields of Turkey, from where the opium went to the Lebanon for processing into morphine, ending in the Corsican-controlled heroin-producing laboratories of Marseilles before shipment to the USA. The film, based on Robin Moore's 1962 book, told how the casual curiosity of two off-duty New York City narcotics detectives, Eddie Egan and Sonny Grosso, led to the biggest heroin haul in the city's history.

FC was full of those twists and turns that underpin the making of many movies. Director William Friedkin, one of the rising stars of New Hollywood, says that every studio passed on the film at least twice before Richard Zanuck gave him $1.5 million to make the film. So although *FC became* a major movie, in Hollywood terms, this was costed as just another low-budget melodrama. By contrast, *FC* producer Phil D'Antoni had spent $25 million on his previous film, *Bullitt* (1968).

Gene Hackman was way down the list of choices for 'Popeye' Doyle. Eddie Egan did not think the relatively unknown Hackman could play him. Egan was a tough, hard-drinking, racist, bad-tempered, workaholic New York narc who earned the name 'Popeye' for his womanising ways. And it took some while for the quiet, urbane Hackman to insinuate himself into what became his best-known role. Roy Scheider, however, was immediately perfect for Doyle's introspective, moody partner, Buddy 'Cloudy' Russo.

Friedkin wanted to find 'the French actor in *Belle de Jour*' for the role of the smooth and outwardly respectable Corsican drug trafficker, Alain Charnier. The casting director signed up the wrong actor, choosing Fernando Rey (who was Spanish) instead of Francisco Rabal, who wouldn't have been any good anyway because he couldn't speak a word of English. Several scripts were ditched, including one by Alex Jacobs, who wrote *Point Blank* (1967), and another by the writer of *They Shoot Horses, Don't They?* (1969) – Rob Thompson. Eventually, they went with a script by Ernest Tidyman, a crime reporter with the *New York Times* and author of *Shaft*.

But in reality it wasn't Egan and Grosso's work which broke the Connection – they simply nabbed a big haul. By 1965 the Corsican chemists were sending over four tons of pure heroin into New York every year. The joke was that corrupt elements in the French intelligence agency SDECE were actually involved in smuggling. In November 1971, in a re-run of *The French Connection*, a Volkswagen Camper driven by a retired SDECE agent acting on behalf of a serving colonel was found to have 45 kilogrammes of heroin stashed away. Eventually, the Turkish government, acting under pressure from the Americans, eradicated the opium crop, forcing the traffickers to look to the Far East for supplies. It was not until 1978 that Marseilles' biggest drugs broker, Jean Jehan, the inspiration for the Alain Charnier character, was finally captured.

Watching most drug war movies is a gruelling experience – no joy, no triumphs, no real winners or losers, just an endless round of murder, mayhem, blood and betrayal. Characters are dragged to the bottom by their ambition, their passions or their weaknesses. Fighting the drug war is a dirty, ugly business, and those who become involved swiftly don the hair shirt of dirty and ugly whatever side they are on. Not that sorting out the good guys from the baddies is always easy. Moral certainties are exposed to scrutiny like a surgeon examining a throbbing heart. Identities become blurred, principles abandoned, lines crossed. Alternative or swiftly changing political agendas protect the bad, leaving the good confused and hung out to dry.

However, *FC* and its equally successful sequel *FCII* (1975), directed by John Frankenheimer, did not hang around to disturb the ironies that beset the war on drugs. It was too busy being a highly effective action movie with one of the best vehicle chases ever shot. Doyle/Egan was a maverick who often trod the lonely path of those who don't play by the rules. He had his weaknesses and he was portrayed paradoxically as an 'addictive-behaviour type', constantly chasing women and drinking. Perhaps this was supposed to explain away the weakest part of the sequel, where Doyle is kidnapped, injected with heroin and turned into an 'instant addict' complete with 'bouncing-off-the-wall' withdrawals inside three weeks.

But he knew exactly where his loyalties lay. He was fiercely anti-drug and convinced himself that if you wanted to make a difference you had to play by a different set of rules from those set out in the police manual – the rules, in fact, of those you were trying to apprehend. Doyle became a modern-day blueprint for all those renegade cop movies where the central character slugs it out with the police chief who is in a constant state of apoplexy at the antics of the employee he knows is both a pain in the arse and the best officer on the force.

The French Connection remains one of the most straightforward of the drug war genre, shot in a time when there was little public debate about the efficacy of fighting the war. Television now marks out the clearest battle lines drawn out in shows like *Miami Vice, Hill Street Blues, NYPD Blues* and, in the UK, *The Bill.* There is little room for light and shade about drugs here. Neither the audience, the advertisers, the network bosses nor regulators would allow it. How soaps deal with drugs, I examine briefly in the next chapter.

Back in the early 1970s, though, the next generation of young directors and actors were busy flexing their artistic muscle. They had grown up during the burgeoning drug culture of the 1960s and the political upheavals of the day and sometimes chose a different set of angels to side with.

Cisco Pike (1971), a well-acted forgotten gem, with uncredited screenplay writing by Robert Towne (*The Last Detail* (1973) and *Chinatown* (1974)), featured Kris Kristofferson in his screen debut as Pike, a failing musician turned hash dealer. He has ambitions of going straight and getting back in the business but is forced into a deal with Gene Hackman, this time as Leo Holland, a corrupt narc who has already busted Pike twice. Holland needs money fast to pay off a $10,000 loan. Pike needs details of prior arrests to 'vanish' as he faces his latest bust charge. Holland offers to change his testimony if Pike can shift in two days the 100 kilogrammes of grass that Holland has stolen.

This is way out of Pike's league, but it is good-quality hash and Pike gets to keep whatever he can make above the $10,000. Despite the quantity, there is still a sense in 1971 of hash dealing as a cottage industry. Pike is a too-trusting hippie dealer getting along, selling to the music business (like infamous Texan doper Doug Sahm and his band, Sir Douglas Quintet) while trying to get his own music scene back together. Pike drifts around doing deals in a film shot in those bright optimistic Californian sunshine colours we see in *Easy Rider* – very different from the gritty realism of *The French Connection* that takes us into the worst of New York's bleak inner-city areas, although both films use hand-held camera techniques to get a documentary feel.

We are always on Cisco's side in the film not just because he is trying to slough off his own bad dealing ways and go legit, but because of the contrast with the hypocrisy of an officer of the law switching sides for his own ends.

At least one reading of *Easy Rider* and *Cisco Pike* would view the main characters as martyrs of the drug culture. Billy Hayes, too, suffers so that others might get high, at the hands of the Turkish police in *Midnight Express* (1975). The background to another true story from the drugs war was American pressure on the Turkish government to eradicate opium production and generally stop drugs flowing out of the country to the USA. Undoubtedly, life in the Turkish penal system was horrific, but Alan Parker's film with an Oliver Stone screenplay overplays Turkish brutality; some of the more sadistic incidents apparently did not take place. The Turks were by and large just following the US line and wanted to make an example of a US citizen to show how 'onside' they were. It is significant that in the film the US government appear to do nothing to help secure Hayes's release, essentially believing that leaving him to rot would show solidarity with Turkey. Having had his already draconian sentence 'upgraded' from 12 years to life, he is only freed by escaping.

However, for a cinematic treatise on drug-driven police corruption, Harvey Keitel's open wound performance in Abel Ferrera's *Bad Lieutenant* (1992) stands alone. What he does on screen is nothing less than heroic; few actors would agree to be seen in such an unwholesome light. Keitel's NYPD lieutenant is never given a name, because right from the start of the film he has already lost all sense of humanity.

He steals coke from crime scenes to resell, takes the proceeds of robberies away from offenders and pockets it. He drinks heavily, smokes crack and visits prostitutes. During the scene where Zoe the hooker (played by Ferrera's co-screenplay writer Zoe Lund) shoots him up with heroin, she compares addiction to vampirism. She knows and understands the lieutenant, she knows about self-medicating pain and self-loathing with drugs. 'Vampires are lucky. They can feed on others . . . We gotta eat away at ourselves 'til there is nothing left but appetite,' she says. From this came the idea for Ferrera's vampire movie *Addiction.*

His real addiction is gambling and he bets with mounting suicidal recklessness on the outcome of a seven-game play-off series between the Mets and the Dodgers baseball teams. As his cocaine paranoia and psychosis grip harder, reality slips away: the lieutenant, in the thrall of rampaging Catholic guilt, hallucinates the figure of Christ moving towards him in a church where a nun has been raped. His howls of pain are subhuman. His massive $120,000 bet fails and now he has nothing to lose.

Harvey Keitel told *Sight and Sound*: 'I was very proud when someone said that it was the best anti-drugs film they had ever seen because there was no moralising in it . . . I believe it is a religious film, because hell is here now and so is the opportunity to know heaven.'[3]

The corruption inherent in the system reaches its apotheosis in *Training Day* (2002). Denzil Washington stars in a debut villain role as Alonzo Harris, leader of a group of maverick undercover detectives, who make many arrests while at the same time helping themselves to large wodges of cash and dispatching anybody who gets in their way. Ethan Hawke is Jake Hoyt as the rookie cop assigned to partner Harris to learn the ropes. Hoyt learns that the ropes can hang you as his 'mentor' drags him further into the mire, starting with the PCP-laced joint Harris forces on him right at the start of the shift to prove he can hack it on the streets.

It is all great fun to watch, with Washington strutting the streets like a Godfather exacting tribute, but surely as comment on police corruption it is so over the top as to stretch the boundaries of plausibility? Apparently not. The film was inspired by real events in the Ramparts district of Los Angeles that made *Training Day* look tame by comparison and has been called the worst police scandal in the history of LA. In 1996 a cop named Rafael Perez joined the LAPD – Community Action Against Street Hoodlums unit. In 1998 he was arrested for stealing three kilogrammes of cocaine valued at over a million dollars from the police evidence locker. In order to plea-bargain, Perez told invest-igating officers about a whole network of corrupt officers engaged in dealing, illegal shootings, frame-ups, beatings, witness intimidation and perjury. One cop was even set up to be murdered because it was feared he wasn't a 'team player'. After covering the story in depth and studying over 50 hours of testimony from Perez, the *Los Angeles Times* concluded in 2000 that 'An organised criminal subculture thrived within the LAPD, where a secret fraternity of anti-gang officers and supervisors committed crimes and celebrated shootings'. Many convictions were quashed and millions paid in compensation. It is just one example of the extreme situations played out in the real drugs war. Nobody has to invent this stuff.[4]

If staying clean is one challenge facing the narcotics enforcement officer dealing with the most lucrative illegal activity on the planet, then the perils of going native when you go undercover are another. Because drugs are viewed beyond the pale by a majority of the population, they become more than the plot devices and drivers for character motiv-ation. They become metaphors to indicate just how far the main character(s) has fallen. It is unlikely that any other illegal activity could put characters in such a dilemma and in a climate where dealers are regarded as worse than murderers, decisions on just how far do you go to get near to them.

Those picked for this work are those most likely to earn the trust of the gangsters they are trying to take down. They may be the ones with the flawed characters, the ones who find it hardest to play by the rules, the mavericks, the loose cannons. And where drugs are involved, the dangers multiply – what happens, for example, if you get too involved with the product?

Rush (1992) was based on yet another true story, this one set in the mid-1970s involving undercover narcotics cop Kim Wozencraft. Pete Dexter (*Paris Trout*, 1991) turned her story into the screenplay about two undercover cops – Jim Raynor (Jason Patric) and Kristen Cates (Jennifer Jason Leigh) – who go native to try to entrap an east Texan drug dealer, Will Gaines, played by Greg Allman.

Patric is the experienced officer who believes that you have to live the life if you want to get ahead – or simply stay alive – in the undercover business. Leigh is the naive foil who goes down that slippery slope with Patric, as the heroin they use to convince those close to Allman that they are genuine, begins to take its toll. And in their adversity, as their addiction grows and they become more dependent on each other, they fall in love. Their visceral, emotionally raw and intense relationship centred on drugs threatens to destroy them both. The signal moment is when they are both forced to shoot up heroin in front of a dealer pointing a gun. The scene is tense and sexually charged with the dealer as voyeuristic onlooker and a scorching, slow-burning Eric Clapton guitar moaning in the background. From that point Raynor and Cates are lovers.

Officers volunteer to become the very people they want to arrest. Being able to 'act out', to sin and get away with it, may be a powerful draw. Raynor is so drawn to the dark side that you almost think he became an undercover cop so he could shoot heroin with impunity.

Good cops going off the tracks is hardly a new concept. But the strong performances here of Patric and Leigh and a good directorial debut for Lili Zanuck offer a powerful take on what can happen when you enter uncharted moral waters, fudge the lines and the doors start closing behind you. At one point Kristen is actually proud that she took a snort of cocaine. But the words of Raynor's boss Dodd come back to haunt her: 'It gets ugly and you get ugly with it.'

The film was chosen for a charity premiere in aid of the UK drugs charity Turning Point in the presence of the Princess of Wales. In her speech she acknowledged that *Rush* 'is not social drama, it is Hollywood [but] vividly shows the fine line between creeping addiction and free choice . . . We should be able to see beyond the gunslinging dramatics of the world of *Rush* to underlying truths common to drug use in any country. In my visits to Turning Point projects, I have yet to meet a villain like Will Gaines, but I have met many unhappy casualties of our own drugs tragedy. I think it is important to remember the differences between negative stereotyping and . . . the reality.' The British tabloids did not take kindly to accusations that they were largely responsible for the stigma that users and their families suffered as a result of the stereotypical press reporting. The *Star* suggested that Diana was no more qualified to lecture on drugs that a 'palace charlady' (5 June 1992), while the *Daily Sport* (5 June 1992) opined that having now championed AIDS sufferers and 'junkies', she needed reminding that 'there are some normal people out there, Di'.

In *Rush* the cops go under because they become users to trap a dealer. In *Deep Cover* (1992) Lawrence Fishburne in his first starring role has to become a major dealer to catch far bigger fish than Will Gaines. He wants the job, but he has some ghosts to exorcise. As a child he witnessed his father killed as he tried to hold up a store and from there developed a stern set of principles for his own behaviour which will have to be compromised if he is to ingratiate himself with the drug-dealing fraternity. His supervisor tells him that psychological profiling demonstrates he is perfectly qualified: 'You score almost like a criminal. You resent authority and have a rigid moral code. But no underlying system of values. Look at all your rage and repressed violence. Under cover, all your faults will become virtues.'

Starting out as a street dealer, he gradually works his way up the hierarchy until he reaches a lawyer who is also a mid-level distributor, played with languid menace by Jeff Goldblum. From there he begins to connect with the South American end of the operation – a major importer, Gallegos – and the ultimate target, a South American politician, Hector Guzman. Working under cover, he breaks all his rules to stay in the game – at one point he has to kill somebody in cold blood. He also begins to enjoy some of the spoils of war – house, car, clothes and the affections of a beautiful woman. Gradually, his perceptions blur at the edges: is he a cop posing as a dealer or the other way round?

There are hints throughout the film of real drug war events – the accusations made by Gary Webb in his 1996 articles for the *San Jose Mercury* and his later book of CIA complicity in Contra coke trafficking and the cat-and-mouse game with Noriega. Eventually, our man gets close to Guzman, but then his federal supervisor tells him to back off because the politics have changed: 'we like him now.' But Fishburne contrives to bring Guzman down anyway with incriminating photos.

The screen has also provided us with a range of dealer personality types. In *Rush*, Greg Allman stalks through the film almost wordless like a black-riding Tolkien ringwraith. By contrast, Nico Brown in *New Jack City* and Tony Montana in *Scarface* are quite literally in your face with serious menace. Less cartoonish is the character of Dwayne Gittens, known as God, played by rap star L.L. Cool J. in Michael Rymer's *In Too*

Deep (1999). Omar Epps plays Jeff Cole, an undercover cop who has to get close to Gittens, the local Cincinatti drug boss. In this excellent film, Gittens is a complex mix of vicious thug, loving family man and community do-gooder while selling drugs to his own people. But he is a lonely man in a business where he trusts nobody. Although appalled by Dwayne's ruthless attitude, Cole gets too close and a friendship begins to develop. The look on Gittens's face as he is led away at the end, staring back at the man he thought was his friend, is almost poignant.

It is perhaps not surprising that after his roles as 'outsiders', Edward Scissorhands and Ed Wood, Johnny Depp would want to take on the true story of cocaine smuggler George Jung in Ted Demme's *Blow* (2001).[5]

Jung grew up in early-1960s Boston, the son of a hard-working but failed small businessman constantly harangued by his wife for their lack of material success. Jung and his friend Tuna flee to California, where they become dope dealers to the beach and surf set. He meets an air hostess, Barbara, and through her hooks up with Derek Foreal, a hairdresser whose business is a front for big-time marijuana dealing. Business is booming until George is arrested and Barbara dies of cancer. While inside, George's cell mate, Colombian Diego Delgado, teaches him all about the coke business: 'I went in with a batchelor's in marijuana and came out with a doctorate in cocaine.' Through Delgado, Jung is introduced to Pablo Escobar, one of the richest and most ruthless drug traffickers in history, and becomes the main conduit for Escobar's cocaine into the USA during the late 1970s and early 1980s. He marries a Colombian girl, Mirtha, they have a daughter, Kristina, and become fabulously rich. But the world of trafficking is full of betrayal, and eventually his partners cut him out of the loop, set him up and he is arrested. Jung jumps bail, tries to get back on the gravy train but is set up again and this time is put away for 20 years. Jung is currently serving out his sentence in the Federal Correction Institute in Otisville, New York, and is not due for release until 2014.

It was a brave decision to make a film with a drug dealer as hero, but left the film open to criticism that it was 'amoral', taking no account of the damage that drugs can do. There were other reasons to attack the film – the Austin Powers wigs, the rushed ending and the over-close homage to *Goodfellas* (to the extent of having Ray Liotta as Jung's long-suffering dad) and *Boogie Nights* – and the unreal depiction of cocaine use itself. People were shown hoovering up large amounts of coke and suffering no obvious effects until they suddenly became basket cases. Nor did *Blow* endear itself to the press when the distributors, New Line Cinema, gave out pocket-size mirrors to promote the film.

One must also be wary of the self-serving nature of biopics based on the life of somebody operating in a hard and very violent environment. In the film, Depp hardly ever draws out a gun, let alone shoots anybody. And we are lured into a view of Jung as victim: he is betrayed by everybody close to him, even his mother. But assuming the account is by and large accurate, the character of George Jung subverts the stereotype of the murderous drug dealer.

Blow showed that Hollywood was prepared to take a risk with a film that offered a view of the dealer as hippie pirate rather than the usual spawn of the devil. It followed on from another film that rather than just offering a sympathetic view of the drug culture suggested that the whole architecture of the drugs war was built on shifting sands. Stephen Soderbergh's *Traffic* (2000) was based on a superb UK mini-series, *Traffik* (1989), and although a first-rate movie and the first American film to cast any doubt over drug war reasoning, it none the less does suffer by comparison with its UK inspiration.

Running at over five hours, *Traffik* is one of the best dramas about the drugs war ever made. Co-produced by Channel 4 and the German company ARD, *Traffik* had time to develop some of the key themes without resorting to cliché and stereotyping. It breaks down into three main story threads.

The first focuses on Jack Lithgow, a minister at the Home Office who goes on a fact-finding mission to Pakistan to see if their anti-drug efforts are sufficient to warrant further aid money.

At the start of the film, a helicopter carries him over fields where his government host tells him that opium has been eradicated, where new crops grow and where hospitals and schools have been built with the Western aid money. The reality, of course, is very different. When he comes down to earth, he is accosted by an opium farmer, Fazal, who tells him that the farmers cannot survive growing other crops, that there are no schools and hospitals, that the aid never reaches the people who need it. Initially dismissive of the arguments, Lithgow comes to learn of the corruption in government and the protection offered to traffickers. He had some early doubts about the integrity of the government when he is taken on a drug bust. Arrests are made but no heroin found; 'perhaps they knew we were coming,' he says.

His host's daughter, an anti-heroin activist, is trying to build a case against Tariq Butt, a major heroin trafficker, and persuades Lithgow to travel to the inaccessible mountain regions where her cousin shows him around. The man tells Lithgow that the people in the region have always traded in contraband: opium is just another commodity and nobody will ever stop it. As Lithgow's moral certainties fall away one by one, he smokes an opium cigarette while the man tries to persuade him to go for the traffickers who make the heroin and leave the farmers alone – although one might ask whether the opium crop would be quite so profitable without the heroin market to sell to.

But growing doubts about granting further aid are strengthened when he finds out that his own daughter Caroline is addicted to heroin. In the full glare of the media, he refuses to sign the aid agreement and is sacked.

The second thread is Fazal's story as an example of the plight of farmers in the developing world. When the Pakistani government go through the motions of cracking down on opium growing to secure British aid, Fazal is driven to work for Butt. But he earns Butt's displeasure, is framed and arrested. To secure his release, his wife is persuaded to smuggle heroin into Britain by body-packing, and she swallows several packets of heroin dipped in honey. Increasingly unwell on the flight as the packets begin to break down, she arrives at Heathrow with her children just as heroin floods her system and she dies a sordid death in an airport lavatory. Fazal is overjoyed to be free, but this quickly turns to horror as he learns what has happened. He seeks out Butt and takes his revenge. Fazal and Caroline are thousands of miles apart, but both victims of the same process.

The final strand is a more routine and less plausible thriller, although very well executed. Karl Rosshalde, a wealthy German businessman, runs an irrigation equipment company doing very nicely in Pakistan on government contracts funded by UK aid. He is also a major heroin trafficker. When Karl is arrested at Hamburg airport, his naive British wife with her cut-glass upper-class accent proves herself to be a very shrewd businesswomen who picks up the threads of her husband's drug business to pay off his debts. Rosshalde has the key witness against him murdered and is released for lack of evidence. But the German detective who arrested him is determined to bring him to justice and manages to place a bug in Rosshalde's house to wait for the man and his wife to incriminate themselves.

The American version, written by Stephen Gagan, contained some excellent performances, especially from Benicio Del Toro, who won Best Supporting Actor at the 2001 Oscars, one of four awards the film picked up. Gagan himself was writing about drugs from first-hand experience. He told *Newsweek* (12 February 2001) that he had gone through the whole chemical concerto, was arrested, but still managed to hold a writing career together, winning an Emmy for an episode of *NYPD* 'composed while on heroin'. The script also captures the utter despair and lack of ideas about how to tackle drugs running right through the US Administration. In one scene, the US drug tsar Robert Wakefield, played by Michael Douglas, travels on Airforce One with representatives from all the various federal law-enforcement agencies back from a trip to see the hopeless situation trying to stop drugs coming across the Mexican border. He gives them an opportunity to think right outside the box, to come up with one single new idea. Everybody looks at the ground – and Wakefield is particularly incensed when he realises that there is 'nobody from treatment' on board the plane.

But although it had less time to develop the story, one has to be slightly suspicious that the whole section about the farmers was completely cut. Instead of South America, where the coca is grown and processed into cocaine, the focus of the film was Mexico, primarily a transit country. With no mitigating circumstances, it becomes the totally corrupt enemy at the gates against which the brave but despairing US must defend itself.

Quoted in the *Traffic* production notes on the Internet, producer Laura Bickford explained the rationale for not locating the film in Colombia. 'We decided to do Mexico because we wanted to do something fresh and we felt we'd all seen movies about Colombian warlords.' She went on to say that since the big Colombian cartels had been taken down, it spread the power around, given the Mexican cartels a bigger piece of the action. The film-makers wanted to reflect this more recent development in the power play of international trafficking. Mexican society was affected as never before. Except we never see this – just a bunch of dodgy policemen and army types, and Benicio Del Toro as the one honest flame in a bushfire of corruption. With the British version, situated in a producer country like Pakistan, you had a much stronger sense of the 'top-to-bottom' impact of the unceasing demand for drugs.

A Mexican general is appointed as his country's drug tsar only for it to be revealed that the reason he is going after one drug cartel is because he is in the pay of another. The downfall of General Salazar and the embarrassment for the US government was no fiction. Drug tsar Barry McCaffrey's cross-border ally, General Jesus Gutierrez, a man McCaffrey described as 'honest', was arrested for working with Amado Fuentes, one of Mexico's most feared drug barons.

However much Wakefield wants his advisers to think the unthinkable, any notion of law reform is out of the question. Two scenes where he is tackled about law reform were deleted from the film. One appears on the DVD where the family are in the car and Caroline asks her father why America doesn't just legalise everything. Wakefield gives a long exposition about the chaos that would ensue if America became the world's drug honeypot. His daughter suggests that wouldn't happen if all the countries legalised at the same time. She is right, of course. All her father can say is: 'I can't see that happening.' Which is also right.

Another scene that didn't even make the DVD involved Ethan Nadel-mann, a real-life drug reformer who heads up the New York-based Drug Policy Alliance. The cocktail party scene involving real politicians remained, but at one point Ethan is introduced to Wakefield and puts to him the point that the drug war is just a war against our own families. This was a particularly tense moment on set because everybody knew that Michael Douglas has a son with drug problems.

Both versions stretch poetic licence when the respective high-profile politicians go looking for their daughters in the mean streets with no security and without the press finding out. But the British take on Caroline's path to addiction is so much more plausible than its American counterpart. Through conversations with her father later on and what we hear in her group therapy sessions at the end, we discover Caroline was an only child whose busy, domineering father had little understanding about what it means to bring up a child in the warm embrace of emotional security. It was left to her mother to overcompensate and Caroline is left unable to cope in the world. Not lacking in intelligence, she goes to Cambridge, but, desperately lacking in self-confidence, she finds that the drugs on offer at parties boost her self-esteem. Heroin works so well for her that she finds she can't do without it, and after a few months realises that she needs the drug every day.

By contrast, in *Traffic* Wakefield's daughter tumbles swiftly from spliff-smoking preppy to heroin-addicted prostitute dragged into degradation by a black dealer – a story 'ripped' straight out of a William Hearst front page. Right at the end, when she is in therapy, we get some idea that she is 'angry' but little else to account for her drug use. One can almost hear the discussions behind the scenes which conclude that in order to get away with questioning the drug war, there has to be something for Mom and Pop to applaud.

Traffik hardly caused a ripple; *Traffic*, on the other hand, had an unprecedented impact around the world. The film was a huge success in Mexico, breaking all box-office records, not least because a Mexican cop was the hero. Colombian cinemagoers actually applauded the film at the end. They felt it demonstrated that for the US to pour guns and money into their country to fight drugs would simply bring more devastation on their heads without doing anything to tackle the issue of voracious drug demand in the US and elsewhere. Thai narcotics police were treated to a special viewing courtesy of the United Nations. The East Asian representative of the UN Drug Control Programme, Dr Sandro Calvini, was quoted as saying that the film 'suggests there is a great need for more transparency in national and international drug control policy and there is a need for more listening, understanding and transparency about what works and what does not work.'

In the USA itself, ABC's flagship current affairs programme *Nightline* devoted five consecutive shows to the subject of drug trafficking, while some senators declared that priorities for drug policy needed to swing away from enforcement to treatment. Drug tsar General Barry McCaffrey, however, was unmoved by all the hoopla created by the film. In a letter to the *Los Angeles Times* (15 March 2001) he wrote: 'All this makes great entertainment. But it is as accurate as saying the Brady Bunch was a portrait of real family life in America. The fact is our national strategy is working.'

Ironically, it was Barry McCaffrey (whose double appears as Wakefield's predecessor) who looked like he might take the next step, again despite the rhetoric. He was actively looking into the possibility of repealing the Rockefeller Laws, securing more money for treatment, and he refused to use 'the war on drugs' handle. But when the Democrats lost, he stepped aside for John Walters, a drug policy hawk, although we have heard little from him as publicity for the war on terrorism has superseded pronouncements on the war on drugs.

One can only be agog that after all the books, articles, papers and conference proceedings on the futility of the drugs war going back decades, it takes a Hollywood blockbuster to open up the debate. But if the door was opened to more reasoned discussion, only a chink of light shone through. The US government admitted in 2002 that a $900 million 'Just Say No'-style ad campaign has been a complete flop – but that they would try again, this time focusing on marijuana. And George Bush has been trying to convince his people that smoking a joint puts money in the pockets of al-Qaeda.

13

E + SF = rave new world

The most significant development in Western drug culture since the late 1980s has been the rise of ecstasy and the rave scene. Originally developed by Merck in 1914 as an appetite suppressant, MDMA was one of many drugs tested by the CIA as a truth drug during the height of the Cold War. It was 'rediscovered' in the 1960s by Alexander Shulgin, a former Dow Chemicals employee who has since become legendary as the creator of many MDMA and LSD-type drugs, all of which he has tried out on himself. Therapists noted the power of the drug to create empathy between people, and MDMA also leaked out on to the streets in the 1980s as a yuppie trip to self-enlightenment. Ecstasy, as it was now known, became especially popular in Texas, where people bought it over the counter in bars and clubs. Then, in 1985, rat experiments suggested that the drug caused brain damage and ecstasy was banned.

No special legislation was required to ban the drug in Britain, because as an analogue of amphetamine it was already controlled under the Misuse of Drugs Act. But that didn't stop it from becoming a firm favourite with British clubbers on the island of Ibiza. Club owners back home opened new all-night dance venues in the late 1980s to capture that ecstasy-inspired summer vibe and happy smiley face. The link between all-night dancing under the influence of a stimulant drug had a long history in the UK going back to the London warehouse parties of the 1920s, when bright young things danced to the beats of jazz and cocaine. The mods picked up the pulse with purple heart amphetamines in the 1960s, while the northern soul crowd and the punks got down to snort up amphetamine powder in the 1970s.

Ecstasy was instrumental in initiating a whole new phase of escalating drug use by UK youth. In the 1980s the substances dominating the headlines were solvents and heroin. These were the drugs of despair, most often used in areas decimated by the decline of Britain's industrial and manufacturing base under Margaret Thatcher. Heroin and glue were perceived as the drugs for losers. E was different. Everybody felt good on E. You needed money to buy it and the lifestyle that went with it – clothes, admission to raves. And few seemed to get messed up. There were some high-profile ecstasy deaths, but for the most part it was seen as relatively safe. This led people to try other drugs around – LSD, amphetamine, poppers (amyl nitrite), ketamine and GHB. Cannabis, too, enjoyed a renaissance, especially when hip-hop kicked in. All very different drugs with very different effects and risks, but the ravers were carried away on a crest of chemical indulgence.

Popular culture was saturated with the imagery and sounds of ecstasy and rave music; it was said that the decline in football hooliganism was due to all the knuckle heads being loved up. But apart from film soundtracks for the likes of *Trainspotting* and cyber geek movies like *Hackers* (1995), little of 'E-culture' found its way to the big screen. The problem for producers and distributors was the relatively benign nature of the ecstasy experience. People enjoyed taking it, and many seemed to benefit from its effects. An E version of *Reefer Madness* would have won plaudits from the mainstream film critics but would have had little credibility with its audience. Financing films about a scene driven totally by young people having a good time on drugs was always going to be tough.

Another problem was actually trying to capture the culture on screen. Rave culture in its widest sense drew on a very broad church. There were the remnants of the 'underground' that kept the spirit of the 1960s alive at Stonehenge and Glastonbury right through to the 'new wave' open-air rave parties. A new breed of punk was born from contact with the festival scene: the so-called rainbow punk – hippies in all but name. They bought trucks and took to the road. They became the core of what became known as New Age Travellers, for whom drug taking was the social cement. By the summer of 1991 the Ibiza and urban club rave scene met the festival-goers and travellers and gave birth to another new philosophy. This was based on the ethos of Spiral Tribe, one of a number of sound systems touring Europe as part of the free party circuit.

So simply showing a warehouse full of extras dancing around to thumping beats and flashing lights acting off their face was never going to be more than a partial representation. But in fairness, trying to corral the rave aesthetic within a tight dramatic framework inevitably led to compromise.

Although the UK pioneered the scene, the US was first out of the blocks with *Go* (1999) over which the shadow of *Pulp Fiction* loomed large. *Go* was directed by Doug Liman, whose debut award-winning movie *Swingers* (1996) was an accomplished comedy about a group of young showbiz ratpackers cruising LA looking for big breaks and willing women.

Go is a fast-paced, well-acted, slick black comedy infused with energy and wit, and a pumped-up techno soundtrack, centred around one night in the lives of LA twentysomethings also in search of a good time on the club scene. Ronna is a hard-pressed checkout girl desperate for cash to avoid eviction who gets embroiled in an ecstasy-dealing scam. The parallel stories involve Ronna's workmate Simon, who persuades Ronna to take his shift so he can party with his mates in Vegas. Things do not quite go according to plan for anybody. The momentum of the film reflects the ecstasy-induced ambience in which it exists, but it remains very hard-edged: there are no huggy sensibilities with this lot.

Another American offering, *Groove* (2000), throbs to much slower bpms and would resonate with anybody who was on the British rave scene in its earliest days. It was a naive but refreshing time, when a new generation was developing a culture of its own, just before the doors of perception opened for business. Written and directed by Greg Harrison, *Groove* was the wow movie of the 2000 Sundance Festival, an ensemble teen comedy set in San Francisco, the crucible of 1950s and 1960s counterculture. In fact, the film speaks to such a particular moment in time and place that one reviewer wondered if it would play even outside the Bay area.

The film starts with the search for a venue south of Market Street by Ernie, the organiser who charges only $2 because he believes that he is fulfilling a service to the community. His main buzz is to get a silent approving nod from a clubber acknowledging his good works. The music is on the button, using the talents of real DJs like John Digwood, but the plot and the characterisation are thin. Harrison is wrestling with the dichotomy alluded to above – trying to establish a sense of time, place and mood and sacrificing those elements that drive a movie forwards. A central plank of the plot is the coming into the light of

David Turner, a computer manual writer whose cynicism about the rave scene is dissolved by a tab of E and the attentions of a woman. Turner represents a sceptical society at large and is won over through a life-enhancing experience similar to that enjoyed by Peter Fonda in *The Trip*.

With magazines like *Time* trying to present rave venues as little more than crack houses with music, Harrison was quite circumspect with the drug content, trying to major on some key health and safety messages, although this is no guarantee of safety from the wrath of the moral guardians.

In 1992 a drug agency in Liverpool produced a leaflet for those attending raves and using drugs like ecstasy. It was the beginning of a general campaign for safer dancing; the agency took the view that, while not condoning use, young people were entitled to information that might help protect them. On its front cover, a British tabloid suggested that parents go around to the agency and chuck the boss into the River Mersey. The funders of the agency came under immense pressure to pull the plug. But within months the same kind of advice was appearing in respectable medical journals like the *British Medical Journal* and *The Lancet*, and soon after that government leaflets carried the same messages. *Groove* carries the harm-reduction messages about drinking fluids to prevent dehydration, not taking drugs on an empty stomach and so on, not least because the clubbers who would make up most of the audience do not have access to that kind of information in the States through official channels.

Somebody almost overdoses, but *Groove* is essentially mellow and accepting of rave culture. The drugs are distributed by a chemist, who tells us all about the brain chemicals serotonin and dopamine, observing that 'to be a successful drug user you've got to be well informed'. No guarantees there, but acting on the right information certainly improves survival rates. The central message of the film is that young people who gather in a spot to dance the night away under the influence of illegal drugs are otherwise law-abiding, don't cause trouble and don't as a rule fatally succumb to the effects of the drugs they are taking.

By far the best British take on rave culture is Justin Kerrigan's *Human Traffic* (1999), which took years to finance and was the first major

British film about E culture more than a decade on from its beginnings.[1] Like its American counterparts, we get a snapshot of the lives of
a group of 20-year-olds, but the vibe is more like *Go* than *Groove*. None
of the characters in any of the films gives a moment's thought to mani-
festoes, and the undercurrent of evangelical self-importance is
mercifully absent. In the opening credits, Kerrigan dips into this with
some Direct Action news footage, but nobody is heard espousing the
cause. In *Human Traffic*, all the characters hate their lives and look
forward to a weekend getting 'more spaced than Neil Armstrong'.

As you would expect, the film is loud and visually arresting, a caul-
dron of energy and excitement, bravura editing, imaginative camera
work and a banging soundtrack. Not everything works, though – the
'alternative national anthem' scene, for instance – and in parts *Human
Traffic* is too self-consciously 'zany' with characters screaming into the
camera and at each other to convince us they are going to have a great
time.

Jip is the focal point of the film, stuck in a clothing store, feeling
shafted by his boss and worrying over a bout of impotence which has
already cost him girlfriends. Jip's mum is a prostitute, working from
home to make ends meet. It would have been easy to make this element
of the story sordid and maudlin. Instead, the relationship between
mother and son and Jip's anger over her exploitation is played with
gentle sadness. Jip's best clubbing friend is the blonde ice-beauty Lulu,
an independent, 'major head-banger', increasingly disenchanted with
feckless men. Koop blags overpriced hip-hop and gangsta vinyl to mugs
in his shop ('This was recorded by a posse of crackheads on Death
Row, right'), while weighed down with jealousy over the antics of his
flirtatious girlfriend, Nina (who has recently walked out of a fast-food
restaurant nightmare), and a father who is mentally ill. Finally, Moff,
the Grade A Party Animal and drug supplier, constantly rows with his
policeman father about his lack of gainful (legal) employment, telling
them that he's not ready yet to be miserable like all his mates.

Some of the put-downs and vignettes of psychobabblers and space
cadets are well observed. For this author, the best scenes in the film are
the suited news reporter telling in 'rave-speak' how the dealing works,
Howard Marks's cameo role describing the art of scoring a toke from a
neighbouring joint, and the scene where Lulu and Nina are being

interviewed by another po-faced media muppet lurking on the fringes of the club scene to conduct an 'in-depth' look at youthful drug depravities. After stringing the interviewer along about how they used to take E until seeing *Trainspotting* 'made them' want to take heroin, the girls cut in: 'We've got to go. We're late for our next hit.'

Kerrigan says he based his script on his own experiences – so, for example, nobody dies from taking drugs. Nina introduces Lee, her 17-year-old brother, to the scene for his first E trip. She has her doubts but rationalises to Lulu: 'He's going to do it eventually, so I reckon he's better off with me than mixing with the wrong crowd.' It could all go horribly wrong – kid brother dies, sister racked with guilt. But he comes through and has a good time.

Kerrigan pastes in a throwback pastiche to the old drug propaganda movies where a doctor tells his shocked audience about the dangers of drugs. Flash to Lee listening to a lecture on the risk of depression in later life caused by ecstasy-induced depletion of serotonin levels in the brain. 'Yeah, all right, fair enough, doc,' says Jip, 'but on the flip side, Lee, you'll feel an overwhelming sense of empathy with people, you'll be able to be intimate with your friends, talk about things you never felt comfortable enough to say before.' The doctor goes on to outline the dangers of overheating and heatstroke. 'Statistically,' counters Jip, 'you're more likely to die from choking on a cabbage leaf, or an argument in a pub, than you are from dropping an E.' 'Your penis will shrivel up,' says the doc, 'and you won't be able to get an erection.' (Jip now silent). 'Anyone who repeatedly takes ecstasy is punching the wall between consciousness and unconsciousness. In later life, instead of reaching for the lasers, you could be reaching for the prescriptions.'

We get a taste of this possible life to come in the kitchen scene at the end of the film. Everybody is totally shattered; the E bonhomie has gone and they can hardly look each other in the eye. The massive comedown at the end of the weekend is partly the downside of taking stimulant drugs and partly the realisation that the weekend is over. Paranoia is coming through the walls; 'the children of ecstasy aren't safe any more. We're no longer all together as one, but separate mental patients . . . all you have to look forward to is unconsciousness. But you can never sleep.' When the party's over, turn out the lights – until the next Lost Weekend, although in the throes of his comedown Moff believes he needs to end The Party for ever.

But the film's real strength is the relationship between the five friends. The heart of *Human Traffic* is the transition for Jip and Lulu from best mates to lovers, and this film does have the human heart and soul lacking in the other films. The irony is that for a film that takes a stand against all the moral panic surrounding rave culture, the ultimate message is very conventional. Love conquers all.

Nowadays 'E' has hyperlinks with the online world: surfing, e-mailing, hacking, spamming, connecting, networking, downloading and crashing. Key pioneers of these technologies revelled in shooting from the hip, taking chances and staring down risk – looking for any stimulus to jump-start the creative process, to come at problems from different angles, including the use of psychedelic drugs.

Jaron Lanier, the dreadlocked computer scientist who coined the phrase 'virtual reality', said: 'almost to a person, the founders of the [personal] computer industry were psychedelic-style hippies . . . Within the computer science community, there's a very strong connection with the 1960s psychedelic tradition. Absolutely no question about it.' Timothy Leary became a huge convert to cyberculture, calling virtual reality 'electronic LSD' and observing: 'It's no accident that the people who popularised the personal computer were Steve Jobs and Steve Wozniak, both barefoot long-haired acid freaks. It's no accident that most of the people in the software computer industry have had very thoughtful, very profitable and creative psychedelic experiences.'[2]

In July 1991 Walter Crin wrote in *GQ* magazine: 'The keys to our economic future are in the hands of Silicon Valley's young computer visionaries. And a lot of those visions are triggered by hallucinogens created in labs just yesterday. Welcome to the Second Psychedelic Revolution.' Crin travelled to the annual Apple computer shindig, Macworld Expo, 'a cybernetic Woodstock, a be-in for the information age'. After two weeks 'deep in the psycho-silicon jungle', he concluded that 'the enemy' in the war on drugs includes 'quite a few of our country's best minds' and wondered if America really could afford to take the 'high' out of high tech.

In the 1999 TNT docudrama *Pirates of Silicon Valley,* Apple founder

Steve Jobs was depicted on an acid trip in which he conceives himself as a conductor of his own cosmic symphony. Bob Wallace, an early Microsoft staffer who owned an online bookshop selling psychedelic titles until he was found dead at his home in 2002, said that his conception of shareware as a formal business application was drug-inspired. Bob Jesse, an ex-vice president of business development at Oracle (second-largest software company after Microsoft), left the company to head the Council on Spiritual Practices that advocates (among other things) responsible use of drugs for religious purposes.

All in all, the similarities between visual representations of virtual reality and cyberspace and the drug experience are too close to be purely accidental. And as youth culture films of the 1960s reflected the drug culture of marijuana and LSD, so the youth films at the end of the century reflect a different drug culture – one where drugs are far more ubiquitous and embracing new drugs on the scene, in particular ketamine.

The drug-inspired SF movie has a dual dynamic often contained within the same film. One is the visual representation of the drug experience like the star gate in *2001*. The second is the link between VR, cyberspace and addiction – the obsessive-compulsive pull of the screen, the keyboard and the world of virtual reality.

VR convinces you that you are in another place by substituting primary sensory data – what you perceive as your normal waking state – with data received and produced by a computer. This is exactly what psychedelic drugs do. By an interaction with brain chemicals, they replace one data set with another. In VR, the body is left behind, leaving an entity of pure mind and energy to roam free and unencumbered by physical restraint. But there is a dystopic trap lurking behind the freedom of VR. Like the ketamine (see below) or the LSD psychonaut, the VR traveller may return in a state of madness and disintegration.

Lawnmower Man (1992) combines the classic Frankenstein story with elements of *Jacob's Ladder*. Pierce Brosnan is Dr Lawrence Angelo, a scientist working on a top-secret project for the government to artificially raise the intelligence of primates using smart drugs and increase their aggression. Early versions of the trials go badly wrong when a brain-enhanced chimp runs amok and kills a human.

Angelo decides to abandon the work on aggression and focus on enhancing intelligence. He turns his attention to Jobe, the simple-minded boy who mows Angelo's lawn, building up his intelligence in a virtual reality environment. The experiment soon spirals out of control. Jobe's capacity to absorb knowledge increases exponentially to abnormal levels. He learns Latin in two hours and quickly outstrips the intelligence of his 'creator'. He develops the ability to read minds and levitate objects. Angelo's paymasters, the CIA, hear of the work; the good doctor's government minder switches the drugs, so that Jobe is now being injected with substances geared to make him violent. He becomes an all-powerful malevolent monster who (ho-hum) plans to take over the world by leaving his physical body, entering the research establishment's mainframe computer and from there to infect every computer and phone line. Virtual reality will become the only reality.

The religious symbolism of drug psychosis runs through the whole film, from the monster's name to the showdown in VR between master and monster when Jobe pins Angelo to a VR cross – reminiscent of a similar scene of the crucified Jessup in *Altered States*. Through his life, Jobe has been in the dark tunnel of ignorance, but is shot into the bright light of knowledge and awareness by Angelo through the technology of VR. At one point it threatens to overwhelm him. For Dr Xavier, the light flooded his eyes; for Jobe, it's the noise of human thoughts flooding his brain that drives him insane. But he becomes addicted to power and knowledge and breaks into the research establishment frantically injecting himself in the neck with the contaminated drug. Kubrick's psychedelic, multimedia, high-tech fascist nightmare is realised when Jobe tells Angelo, 'You need to be led. It's a basic need.'

The dystopic/addictive dynamic of VR is also explored in Kathryn Bigelow's *Strange Days* (1995) and David Cronenberg's *Existenz* (1999). Cronenberg's rather weak exposition on runaway technology centres on the dangers of game addiction where the players who can't get enough of alternate realities are fitted with a bioport in the base of their spine for the game to be shot directly into the neural network of the brain.

Strange Days stars Ralph Fiennes as Lenny Nero, ex-cop turned street hustler who trades in illegal SQUIDS – Super-Conducting Quantum Interface Devices. Street people like hookers and burglars are paid to have sex or commit crimes while wired up to mobile headsets. Their experiences can then be downloaded on to disks, for straight people to enjoy a vicarious thrill – at a price. Nero is the high-tech dealer in altered states of consciousness offering a smorgasbord of VR jollies who tells one hesitant punter: 'I can get you what you want. You just have to talk to me. I'm your priest, your shrink, your main connection to the switchboard of the soul. I'm the Magic Man, the Santa Claus of the subconscious. You say it, you even think it, you can have it.'

In 1962 Calvin Stevens, working with US pharmaceutical giant Parke-Davis, came up with a drug codenamed CL369, later named 'ketamine'. The new drug was given to a human subject for the first time in 1964 by Dr Edward Domino, who described to his wife how the subject was fully awake but just 'not there'. The drug was important as a replacement anaesthetic for phencyclidine (PCP or, as it later became known, 'angel dust'). Many patients given PCP to sedate them reported all kinds of disturbing hallucinations as they came round after surgery. Because it is quick-acting, ketamine also became popular in battlefield surgery and was mentioned a couple of times in the TV series of *M.A.S.H.*

But ketamine turned out to be a very strange drug indeed. Not only was it an effective anaesthetic but it had other effects similar to psychedelics, amphetamine and heroin. It is probably also the only addictive psychedelic with fast-building tolerance.

One of the most dramatic effects of ketamine is a re-creation for some users of what is known as the near-death experience (NDE). Non-drug-induced NDE is most often reported by those actually on the point of death who, for example, survive major traumas like heart attacks or surgery.

Those who have experienced ketamine-induced NDE feel they have left their body and travel at great speed through a tunnel to a source of light. Convinced they are dead, they experience telepathic communication with God, enter other realities and alternative universes that appear more real than normal consciousness and reality. Nothing is real except the self and the sense that there is no reality to return to. This is close to what Eddie Jessup feels in *Altered States* as he journeys deeper into his own 'back catalogue', because Jessup is modelled on Dr John Lilly, who not only pioneered the flotation tank but was a regular ketamine user into his eighties right up to his death in 2001.[3] He wrote of his drug experiences in *The Scientist: A Novel Autobiography* (1978).

Over many decades, John Lilly consumed frightening amounts of ketamine – at one point he was injecting himself every hour, 20 hours a day for a month. Even as a child, Lilly experienced a number of mental disturbances – out-of-body experiences and visits by guardian angels.

He worked with sensory deprivation in the flotation tank for ten years, then combined this with LSD in 1963. His first experience with ketamine came when a young doctor friend, Carl Enright, injected him as a cure for migraine, after which he believed that beings told him to carry on taking the drug for 'educational purposes'. He went on a 13-month binge, during which he came to value internal realities over the external world. He believed he was connected to a solid-state civilisation in charge of the earth's computers. Another time, he nearly drowned in a pool and, once resuscitated, thought the year was 3001. His wife begged him to get help, but he refused. He was in a cycle of chronic ketamine use, followed by collapse and resuscitation, only to return to the drug. He was convinced that the world would be taken over by this computerised alien evil force and tried to warn the President. He refused to acknowledge that he was addicted, referring simply to 'a repeated use trap'. Lilly said of the Beings: 'When you take the drug you enter into their consciousness.' In other words, under the influence of ketamine, you imagine the drug is a door into a world that already exists, that is hidden from waking consciousness, unlocked only by ketamine. It's a world of morphing body shapes, swirling vortex, mythical and religious visions, becoming God and contact with a higher self. Real life is actually the dream – the ketamine vision is what life really is.

Contact (1997), starring Jodie Foster, contains one interesting episode where she is sent spinning across the universe inside an alien craft, without actually leaving earth. The special effects are similar to those described by users as falling into a 'ketamine hole', resembling the NDE. The story was written by Carl Sagan, whose use of psychedelic drugs became widely known after his death in 1996. The perception that one has crossed the universe is a known ketamine effect described by John Lilly as being part of a 'thin sheet of consciousness that is distributed around the galaxy'.[4]

But probably the most realised synergy between drugs and cyberculture – cyberdelia – comes with *The Matrix* (1999). The film spawned whole websites devoted solely to interpreting and picking apart every detail of the film. Message boards teem with analysis and comment. The most common metaphors associated with the film are biblical: a cyberpunk parable (as one intricate analysis put it), Neo as the Messiah, Trinity, Zion, a craft called Nebuchadnezzar and so on. The drug dimension to *The Matrix*, though, has been curiously overlooked. Nobody says too much about it. Obviously, Warner Brothers would not want to play up the drug angle. Fans, too, are wary of any analysis that might cheapen what some of the more zealous elements seem to regard as a quasi-religious and metaphysical experience. But like it or not, there is an interpretation of the film which grounds it securely in the drug/cyber culture of the twenty-first century.

The whole premise of the film revolves around the nature of reality, the space between waking and dreaming. Here are John Lilly's evil solid-state entities ruling the world, dominating humans. And here is the world of another ketamine traveller we have yet to mention. Lilly's cold unemotional experiences dominated the thinking on ketamine because he was well known. Less well known, but published in the same year as Lilly's book, was Marcia Moore's *Journeys of the Bright World*.

Marcia Moore was a Harvard graduate and a leading writer on astrology and yoga. She wrote that her ketamine journey appeared to go through certain stages, the highest of which was said to be the 'cosmic matrix', described as a state of purely transcendent being. She also described how prolonged use of the drug resulted in fragmentation of her personality into sub-personalities that grew a life of their own. Gradually, she was injecting the drug several times a week and acknowledged that a psychological tolerance was building up. But she was convinced she could gain control over the drug and, despite her husband's concerns, she wouldn't stop using. The boundaries between her existence under the effects of the drug and her normal waking state became increasingly blurred, which she interpreted as the drug telling her to 'let the soul seep through'.

By February 1978 she was injecting daily and sleeping only three hours a night. Aged 50, she disappeared from her house on 14 January 1979. Her husband travelled the world for a year looking for her. Her skeleton was found in the spring of 1981 at the spot where she had frozen to death after injecting herself with all the ketamine she had.

In *The Matrix*, Neo, too, sleeps little: he is hooked on cyberspace. He wakes from a dream telling him that the legendary cyber-bandit Morpheus (morphine) – the Roman god of sleep – has been looking for him, as he has been looking for Morpheus. Both are on a journey. Neo is told to follow the white rabbit. Like Marcia Moore's relationship with ketamine, cyberspace calls to Neo, determining his destiny.

But if Neo is a messiah, the One, he is also a techno-pusher, dealing in illegal software. There is a knock on the door. He opens it cautiously, and there stand some friends come to buy virtual kicks from the Internet candyman. Two thousand dollars are passed across to Neo. He secretes the money away inside a book in exchange for computer disks. Neo's dream has left him in a confused state: 'You ever had that feeling that you're not sure if you're awake or still dreaming?'

'All the time,' says Choi. 'It's called mescaline and it's the only way to fly.'

Choi thinks he is in the real world – and needs to escape from it. All he is escaping from is a dream created by AI. The world is one large dose of soma, although this is not enough for all.

They invite him out clubbing; Neo declines until he sees Lewis Carroll's white rabbit tattoo on Dujour's shoulder and, like both Alice and Dorothy in *The Wizard of Oz*, Neo is about to be flipped into another dimension. But not before he has met Morpheus.

They meet at the Hotel Lafayette, room 1313. Lawrence Fishburn is kitted out like a stereotypical black crack dealer – long black trench coat, fashionable shades. He, too, is a techno-pusher, but what he has to offer is infinitely more life-changing. Like Lenny Nero, Morpheus draws Neo into the net, seductively, but, unlike Lenny, with quiet authority, not hustler schtick. He tells Neo that he knows the young hacker has always felt something wasn't quite right with the world; it was somehow out of register. What Morpheus is offering is that ultimate addictive drug, the one we all want but at the same time shy away from for fear of what it might reveal – the Truth. And how does Neo get there? The dealer offers a choice: 'You take the blue pill, the story ends.

You wake up in your own bed and believe whatever you want to believe. You take the red pill, you stay in Wonderland and I show you how deep the rabbit hole goes.'

Right at the start of the film, we are shot down the tunnel into the bright light of a policeman's torch. Wired up, Neo takes that trip again, only this time he is reborn in real time – not 1997, but something closer to 2197, as Lilly thought it was 3001. He is in a womb-like state, bald, naked and bio-technically wired into the Matrix. But he is rejected, swilled down another dark tunnel only to be rescued by Morpheus and his team. After that, the Truth will out. Neo flips between the reality of a boring job and a life spent hacking (except, of course, he is only a cyber-terrorist because the controlling AI allows him that escape) and another reality far more terrifying and dangerous – but somehow more alive. Even Agent Smith, perhaps becoming more human, wants out, but he, too, realises – as do all those on the run from reality – that you cannot run from yourself.

14

Pulp frictions

America has some of the most vocal and well-organised drug reform activists. At state and city level, mayors and governors have expressed both their concerns about the conduct of the drug war and supported attempts at law change. At a federal level, however, the government is implacable in its prohibitionist stance. For the Bush Administration and the Office of Drug Control Policy, marijuana remains no less the evil weed of youthful destruction than it did in the days of Harry Anslinger.

For some other countries, the debate about drugs is no longer simple. In truth, it never was – only the media and politicians chose to ignore the complexities of a straightforward message that all drugs are evil and should be banned and all users are criminal reprobates. Things are changing. You are unlikely to be prosecuted for possession of small amounts of any illegal drugs in Holland, Spain, Portugal, Italy, Germany and Belgium, and in the UK cannabis will be reclassified as a less dangerous drug under the Misuse of Drugs Act.

Yet as the debate opens up, doubts and concerns rise to the surface. Many young people don't take any illegal drugs. Not all opinion polls support a move to liberalisation. There is confusion over the jargon of reform – legalisation, decriminalisation, depenalisation. Hardly a week goes past without another new scientific report on ecstasy claiming calamitous brain damage awaiting the current generation of users. Is the new research on E just LSD horror stories of the 1960s rewritten for the rave generation or might it all be hideously true – chronic depression and misery for thousands in the future?

Some of the confusions that pervade the drugs debate are manifest in films already discussed. *Traffic* meshes a radical statement about the drugs war with crude 'slippery slope' melodrama. *Blow* sympathetically portrays a major cocaine trafficker who just wants his family to love him while mixing with the most vicious of traffickers. In the midst of the hoo-ha about heroin chic, *Realm of a Dream* uses a sexy Lolita-type junkie to remind us that there is little that is cool about addiction, but pulls us into an over-the-top Hammer House of Horrors to make the point. Are there any consistent trends we can point to which reflect the climate of drug use beyond the darkened cinema?

The most dramatic sea change in the depiction of drug use on screen has been the change in attitude towards smoking marijuana. The changes here have been both blindingly obvious and significantly more subtle.

Police and Federal Narcotics Bureau propaganda that marijuana turned degenerate blacks and Mexicans into homicidal maniacs became unsustainable once the drug was adopted by white middle-class students in the 1960s. This allowed film-makers to take a more light-hearted approach to the drug from Peter Sellers's *I Love You, Alice B. Toklas* (1968) onwards. *Easy Rider* established two important contexts for the drug: first, that smoking marijuana was a political act in its own right, marking you out as anti-authoritarian, and for most smokers that was the extent of their political activity. Secondly, that smoking was a social activity that could help create a bond between people who might be complete strangers or in other circumstances be mutually hostile. From that point, films involving marijuana have mainly followed these two tracks – hydroponic slapstick or social glue.[1]

Tommy Chong and Richard 'Cheech' Marin built a career out of dope humour. *Up in Smoke* (1979) was the first and best of a one-joke series of six films ending in 1984 with the dreadful *Cheech and Chong's the Corsican Brothers*. The most famous and funniest scene in the series occurs in the first film when their car fills with the smoke of a massive joint and they can't see where they are going. But like all subsequent attempts to build a whole film around smoking marijuana – the question is, where do you go from there? There are only a limited number of chuckles to be had from getting silly on sinsemilla. Two 1997 American movies, *Half-Baked* and *Homegrown*, and the British movie *Saving Grace* (1996) were about the 'best' of a lame bunch. *Saving Grace* starred Brenda Blethyn as a widow who has to pay off debts and decides to go into the growing business. All that grows is our disbelief as the film quickly slides into *Carry On Toking*.

The best dope moments are small flashes of deft humour. Two

examples will suffice. First, *Play It Again, Sam* (1972) when Woody Allen climbs into a cab just vacated by dopers and immediately crawls out, coughing and wheezing. The second is the Camberwell carrot scene for *Withnail and I* (1986). This film is considered in more detail in the next chapter, but this moment concerns the dealer Danny, who uses 12 papers to roll a massive volcano-like joint. Marwood (the 'I' character who tells the tale) says: 'It's impossible to use 12 papers on one joint.' Says Danny: 'It's impossible to make a Camberwell carrot with any less.' 'Who says it's a Camberwell carrot?' 'I do,' says Danny very slowly. 'I invented it in Camberwell and it looks like a carrot.'

But although by the 1970s smoking dope had become an unremarkable activity for many young people, film-makers looking back to that era have tended to identify the dope smoker as a barely coherent space cadet, victim of the new marijuana bugaboo – 'amotivational syndrome'. This is a condition supposedly linking cannabis smoking with chronic underachievement, especially at school. There are those who spend their days almost permanently stoned and for whom any movement off the couch is a major achievement. But these are people who, for whatever reason, decided to drop out: heavy cannabis smoking merely confirms them in their inactivity. As an ex-hippie still living in the 1960s, Jeff Bridges as the Dude in *The Big Lebowski* (1997) presents a masterclass for the workshy, but shifts into gear when he has to. The only recent film to implicate dope smoking more directly with failure was *Wonder Boys* (2000). Michael Douglas plays a middle-aged blocked writer whose creative demise is laid squarely at the feet of too much dope. He symbolically stubs out a joint on the floor at the end.

The updated version – the Generation X stoner – is a very young Sean Penn as Jeff Spicoli in *Fast Times at Ridgemount High* (1982), but with an interesting twist. Yes, he is a complete no-hoper – falling out of his smoke-filled van at school first thing in the morning with his mates, already stoned. But this apparently dope-addled dimwit is also a surfer – and not just any surfer, but a champion in a sport requiring perfection in timing and coordination.

Richard Linklater continued to give the 1970s generation its voice with his low-budget but highly successful *Slacker* (1990) and followed it up in 1993 with one of the best coming-of-age teen movies since *American Graffiti* (1973), the autobiographical *Dazed and Confused*. Linklater told *High Times* (February 2002) that the film 'was about growing up at that particular time in the 70s, that feeling of being stuck and having no options. Doing drugs was the only way for kids to express a general fuck you to the small town they were stuck in. The one thing you don't have in those teenage years is freedom.' There was a relentless honesty about *Dazed and Confused*: the kids are selfish, sadistic and hedonistic; there is no political agenda here, just drugs, booze and the love affair with heavy rock which dominated 1970s small-town America. The heir to the 1950s beat and the 1960s dude is Slater, played by Roy Cochrane. But like Spicoli, stoner appearances can be deceptive: Slater is obviously highly intelligent and full of schemes and ideas.

But dope smoking in movies can be more than just a vehicle for sight gags or the outcropping of teenage rites of passage. Use of marijuana in *The Breakfast Club* (1985) is not specifically played for laughs.[2] Five students are thrown together in detention. They represent a range of character types you would find in any high school – the rebel, the brain, the jock, the recluse and the prom queen. At first they all make clear their contempt for each other, but then they start smoking the dope that Bender the rebel has sneaked in. Soon insults are replaced by serious conversation. They realise that none of them is happy at home, they begin to see the people beneath the stereotypes, shed tears together and end the detention as friends. Without the dope, they would have continued to trade put-downs and jibes until they went their separate ways.

Adults in the working world have a similar experience in *Nine to Five* (1980) as Lily Tomlin, Jane Fonda and Dolly Parton find common cause through joint ventures. Tomlin is a senior office manager gagging for promotion, Parton is PA to the boss, Franklin Hart, while Fonda is the new girl in the typing pool. Lily Tomlin is outraged because the boss has taken credit for a report she has written. Her son tells her to chill out and offers her a spliff that she reluctantly smokes. He then slips another in her purse.

At the office, the three women hardly talk to one another, but they all ship up at a bar to drown the sorrows caused by office politics and the antics of Hart. Lily Tomlin discovers the joint in her purse and they all repair to Dolly Parton's house. They giggle a lot, eat a lot to combat the munchies and, under the spell of dope camaraderie, plot the downfall of the boss and become firm friends.

Dope is also used to help friends reconnect in *The Big Chill*. These old college mates assemble for the funeral of Alex, who has committed suicide. They've all joined the establishment, but Nick deals drugs. During the course of the film they all smoke dope, but still disapprove of how Nick earns his money. They smoke dope to deal with the sadness over Alex's death, to ruminate on unfulfilled ambition, to deal with crises in their lives and to loosen themselves up enough to allow disclosure to the others and generally to find common cause. But nobody makes a big issue out of it – they just smoke. Going through his mid-life crisis, Kevin Spacey as Lester in *American Beauty* (2001) reaches for the weed – symbolic of the past he wants to recapture as the horrors of suburban life close in.

Most movie-makers will want to reflect the society around them – and the use of drugs by young people is seen as one of the more troubling aspects of modern society. Not surprisingly, the drug content of films has risen substantially in recent years – whether as the focus of the film, as in *Traffic* or *Blow*, or unremarked on, like the dope smoking in Larry Clarke's *Kids* (1995) – a highly controversial docudrama for its sexual rather than drug content.

The 'normalisation' of drug content in films has led regulators to worry that this might encourage the use of drugs – encapsulated in part by the concept of 'heroin chic'. This accusatory term points the finger at the media for exploiting the physical imagery of chronic heroin use to sell fashion and film and its attendant merchandise. Fashion designers like Karl Lagerfeld picked up on the visual imagery of 1990s culture – young people who deliberately made themselves up to look like the emaciated heroin addicts of government posters – 'corpse white concealer and lipstick in shades of oxygen-starved blue.'[3] Amid tales of young fashion models hooked on cocaine and heroin to attain the right body shape and image and to deal with the pressures of the business, fashion magazine editors took to the platform of drug debates to defend the industry against accusations of vulgar and cynical exploitation.

Within film, much media criticism was levelled at *Pulp Fiction* (1994) for the scene where John Travolta shoots heroin and then drives off with a big smile on his face. Uma Thurman is portrayed as a cool and glamorous user of cocaine, although she goes through a particularly nasty overdose, revived only by having a syringe full of adrenalin slammed into her chest.

The mounting use of drugs of all kinds in mainstream films reflecting escalating drug use in society at large led the regulatory bodies in the UK to commission research during 2000, conduct opinion polls and review guidance on the depiction of drugs on film and TV.

The Broadcasting Standards Commission (BSC) produces codes of practice on standards and fairness relating to television and radio and adjudicates on complaints about unfair treatment by the broadcast media.

In February 2000 the BSC condemned the producers of TV soaps and dramas for making drug taking appear fashionable and common-place. A BSC source was quoted (*Daily Express*, 13 February 2000) as saying: 'Programmes can give the idea, intentionally or not, that an enormous number of people are using drugs. That can easily send the wrong message.' Leaving aside the fact that large numbers of people *do* use drugs and the critical cul-de-sac of the 'wrong' or 'mixed' message – inevitably within the contexts of contemporary story lines depicting crime, hospital emergencies and dramatic personal circumstances, drug use will often figure. But unless the premise is that simply showing or referring to drug use on the glamorous medium of TV is by defi-nition to glamorise it, the accusations of the BSC are wide of the mark. If anything, most TV depictions of drug users are as stereotypical as any other form of anti-drug propaganda, focusing as they do on the 'worst-case scenarios' demanded by high drama.[4]

BBC's prime-time soap, *EastEnders*, is a good example. Currently broadcast five times a week (including an omnibus show at the weekend), *EastEnders* plays out the real-life dramas that can affect ordinary people and commands significant portions of the viewing audience with each broadcast. The programme has dealt sensitively with a whole range of personal issues – rape, homosexuality, HIV and AIDS, relationships between older people, teenage pregnancy and (less successfully) racial prejudice. But when it comes to drugs, the programme falls back on tired old stereotypes. All the characters who have become seriously involved with drugs have been utterly unsympathetic with no saving graces: Nick Cotton (thief, liar and murderer – often dressed in black), Steve Owen (murderer, liar and general bad egg), Janine Butcher (prostitute, liar and thief) and Cathy Beale's long-lost daughter – a very weak character with very low self-esteem, always moaning about life's raw deal, who eventually dies of a drug overdose. In a very brief nod to the debate about the therapeutic potential of cannabis, there was a comic interlude where Dot Cotton is given dope to relieve her glaucoma. On a much earlier occasion, Michelle Fowler goes with friends to Amsterdam. She is passed a spliff by one of her friends in a Dutch coffeeshop, but turns it down. Why? Because she is set up as a popular character struggling against the odds of bringing up a child on her own and unable to reveal the name of the father.

The BSC's warning to TV programmes was taken from a report not eventually published until April 2000. *Knowing the Score* (in association with the British Board of Film Classification, BBFC) surveyed different groups of people and their attitudes to the depiction of illegal drug use on film and TV. A total of 170 males and females aged 11 to 35 were interviewed, whose drug-using career ranged from never used to ex-use and current heroin use. The researchers also interviewed workers in the drug treatment and drug education fields. Different age groups and use groups were shown different 'trigger' images – everything from Robbie Fowler, the then-Liverpool footballer, censured for 'sniffing' along the painted white line of a football pitch during a match, to uncut versions of *Trainspotting, Pulp Fiction* and *Bad Lieutenant.*

The statements made by the BSC to the press in February reasonably reflected the views of those interviewed in that programmes should not suggest that everybody was 'at it' because even for many young people illegal drugs are not part of their normal life. And if 'glamorising' drug use means suggesting that shooting heroin is a positive life choice, then none of those interviewed would sign up to that. But the respondents also fed back views that were less widely reported: not all drugs carried the same risk, most depictions of drug use were not credible because they majored on the downside – and that there was little to be 'learned' about the techniques of using drugs from watching the screen, big or small. These were views expressed both by non-users as well as users.

What is clear from the survey is that, contrary to predigested popular views, film and TV played no discernible role in determining the drug careers of those who went down that route and (in generally portraying the negative aspects of drug use) no obvious role in dissuading non-users from steering clear. Of course, few people would admit to being directly influenced by films or TV as few would admit to being influenced by advertising, and perhaps the subliminal effects are more pervasive than we can accurately track. But in any case the genesis of drug taking is well evidenced in the literature – very much to do with personal, social and environmental circumstances, peer preferences (rather than peer pressure), values and standards set within the family, early onset of alcohol and tobacco use and so on.

For this group of interviewees, film was more likely to portray realistic images of drug use than TV, which by contrast is transparently sending out the anti-drug message through a medium much more regulated and more vulnerable to political pressure than the movie industry. Even so, they thought that, some odd scenes apart, drug use in films like *The Basketball Diaries* was more likely to put people off.

Regulation of film, video and DVD content is the job of the BBFC. They are an independent body funded by the fees they charge to rate content for general release. Tracking back through the BBFC's annual reports, we can see how the climate of drug use in society at large has affected BBFC judgements on acceptability. In 1986, for example, it passed uncut some comic references to cocaine sniffing in *Crocodile Dundee*. By 1987, for the video release, it demanded the removal not only of people sniffing the drug but the dialogue spoken by the sympathetic leading lady that (according to BBFC examiners) appeared to advocate use. But overall, the BBFC has been very fair to drug movies and has not regularly insisted on unwarranted cuts. In its 1989 report there was praise for *Drugstore Cowboy* as 'serious and accurate' and in 1995 for *Trainspotting* and its 'unflinching . . . cool look at the price of addiction'. The BBFC's main concerns are those scenes showing actual techniques of using drugs (invariably the process of injecting) and the degree to which vulnerable or impressionable people might learn in the privacy of their own homes with a video which can be replayed. With this in mind, the BBFC asked this author to convene a panel of professionals and users to view *Trainspotting* and judge whether cuts should be made. Our decision was to leave it uncut, although we knew that the BBFC would have a problem with the camera dwelling on the syringe sequences. We reported back that, moving beyond the detailed mechanics of the film, the essential message was that to get out of the drug life you could fund it by becoming a drug dealer and then ripping off your mates – a point raised by a number of those interviewed for the *Knowing the Score* study.

In the light of the current drug scene, the BBFC, too, felt constrained to investigate public and professional opinions about drug use on screen. By 1999 the BBFC decided it was time to introduce guidelines so that those presenting films, videos and (now) DVDs to the BBFC for ratings would have a better idea in advance where potential problems might lie. Draft guidelines were issued and various panels convened in June 2000 to discuss different subject areas, including one on drugs involving myself and others in the drugs field.

Generally, we felt that the BBFC had got it right through the ratings from U to 18 and little change was required from the draft to the final guidelines. But one passage in the guidelines shows just how deep the fear of drugs runs in society – the one that details why, if cuts are not possible, a film might be rejected outright by the BBFC. 'The following are of greatest concern: graphic rape or torture; sadistic violence or terrorisation; illegal or instructive drug use; material likely to incite racial violence; portrayals of children in a sexualised or violent context; sex accompanied by non-consensual pain, injury or humiliation; bestiality, necrophilia . . . '

In finalising their guidelines, the BBFC also surveyed the general public. The results reflected that the rise in drug use and the amount of debate this has generated about reform bring to the surface a groundswell of public unease. Over half the sample agreed with the statement that 'films should be allowed to portray drug use in a realistic manner'. Yet the portrayal of drug use was considered more offensive than any other classification issue – sex, violence, nudity, blasphemy and language – and the guidelines on drugs were regarded as not strict enough, even for films rated 18. What this now means in practice is that 18-category films are less likely to be cut for sex and violence but more likely to be cut for drug content. John Travolta's heroin scene in *Pulp Fiction* would now not be allowed.

As well as regulatory bodies monitoring drug content, governments on both sides of the Atlantic have sought to influence programme-makers to include even more overt anti-drug messages. In a typically understated British way, our first and only drug tsar, Keith Hellawell, simply wrote to the producers of the major UK TV companies 'urging them to play a more positive role in the fight against narcotics' (*Sunday Express* 13 February 2000). The US government did more than just write letters.

During the 1960s J. Edgar Hoover personally endorsed and controlled the content of ABC's crime series *F.B.I.* and a Hoover representative was on the set of every show to make sure there were no deviations. The White House has a long track record of 'reminding' film and TV executives about their role in the war against drugs. In 1970 Richard Nixon told them: 'The scourge of narcotics has swept the young generation like an epidemic . . . If the nation is to survive, it will have to depend on how you gentlemen help raise our children.'[5] In 1981, during the week of Ronald Reagan's inauguration, stand-up comedian Argus Hamilton appeared on Johnny Carson's *Tonight Show* doing coke and dope jokes. Nancy Reagan went ballistic and gave the network a severe dressing down. 'There will be no more drug humour on television. It's over,' she raged. The First Lady was giving immediate notice that 'Just Say No' had arrived. She went on to lecture 1,300 members of the Academy of Television Arts and Sciences and then met privately with all the major studio heads.

The media bosses were happy to play their part in keeping 'on message' about drugs. Anti-drug public information clips appeared in movie houses all over the States; there was a sudden proliferation of TV documentaries about drug busts and crack. More sinister was the spectre of censorship; scripts that had drugs in their first draft had no such references in subsequent versions. While three strong anti-coke movies were released between 1987 and 1988, casual cocaine use was removed from the script of Jim Crumley's *Dancing Bear*, while no studio would even read a screenplay based on Robert Ward's novel *Budding Prospects* about three friends tricked into looking after a dope farm. Drug references were cut from films at the scripting stage, even when use was shown in a negative light. Kim Basinger's drugs and drink bender in *Blind Date* (1987) was first reduced from coke, acid and booze to antihistamines and booze and finally just alcohol. It wasn't that Hollywood had suddenly seen the light or donned the hair shirt of moral rectitude; like the old days of the Production Code, they just wanted to get the politicians and the media off their backs in case anybody thought federal control was a good idea.

But everyone in Hollywood knew that this was just another fashion. As one Hollywood writer said at the time: 'This is not a new McCarthy period. Studios will ultimately be guided only by the marketplace. Eventually, a drug script will come in with big revenue potential. All that will be necessary then is to provide the audience with the moral and aesthetic justification to come in and see the freaks. And they will, even if the freaks are druggies. And if that movie makes it, then it will be a whole new ball game.'[6] He was right – although it wasn't until the release of *Traffic* that a full-on Hollywood drug movie hit paydirt at the box office. By then the government were at it again.

Under the Clinton Administration, Nancy's threats were replaced by Bill's dollars as the government bought airtime for anti-drug ads. In 1997 Congress approved a proposal from General Barry McCaffrey, the drug tsar, that he should spend $1 billion-worth of taxpayer's money over five years buying ad time on TV. Congress said yes, but what they didn't know was that McCaffrey had struck a secret deal with the networks. They were supposed to provide a free ad for every one paid for by the government. Trouble was that this meant giving up valuable advertising revenue. So McCaffrey suggested that the companies could buy credits – the more anti-drug messages went in the programmes, the more extra revenue they could earn. Shows that had their scripts vetted to pump up the anti-drug content included *ER* and *Beverly Hills 90210*.

The tsar was hauled up before Congress in October 1999 to explain what was going on and was heavily criticised by Congress, civil liberties organisations and sections of the media who raised the spectre of federal censorship and state-sponsored propaganda. In the face of all the flak, the tsar's office cut the overt link between script approval and funding – but it still went on. Network bosses leaned on their producers to make sure they toed the drug strategy line, thus ensuring the government cash cow kept delivering.[7]

During 2002 McCaffrey's successor, John Walters, announced that the five-year ad campaign had been a complete flop. The new plan was to do it all over again. The failure of this and many other similar high-profile anti-drug initiatives should come as no surprise. There is no evidence that what people see on the screen influences their behaviour one way or the other. Most likely, all film and TV does is to confirm people in their existing opinions and preferences. There will be those (the majority) for whom the sight of somebody injecting drugs will be disgusting, and for others it will validate them in their maverick status. Just as users flocked to see *To the Ends of the Earth* in 1948, so the heroin users in the BSC survey had seen *Trainspotting* a number of times. Many clubbers will relate to *Human Traffic* as powerfully evocative of the good times to be had under the influence of ecstasy; others will see just a boring bunch of sad individuals playing Russian roulette with their lives.

15

We failed to paint it black

I attended a drug conference once where a speaker said: 'I usually begin my speeches with a joke. But not only could I not think of one about drugs, but the subject is far too serious to make jokes about.' Now I would have to disagree here. Of course, it is a serious subject – drug use can be very dangerous and devastate the lives of individuals, families and communities.

But alcoholism is also a very serious subject – thousands die every year from the direct and cumulative effects of chronic drinking; many more thousands die in drink-related road accidents; most domestic violence, date rape and public disorder is the result of too much booze. Yet this has not prevented comedians from W. C. Fields to Billy Connolly from making a career poking fun at alcoholics. The impact of humour has not been lost on alcohol manufacturers either. Most adverts for alcohol are humorous and/or surreal and weird. Research shows that the adverts we best remember are the funny ones – which probably explains the appearance of John Cleese some years ago in government-sponsored anti-tobacco advertising. The point is that while there is a danger that humour can trivialise a subject, it can also 'domesticate' it. If we can laugh at something, it probably means we don't feel too threatened by it. This would be a fruitful path for public information and education about drugs. We might better understand and control our fears about drugs – and so react less violently – if we felt they were an appropriate subject for a good chuckle.

Which is why I am going to use these last few pages to nominate my two favourite 'substance-orientated' films of all time. They are both comedies, albeit of the darkest hue. One is American, the other British, but both have a similar theme, one that crops up in many of the drug films in this book. They chronicle the escape from the madness, absurdities and frustrations of 'normal' everyday life and the death of dreams – to another reality influenced by the effects of drugs and alcohol.

In 1971 Hunter S. Thompson was on assignment for *Rolling Stone* covering the story of the death of Chicano journalist Ruben Salazar the previous August. Salazar was sitting near the doorway of the Silver Dollar Café in East LA when an officer of the LA County Sheriff's Department fired a tear gas bomb through the door and blew half of Salazar's head off. Thompson's main contact for the story was an old friend, Chicano civil rights fighter and lawyer Oscar 'Zeta' Acosta. But Acosta was surrounded by other heavyweight Chicano militants, who were extremely distrustful of a white journalist hanging around asking questions.

Thompson and Acosta needed some space to talk, and Thompson himself needed a break from writing all night close to the action where death walked behind him. Another friend, who was working for *Sports Illustrated*, came to the rescue. Thompson was offered an all-expenses trip to Las Vegas to write a short caption piece of no more than 250 words on the Mint 400 cross-desert bike race. He took Acosta with him and wrote up their adventures as the semi-fictional *Fear and Loathing in Las Vegas*, published not by *Sports Illustrated*, who turned the original piece down, but in two instalments for *Rolling Stone* in November 1971.

F and L wasn't just an account of a road trip to Las Vegas. It morphed into a piece of mad dog journalism, a wild trip of drug-induced paranoia into the nightmare lurking at the bottom of the pot right at the end of the 1960s rainbow – 'a savage journey into the heart of the American Dream', as the book was subtitled. A tale about the death of hope.

In the book, Thompson describes mid-1960s San Francisco as 'the kind of peak that never comes again . . . a very special time and place to be part of. Maybe it meant something. Maybe not in the long run . . . but no explanation, no mix of words or music or memories can touch that sense of knowing that you were there and alive in that corner of time and the world . . . You could strike sparks anywhere. There was a fantastic universal sense that whatever we were doing was right . . . '

Within five years it had all gone – and America was left in 'this doomstruck era of Nixon. We are wired into a survival trip now . . . This was the fatal flaw of Tim Leary's trip. He crashed around America selling "consciousness expansion" without ever giving a thought to the grim meat-hook realities that were lying in wait for all the people who took him too seriously.' The result, as Thompson saw it, was that the Acid Culture were hung out to dry, 'a generation of permanent cripples, failed seekers', who made the basic error of assuming that 'somebody . . . or at least some force is tending the light at the end of the tunnel'.

So with the Alternative American Dream shattered, Thompson was left with the original one – the one that celebrated greed, avarice and ambition. And where better to find that than Las Vegas, a huge slot machine in the desert built with Mafia money and as bizarre a place as you are likely to find anywhere on the planet. For Thompson his trip was only half-jokingly 'a vile epitaph for the drug culture of the 1960s . . . The whole twisted saga is a sort of atavistic endeavour, a dream trip into the past, that was only half successful.' Thompson once said about drugs and booze: 'I rely on my medicine to keep totally twisted. Otherwise, I couldn't stand this bullshit.' Small wonder then, that to deal with the craziness of Las Vegas, Raoul Duke and Dr Gonzo make this a trip of inner space which quickly descends into horrific, swivel-eyed, drug-demented chaos and violence.

Small wonder, too, that Martin Scorsese, director of American Dream seekers like Travis Bickle and Jake LaMotta, wanted a crack at the film. For Oliver Stone, *F and L* would have been a fitting climax to his 1960s oeuvre. And you don't need to be a genius to work out why John Belushi relished the idea of playing Thompson. Bill Murray and Peter Boyle did take it on in *Where the Buffalo Roam* (1980), by all accounts a failed attempt to merge two Thompson books, *Fear and Loathing in Las Vegas* and *Fear and Loathing on the Campaign Trail.* The film may also have taken from Oscar Acosta's own book, *Autobiography of a Brown Buffalo,* published in 1972.

The film, finally released in 1998, first took shape under the directorship of Alex Cox, best known as writer/director of *Repo Man* (1983) and *Sid and Nancy* (1986). He also directed the Spanish-produced *Highway Patrolman* (1991), a very well-observed portrait of a young Mexican policeman who begins his career full of high ideals about combating crime and corruption and ends up full of rage and depression about his own weaknesses.[1]

Hired in January 1997, Cox wrote a script with Tod Davies, budgeted at $5 million, and brought in Johnny Depp to play Raoul Duke and Benecio Del Toro as Dr Gonzo, both destined for key roles in major drug films to come. But the project stalled because Cox and Thompson couldn't get along. The story goes that Thompson wanted to watch football all the time, which Cox hated; he cooked sausages for the vegetarian director and further offended Cox by marking the entrance to his house, Owl Farm in Aspen, Colorado, with a blown-up doll lying in the road covered in fake blood. But more substantially, Cox had a different vision from Thompson, who was not impressed by the idea that the film should incorporate animation.

Cox was sacked by the producers in the spring of 1997, who then turned to Terry Gilliam. With his *Monty Python* credentials, surreal extravaganzas like *Time Bandits* (1981), *Brazil* (1985) and *Baron Munch-hausen* (1989) and two films dealing with madness, *The Fisher King* (1991) and *Twelve Monkeys* (1995) under his belt, Gilliam's arrival boded well for the project.

Gilliam deliberately kept his distance from Thompson; Depp did exactly the opposite, staying several weeks in Aspen learning how to be Hunter S. Thompson: 'my goal was to steal his soul,' he said later. Within a few days, Depp was exhausted trying to keep up with a man who never rests. He crept away to a secluded part of the house to catch up on some sleep, read a book, have a smoke. It wasn't until many cigarettes later that he realised he was sleeping in the basement room where HST kept gunpowder. For all his mid-1960s sensibilities, HST is no flower child. Squirreled away in his fortified compound, he has enough guns, ammo and provisions to hold out against the Feds should they come knocking for any reason – or to survive in the event of war.

Gilliam scrapped Cox's script and worked for ten days on a new one with Tony Grisoni and then got into a huge fight with the Writers' Guild of America, who wanted to assign sole credit to the Cox/Davies script. Eventually, all four names appeared, but it led Gilliam to ceremonially burn his WGA card outside a Barnes and Noble shop in Manhattan. Shot in 56 days on a budget that crept up to nearly $19 million, the film was still costed very modestly by Hollywood standards.

The film opens on a fire-apple-red open-top convertible barreling down the highway. The drugs are kicking in and Raoul Duke is being dive-bombed by imaginary bats. He stops by the roadside and voice-overs a description of all the drugs stashed in the boot: 'We had two bags of grass, seventy-five pellets of mescaline, five sheets of high-powered blotter acid, a salt shaker half-full of cocaine, and a whole galaxy of multicoloured uppers, downers, screamers, laughers and also a quart of tequila, a quart of rum, a pint of raw ether and two dozen amyls. Not that we needed all that for the trip, but once you get locked into a serious drug collection, the tendency is to push it as far as you can.' We are in the land of serial drug appetites.

It's a lifestyle most people would run a mile from. But the lurid fascination and vicarious thrill of such a public display of manic self-destruction and Gilliam's rendering of Thompson's glorious sense of the absurd glue you to the screen. You can hardly believe what you are seeing.

Hotel rooms are destroyed on an epic scale. Cars are driven until they fall apart, all manner of Vegas citizenry offended, terrorised or simply bemused. Despite the breadth of the pharmacy they carry with them, it's the acid and the mescaline that really do the damage. Gonzo gets the fear, can't get off a slowly revolving casino bar and later, as he wallows fully dressed in a hotel bath, demands Duke kill him by throwing their tape machine into the bath as Grace Slick hit the peak of *White Rabbit*. And that's when he isn't brandishing a gun or a knife in the grip of psychedelic paranoia. For Duke, the whole reception area turns into a mass of seething reptiles and lizards – very appropriate, as the film opened the same week as *Godzilla*. Less dangerous than Gonzo, but equally full of psychotic raving, Depp becomes Thompson. He wears his clothes, drives his car, clamps the trademark cigarette holder between his teeth and hops and sways through the film like a spider walking on cut glass, like David Carradine in *Kung Fu*, delicately not creasing the rice paper. It was Thompson who cut Depp's hair off for the part. Benecio Del Toro, on the other hand, put on pounds of weight for the role and rampages through the story like the buffalo of Acosta's autobiography.

The camera work and lighting deliberately establish the drug ambience – the non-defined world of ether, the rising and falling light levels of the amyl experience. Gilliam explained: 'The whole film is shot with extremely wide-angle lenses and so it all looks disorienting . . . and the camera is tilted an awful lot of the time, so the horizon is never very level, and the camera floats . . . And I think it all adds up to a pretty disquieting experience for a lot of people!'[2]

But this is Las Vegas; as Thompson said: 'In a town full of bedrock crazies, nobody even notices an acid freak.' In the Circus-Circus Hotel, trapeze artists swing overhead of those playing the tables, chimps and clowns roam about, hustlers shout in your face, screaming about the benefits of having your face projected on to the side of a Las Vegas building for a reasonable sum. The lights flash, the noise is constant, the place never shuts.

'Vegas is a truly depressing place,' said Gillian. 'I think I was there for five weeks in all. It just gets to you, it's non-stop. It really is the American Dream and all of America is there. I don't know what Vegas is because it's a total disconnection from any reality that exists on the planet. Nothing has any meaning, it's all ersatz, everything is pretending to be something, but it has no reality. Even the architecture doesn't have meaning – they'll have an Egyptian column on a Romanesque arch . . . there's a good Italian restaurant . . . called Il Formato, and they ask you, "Do you want to dine in or out tonight, sir? You can sit inside where there's a ceiling above you, or you can sit outside where there's still a ceiling above you, *painted* blue." It's just bizarre!'[3]

He compared Vegas with Bad Boy's Island in *Pinocchio*: 'It's beautiful and it's got everything, yet there's a rot at the centre which is actually destroying something. *Fear and Loathing* is about an anarchic quality, a sense of madness, of pushing things, including yourself, to the limit.'[4] The destruction of rooms and cars attacks the heart of America – everything that is precious in the American Dream – which is under-mined by drugs because (unless you are a rich dealer) overindulgence is almost guaranteed to ensure that you won't acquire the material wealth to realise the Dream.

At one point Duke has had enough and, finding Gonzo has fled, leaving him with a hotel bill he cannot pay, he flees into the desert. He phones Gonzo in a rage only to be told that he must return to Vegas immediately and check in to the Flamingo Hotel, where he is supposed to report on a national police drug conference for *Rolling Stone*. He arrives with a caseload of drugs, calmly walks through the lobby and checks in. He gets to his room to find Gonzo already holed up with an underage girl who only paints portraits of Barbra Streisand.

They attend the conference where the guest speaker is L. Ron Bumqvist, a deranged Groucho Marx lookalike 'drug expert' who announces to the assembled throng of police chiefs and district attorneys that he has identified a typology of marijuana smokers. He solemnly declares that the smoker starts out straight and progresses to 'groovy' with aspirations to be 'cool'.

The conference is then shown a ludicrous film about drugs for narcotics officers which crystallises the reality gap between the world of drug law enforcement and the drug culture:

> KNOW YOUR DOPE FIEND. YOUR LIFE MAY DEPEND ON IT. You will not be able to see his eyes because of the Tea-shades, but his knuckles will be white from inner tension and his pants will be crusted with semen from constantly jacking off when he can't find a rape victim . . . The Dope Fiend fears nothing. He will attack for no reason, with every weapon at his command, including yours . . .

Before *Fear and Loathing* opened, Gilliam said: 'I don't think there's going to be a middle ground on it.' How right he was. This is unquestionably a love/hate movie – and for the most part, when it was released in May 1998, the mainstream film critics hated it. But in the run-up to Cannes things looked good – the studio loved it and there was even talk that the film might win the Palm d'Or. But everything went hideously pear-shaped and the press tore the film to bits. Gilliam says he wanted desperately to get his thoughts about the film across and promote some challenging questions, but 'some journalists didn't want to interview us because they didn't like the film – how pathetic'.[5]

Most thought it was just a pointless mess which celebrated the worst excesses of drug abuse, and many believed the film should be consigned to the 'worst film ever made' category. One critic took a cheap shot at Johnny Depp for appearing in a drug-addled movie when River Phoenix had overdosed outside his club.

Barbara Shulgasser of the *San Francisco Examiner* (22 May 1998) missed the point entirely. What Thompson called 'a vile epitaph' to the 1960s she thought was a celebration not just of the 1960s but of the hedonism of pre-Nazi Germany: 'The joke is that to idealize an era liberated by the birth control pill and easy access to mind-altering substances is to turn a blind eye – talk about Germany in the '30s! – to the destruction that inevitably followed that time. Yes, the United States of the 1960s and '70s was gripped by a goodhearted passion to end a bad war, to free women from stereotyping and to equalize the social status of the races, but some of the subtle consequences of the changes that began in that era include today's rampant teen pregnancy, rife drug abuse, a failing education system and a rising crime rate fed by all of the above.'

Gilliam himself concluded: 'I think in the end we've made an anti-drug movie, although not everyone agrees with me. But even if it's not anti, at least it's an honest film about drugs in the sense that you get the ups and downs, the goods and the bads – the whole thing; you're put through the intensity of what drugs are all about.'[6]

Depp said about the drug content: 'When you see this film and you see what these guys ingest . . . it's not like I watch it and go, "Jesus. What a good idea. Let's get really high and puke." This is like the drug nightmare. What were people expecting – *Peter Pan*? This is *Fear and Loathing.*'

In defence of accusations that the whole thing was a tale of lovable rogues on an amoral drugfest, Gilliam pointed to the North Vegas café scene. Gonzo and Duke are in a café late at night. They are the only customers for the sole waitress to serve. Duke writes a note for her on a napkin: 'Back door beauty?' – a reference to anal sex. The waitress is furious and orders them out, until Gonzo pulls a knife, cuts the telephone wires and frightens the poor woman half to death. Gonzo gives her $5 for a whole lemon meringue pie and walks out. Duke follows after him, having done nothing to intervene. She is still trembling when they leave, rooted to the spot, unable to move.

'We felt we still had to make some kind of moral judgement in this whole thing; a lesson had to be learned somewhere, otherwise it's just rampaging around with no point.'

It could be that all the crashing around, trashing bedrooms, challenging authority and convention – in that most conventional of all-American towns – *is* the rebellion of the 1960s. The knife-wielding café scene, on the other hand, represents something much darker – the stabbing of Meredith Hunter and Sharon Tate – and with Nixon's image floating across the screen and the war booming from all the hotel TVs – the stabbing of America by politicians who dragged it into a war they could never win.

On another tack, Gilliam thought the book was 'about the despair of the American Dream never coming true'. But it does – as they sit at the revolving bar of the Circus-Circus, Gonzo sweating from the horrors, Duke says that Gonzo can't quit because they came searching for the American Dream and here they are at its vortex. Thompson knew full well what the American Dream was, where to find it and what it smelled like.

It was probably no coincidence that cartoonist Ralph Steadman, who illustrated Thompson's book, also created the poster artwork for *Withnail and I* (1987) – the British *Fear and Loathing* written and directed by Bruce Robinson and based on his early life as a drama student. He later won an Oscar nomination for his screenplay of *The Killing Fields* (1984) and played the enigmatic rock star Brian Lovell in *Still Crazy* (1998). But he will be best known for the creation of the ramshackle, self-obsessed, crazed wannabe star, Withnail, and his permanently paranoid sidekick Marwood, the 'I' who narrates.

Like Thompson's story, the plot is simple. Set in Camden, north London, in 1969, Withnail and Marwood are two destitute out-of-work actors living in grinding poverty surrounded by rubbish, mountains of washing-up and a landlord hungry for rent.

Marwood escapes from the flat one Sunday morning to a nasty café in Camden: 'The café is a hovel. Grease and fumes and ketchup bottles with blackened foreskins. Some horrible faces in here. MARWOOD watches an old woman eating – her fried-egg sandwich ruptures. Loathing and fascination. Loathing wins it and he turns away.'

Withnail and Marwood have both crashed to the ground after a three-day amphetamine jag: 'Speed is like a dozen transatlantic flights without ever getting off the plane. Time change. You lose. You gain. Makes no difference so long as you keep taking the pills . . . But some time or other you gotta get out. Because it's crashing. And all at once those frozen hours melt through the nervous system and seep out the pores.'

It is all too much, so they decide on a bit of R&R in the country, courtesy of Withnail's eccentric gay Uncle Monty, who owns a cottage in the Lake District. Totally unsuited to the alien environment of country living, they struggle to survive. Unknown to Marwood, in order to secure the cottage Withnail has intimated to Monty that Marwood is also gay and would not repulse Monty's advances. This sends Monty scurrying northwards in the middle of the night. After a grim 48 hours in rain and muck, terrorised by imaginary dangers and Marwood fending off both an angry bull and the predatory Monty, they flee back to London in a decrepit Jag with bits missing.

Withnail was based on Vivian McKerrell, one of Robinson's fellow students at the Central School of Speech and Drama:

> I met him in 1964 in our first year in drama school. He wore a blue suit and shades and looked like Marlon Brando. Everyone thought he was going to be a star . . . Everyone loved Viv. He wasn't a bad actor (though when we left Central School he hardly ever got a job). Wasn't a bad writer either (although I don't ever remember him writing anything). The reality is that if he had acted or written he wouldn't have excelled at either because the interest wasn't there. What Vivian was brilliant as was being Vivian.[7]

'It came as quite a freight train of shock to him as he was getting older that it hadn't worked, and consequently he got stuck in 1968 for the rest of his life.'[8]

The name Withnail was an accidental misspelling of Withnall, Jonathan Withnall, a friend of Robinson's father, an upper-class rogue with an Aston Martin and a massive drinking problem. But the name was quite apposite – vicious and barbed, like the humour.

Withnail is a wild, cowardly dandy, self-pitying and venal, yet at the same time dignified and charismatic. There is a House of Usher feel to Withnail as he slowly falls apart under the effects of alcohol and drugs. He is a classic figure of British comedy, in the tradition of Tony Hancock and Harry H. Corbett as Harold Steptoe semi-tragic figures with grand ambitions who feel the world owes them something for their greatness but whose dreams will always turn to dust. We laugh because they fail. The comedy of desperation.

In essence, *Withnail and I* is all about a fading relationship at the fading end of a decade of broken dreams – a time and place on its last legs. Danny the Dealer is the emblematic figure of the period who philosophises on life in a slow, precise drawl from the depths of drug-soaked synapses.

Marwood says of Danny that he has 'dedicated his adult life to drugs. And it shows. He is a wreck. About 60, except he's 26'; 'Head-hunter to his friends. Head-hunter to everybody. He doesn't have any friends. The only people he converses with are his clients and occasionally the police. The purveyor of rare herbs and prescribed chemicals is back. Will we ever be set free?'

But Withnail doesn't need Danny – he can self-destruct all by himself. At the start of the film, Withnail awakes to the awful realisation that they have run out of wine. In his desperation Withnail squirts lighter fuel down his throat and then demands that Marwood hand over his anti-freeze. Marwood through genuine concern tells Withnail that he should never mix his drinks. Withnail collapses in a hysterical heap before vomiting over his flatmate's boots.

When Marwood finally leaves Withnail for a job in Manchester, you know Withnail will not survive. Describing his failed acting career earlier on in the film, Uncle Monty wistfully remarks: 'It is the most shattering experience of a young man's life when one morning he awakes, and quite reasonably says to himself: "I will *never* play the Dane." When that moment comes, one's ambition ceases.' At the end, Withnail proves what a compelling Hamlet he could be if only some-body gave him the chance. Sadly, the only creatures to hear his soliloquy are a pack of wolves at Regent's Park Zoo. You feel he will go down in a torrent of booze and drugs, and this is precisely what hap-pened to the real-life Withnail. McKerrell introduced Robinson to Verlaine, Rimbaud, Baudelaire – all the French literati who went to the edge with drugs and booze just to see if they could pull themselves back from the brink and galvanise the creative muse at the same time. Except for Vivian there was no creative muse, just frustration and regret.

Much of which comes out through the sax of King Curtis and his rendition of 'Whiter Shade of Pale'. In the hands of Gary Brooker and Procol Harum, the song came to symbolise the halcyon days of flower power. King Curtis's arrangement is very different – bittersweet, soulful and full of sadness. The song, a perfect choice for the film, was recorded live at the Fillmore in New York. A week after the album was released, King Curtis was stabbed outside his apartment on 13 August 1971. More knives at the end of the decade of peace and love.[9]

In philosopher mode, Danny the Dealer bemoans the sight of Woolworths selling hippie wigs. 'The greatest decade in the history of mankind is over.' He quotes his business partner, Presuming Ed, with whom he hopes to start a thriving enterprise selling dolls that shit themselves and who 'has so consistently pointed out, we have failed to paint it black'.

But was it all a colossal illusion? Did all the dopeheads dupe themselves that anything they did made a difference? It may well be that communal spirit was all in the head. If these films are about anything, it is about the alienation of those times. Crowded on the floor in a joss stick fug tripping to the Stones was never really a communal experience: everybody was surfing their own inner space. Sergeant Pepper's Band was for Lonely Hearts, Eleanor Rigby was all by herself and Dylan was on 'Desolation Row'.

They were heady days – Vietnam War demos, timeless music, the underground press, mad clothes and pre-AIDS sex. It was also a con trick – capitalism in an Afghan coat, exploiting youngsters with too much money to spend. But did any of it make any difference? Was it the dawning of the Age of Aquarius? Thompson would argue that it doesn't matter – the important thing was that it *felt* like something was happening. But that was over 30 years ago – are classic songs and reruns of *Woodstock* the only legacy?

William James said in discussing a nitrous oxide trip that our normal waking, rational consciousness is 'but one special type of consciousness' only separated from other types by 'the flimsiest of screens'. Because alternate realities are so close at hand and reached through microgrammes of a cheap chemical, there is no reason why they should be any more profound than the one that faces us when we wake up in the morning. But the very fact that they exist and millions of people have gained access to them has released the genie of cynicism against the notion of one truth or a single world view.

Undoubtedly, cynicism about government and politicians was accelerated by the fact that not only were many more people in the 1960s experiencing other ways of looking at the world through marijuana and LSD, but that the government were trying to close those doors by ever more draconian drug legislation. The effect was subtle, because direct political action is hardly facilitated by being stoned – one reason why the far left of youth politics was always anti-cannabis. But the existence of another world view was reason enough for people to become increasingly suspicious of what was being done in their name, and this is perhaps one of the abiding legacies of the 1960s.

There is a now a deep-seated belief publicly expressed with increasing and unprecedented regularity as one scandal after another is exposed that most of the individuals, agencies and businesses on whom we rely, whether in the private or public sector, cannot be trusted. 'They' are not going to sort things out on our behalf because 'they' are now revealed as incompetent, corrupt or powerless. From the environment of altered states come counter and opposing views. Perhaps this is one of the many subtextual layers of the drugs war – the battle for the control of truth and reality joined in earnest when a new generation, full of fear and loathing, began marching to the beat of a different drummer.

Appendix:
US classroom 1960s scare movies

The adult commercial drug movies like *Psychedelic Sex Kicks* (1967) and *The Acid Eaters* (1968) had their counterparts in the classroom; the 1960s was also boom time for cautionary drug 'education' films. These were a subset of classroom movies known as mental hygiene films that first emerged in the 1940s as a direct response to the perceived threat of juvenile delinquency. They were conceived as preventative medicine, like vaccines, to mould behaviour, to inculcate the notion that the selfish and delinquent would be at best unhappy and at worst (as it often was with the drug films) dead. There were films showing young people how to be popular, how to fit in, rigid rules and regulations for acceptable behaviour in an era that revered conformity, the pitfalls of dating and all the ways you can die a horrible death, from sex outside marriage and drink-driving to drugs. Paradoxically, while the 'fitting in' films encouraged young people to be like their friends, the drug films warned against peer pressure and running with the pack. Drug use was not surprisingly portrayed as well beyond the pale; drug users were entirely to blame for their predicament. It was never the fault of the pressures to conform, indifferent parenting or other social circumstances – just weak pathology, whose outcome could only be tragic. The classic 'Drugs Are Bad' drug education episode in *South Park* neatly sums up the level of sophistication of most classroom drug movies.

There were two basic setups. One was 'the cautionary tale', beginning as early as 1951 with *Drug Addiction* (cannabis leads to insane giggling leads to carving your face up with a broken bottle) and *The Terrible Truth* (cannabis leads to heroin leads to a really grim hairdo). More than 15 years on and nothing had changed much in terms of a reality check with *Narcotics: Pit of Despair* (1967), *Drug Abuse: the Chemical Tomb* (1969) and *Keep off the Grass* (1970) among many films produced at the time. About *Narcotics: Pit of Despair*, Ken Smith in his history of mental hygiene movies said, 'It's a crowded field, but this may well be the stupidest drug film ever produced', and demonstrates that these films were no more educational or accurate than the exploitation movies showing up the road in the drive-in – the only difference being that the women kept their clothes on.

The film starts with those damned bongos – so we straight away know that dirty deeds are afoot. John is the all-American track hero with the smart sports car and cute girlfriend. But he has a 'friend' called Pete. Now Pete sports all the signs of bad influence – he has a beard *and* he wears a turtleneck sweater. For reasons best known to himself, Pete decides to get John involved in drugs. John falls for it (again we don't know why, other than John isn't wild about doing his homework). And like Alice in *Alice in Acidland*, John goes to a 'wild party'. We know it's wild because of the crazy Hammond organ blasting away. John is introduced to Helen, 'the hip chick of the gang', who waggles her boobs in his general direction and entices him into the garage for a spliff. Or, as the script informs us, 'the place where the grasshoppers are really blasting' when John can 'take a trip from Squaresville', 'get with the countdown' and so on. One toke gets him immediately shooting up heroin, and from there it's 'goodbye track star and girl-friend' and 'hello nicking the family silver'. Eventually, the police intervene, John is admitted to hospital, Pete is in prison and we look set for a happy ending – the classic three Rs of the moral tale: Revolt, Ruin and Rehabilitation. But no – John is out of hospital and straight back to the bongo music as he wonders if Pete is out of prison again. He decides to drop by and see. THERE IS NO END says the title over an image of a spitting cobra. Fortunately, there is an end to this terrible film. But as Smith says, it was a crowded field and most of them are uniformly awful, produced at a time when millions of young people were smoking cannabis and clearly not drifting into heroin use. One film, *Weed* (1971), did manage to be halfway sensible about cannabis, suggesting that getting a criminal record was likely to be the most damaging outcome of smoking dope.

The other type of classroom drug short was the 'drugs and the body'-type medical film which purported to be scientific in its presentation but was simply anti-drug propaganda aimed at scaring kids witless.

Claims of youngsters running into traffic thinking they were God or going blind by staring into the sun on LSD were common tools in the fright armoury. And some might argue that if the 'drugs equals scrambled brains' movies actually did scare kids off, it might have been justified. Except that every piece of research into drug education showed that it didn't work and still doesn't – or if it did, the decay factor was significant. In other words, the effect of the films would not have lasted much after they were seen. Good examples are the TV documentaries on the dangers of smoking showing bell jars of diseased lungs. Smokers may be shocked, some resolve to give up or cut down, but the impact is short-lived, decaying after a few weeks.

And what of the people who made these films? They appeared to be well meaning enough, anxious to make a difference – but were totally misguided in their efforts. Yet because they were dealing with dark and difficult subjects, they were left to sell their wares direct to the classrooms with no educational checking system in place. But then, when it came to drugs nobody would challenge many of the claims, mainly because, however wild and wacky, teachers and parents always wanted to believe the worst about drugs.

The three main companies involved were Coronet, Encyclopaedia Britannica and the king of the cautionary tale, Sid Davis. Coronet was the brainchild of publishing millionaire David Smart, who founded *Esquire* and the magazine which later became *GQ*. Hugh Hefner was a young employee who picked up on Smart's flamboyance and grandiose imagination. Smart's main interest in educational films was 'social guidance', getting the youngsters of America to behave in the way their parents would wish rather than the cautionary tales of teenagers gone bad. He ceded that ground to his main rival, Encyclopaedia Britannica, which made *Drug Addiction* in 1951. But it was the films of Sid Davis more than any others that tried to bring home to teenagers the horrible fate that awaited them should they deviate from the straight and narrow.

Davis had a Hollywood career of sorts, as a John Wayne stand-in, but like many in the industry he wanted to direct his own films. Davis was deeply affected by a news story about a young girl being molested, and he asked John Wayne for the money to make a 16-millimetre classroom film about child molesters. Wayne agreed, and in 1950 *Dangerous*

Strangers was released. Hyped up like the old-time exploitation movies, the film sold well and Davis realised he was on to something. From then on, Davis became the Dwain Esper of the classroom. He dealt with the subjects nobody else would, from social anarchy to drugs, and he could say what he liked without any challenge, such as the accusation in *The Terrible Truth* that the Russians were flooding the West with drugs. There were no shades of grey in Sid's movies – everything was black and white, good and evil, and whatever happened to the adolescent it was always his or her fault for stepping out of line, disobeying parents or hanging out with the wrong crowd. Davis made over 150 ten-minute films, many warning against the stupidities of juvenile delinquency and dropping out. The dénoument was predictable – often kids killed in car wrecks or killing others.

*

References and notes

Introduction

1 Stevenson, p. 5.
2 Bernstein, M., and Studlar, G., *Visions of the East: Orientalism in Film*, Tauris, 1997.
3 For example, Ross, S. J. *Working-Class Hollywood: Silent Film and the Shaping of Class in America. Princeton University Press, 1998.*

Chapter One

1 Jonnas, p. 18.
2 Levinthal, p. 564.
3 Jonnas, p. 20.
4 Mandel. (Web article – see bibliography)
5 Swanberg, p. 196.
6 Ibid.

Chapter Two

1 Bryson, Bill, *Made in America,* Black Swan, 1998, p. 298.
2 Brownlow, *Behind the Mask of Innocence,* p. 97.
3 Gay, p. 136.
4 Ibid.
5 Friedrich, *Before the Deluge,* p. 12.
6 Phillips and Wynne, p. 83.
7 Gay, p. 110.
8 In *Hollywood Babylon,* Anger quotes a doctor who suggests that film stars deliberately took drugs because it gave their eyes a certain hard brightness that improved appearances in front of the camera.

Chapter Three

1 Authorities differ on this point. Some cite Florence Lawrence, 'the Biograph Girl', as just beating her namesake to the punch as the first movie star.
2 Monaco, p. 135.
3 Brownlow, *Behind the Mask of Innocence*, p. 107.
4 Silvester, p. 46.
5 Ibid., p. 215.
6 Ibid., p. 255.
7 Brownlow, p. 108.
8 Silvester, p. 173.

Chapter Four

1 Courtwright, *Addicts Who Survived*, p. 68.
2 Black, *Hollywood Censored*, p. 9.
3 DeGrazia, p. 23.
4 Starks, p. 54.
5 Black, *Hollywood Censored*, p.39.
6 Doherty, p. 3.
7 Bernstein, p. 6.
8 In *The Last Tycoon*, F. Scott Fitzgerald has his Irvin Thalberg movie mogul character say that a priest needs to be hit in the script. 'I've talked to Joe Breen. Priests have been hit. It doesn't reflect on them.'
9 And a historian of animation told me that it was well known in Hollywood circles that what made Popeye strong wasn't the leaf of the spinach but the leaf of the coca.

Chapter Five

1 Feaster and Wood, p. 8.
2 Ibid.
3 Schaefer, p. 13.
4 Bonnie and Whitehead, p. 17.
5 The Harrison Act had dramatically swollen the prison population with those whose only crime was to be addicted to drugs. Although fervently anti-drug, Congressman Stephen Porter of Pittsburgh put forward a bill to establish special 'narcotic farms' at Fort Worth and Lexington where

users might receive specialist treatment. The bill was passed in January 1929, but Porter did not live to see the farms opened. He died on 27 June 1930.

6 Feaster and Wood, p. 72.

7 Schaefer, p. 122.

8 The *San Francisco Call* (24 June 1895) wrote about a 20-acre hash farm run by unidentified Middle Eastern nationals near Stockton supplying 'Arabs' and 'Turks' living in San Francisco. Dale Gieringer calculates that this one farm could have produced something like 500 to 1,000 pounds of hash – enough for up to half a million doses and rather more than the needs of the Middle Eastern community of SF, however large. 'The forgotten origins of cannabis prohibition in California', 1999, 26(2), pp. 237–288.

9 Professor Lester Grinspoon goes into the etymology of the story in some detail in *Marihuana Reconsidered.*

10 *Variety* audience figures show that the film had an 18-day run in Minneapolis in late September and early October 1936, earning $8,000, which roughly means 25,000 admissions, and had a first week described as 'huge'. A three-week run at Chicago's Garrick Theater in early 1938 pulled in nearly $23,000, or around 45,000 admissions. Schaefer, p. 235.

11 Quoted in Crowther, p. 390.

12 McWilliams, p. 101.

13 Schaefer, p. 125.

Chapter Six

1 Lewington, M., in Cook, J., and Lewington, M., pp. 22–4.

2 Some of the detail which follows on the making of *The Man with the Golden Arm* comes from Black (1997), pp. 151–5.

3 There was a connection between Sinatra and John Garfield, the original choice for Frankie Machine. Sinatra's *Young at Heart* was a remake of the film starring Garfield called *Four Daughters* (1938). Warner's had put retreads on their film and turned it into a musical for Sinatra and Doris Day.

4 Pickard, p. 93.

5 Pickard, p. 90.

6 Bing Crosby was warned against playing an alcoholic in *The Country Girl* (1954) but decided the film was more about regeneration than alcoholism. But Ray Milland in *Lost Weekend* (1945) had already opened

the door for stars to play alcoholics: James Mason, Judy Garland, Edward J. Robinson, Burt Lancaster, Jack Lemmon, Grace Kelly and Susan Hayward were just some of those who took on the challenge with no obvious detriment to their careers.

7 In 1962 United Artists went back to the PCA to ask Shurlock to grant production seals for both *The Moon Is Blue* and *The Man with the Golden Arm* well after both had finished their cinema runs. UA had one eye on television leasing rights, and the networks were reluctant to show non-seal films. The PCA complied and granted both films their production seals. Schumach, p. 70.

8 DeGrazia, p. 249.

9 Robertson, p. 118.

10 It was the same heroin users portrayed in Anderson's documentary who began to arrive in Britain when they heard how easy it was to obtain heroin from doctors. Some suggested that it was this group who helped to change the face of British addiction from those among the middle aged and middle class whose problems started with their doctor to Bohemian and youthful working-class hedonists.

11 The deadly item in *Kiss Me, Deadly* (1955), one of the most famous of the American film noir movies, was originally drugs, but code restrictions (pre-*Golden Arm*) forced the change to radioactive materials. Similarly with Sam Fuller's *Pick-Up on South Street* (1953), Dwight Taylor's original drug story becomes a spy thriller. Cameron, p. 243.

12 Starks, p. 81.

13 Zinneman, p. 151.

14 Jackie McLean, a real-life user and top alto player, is one of the musicians in the flat.

Chapter Seven

1 Biskind, p. 20.

2 Gollin, p. 170.

3 King, Stephen, *On Writing*, New English Library, 2000, p. 40.

4 Corman, p. 132.

5 Ibid., p. 135.

6 The whole point of exploitation movies was to wring the subject matter dry until the audience dried up. AIP quickly followed up on their success with *The Devil's Angels* (1967), produced by Corman with John Cassavetes in the starring role, *Born Losers* and *Rebel Rousers* (with Bruce

Dern, Jack Nicholson) all in the same year. Nicholson also starred in *Hell's Angels on Wheels* (1968) as the gas station attendant who decides to hang out with the Angels. Bruce Dern, Harry Dean Stanton, Dean Stockwell and *High School Confidential* star Russ Tamblyn also had their names in the saddle.

7 Corman, p. 148.

8 In 1968 Nicholson and Dern both appeared in an acid movie, *Psych Out*, in which Susan Strasberg, another star of *The Trip*, plays a deaf girl searching for her LSD-addled brother (Dern) in Haight-Ashbury who had sent her a postcard declaring: 'God is alive and well and living in a sugar cube.'

9 Phelps, p. 123.

10 Hunnings, N., review of *Film Censors and the Law, Sight and Sound*, winter 1967/68, p. 50.

11 Corman, p. 131.

12 Elements of the competing stories are covered by Peter Biskind's *Easy Rider Raging Bulls* and Lee Hill's essay 'Easy Rider', with counterpoints offered by Dennis Hopper in many of his recent magazine interviews.

13 *Telegraph* Magazine, 4 September 1999, p. 28.

14 *Observer* Magazine, 14 January 2001, p. 13.

Chapter Eight

1 Corman, p. 117.

2 The film also demonstrated the important point that people's drug experiences are often the product of what they expect to happen. This might be the result of past experiences or simply based on what they have read or heard about.

3 Walker, p. 175.

4 Brown, p. 6.

5 Ibid., p. 70.

6 Herr, p. 50.

7 Cowie, p. 147.

8 French, p. 76.

9 Sam Bottoms, who played Lance, said he actually played out the bridge scene whacked on speed, booze and dope. French, p. 76.

10 The whole section of the plantation following the death of Chef was cut from the original film but has now been restored in the director's cut version, *Apocalypse Now Redux*, released in the UK in 2001.

Chapter Nine

1 See Appendix for an overview of films in the 'mental hygiene' genre.
2 Epstein, p. 109.
3 Marlowe, p. 56.
4 Like the junkie bandits in *Killing Joe* (1994) or James Woods as Mel in Larry Clark's *Another Day in Paradise* (1998).
5 Denzin, p. 10.
6 For those interested in reading around the whole subject of the nature of addiction and the lives people lead, there are some recommended books. One of the most challenging books on addiction in recent years is by John Booth Davies called *The Myth of Addiction* (Harwood, 1992), in which he attacks the notion that addiction *happens* to people through the intervention of outside forces beyond the individual's control. Stanton Peele's books, especially *The Meaning of Addiction* (Jossey-Bass, 1985), also challenge conventional wisdoms, most controversially for an American book the 'addiction as disease' theory on which the whole ethos of Alcoholics and Narcotics Anonymous is based. The best non-fiction accounts of the heroin lifestyle include *The Heroin Users* by Tam Stewart (Pandora Press, 1987), who recounts her life on the streets of Liverpool, and *How to Stop Time: Heroin from A to Z* by Ann Marlowe (Virago, 1999). The novels by addict writers William Burroughs and Alexander Trocchi (*Cain's Book*, Grove Press, 1960) are must-reads, along with Irvine Welsh's *Trainspotting*.
7 Yacowar, p. 39.
8 Raoul Julia has a small part as the artist who gets Helen pregnant, and Warren Finnerty, who played both Leach in *The Connection* and the farmer who allowed Peter Fonda use of his barn to change a tyre in *Easy Rider*, features as one of Bobby's heroin acquaintances.
9 Yule, p. 44.
10 This view of the heroin life on the streets is taken from a study by Edward Preble and John Casey, undertaken on the streets of New York in 1969, not long before the film went into production.
11 Marlowe, p. 130.
12 Apropos of nothing at all, three actors from *The Sopranos* are in this movie: Lorraine Bracco (Tony's psychiatrist) plays Carroll's mother, Michael Imperioli (Christopher Moltisanti) is Jim's friend Bobby who dies of cancer, and Vincent Pastore, the traitorous Pussy Bonpensiero, has a bit part.
13 The film was placed tenth in a 1999 British Film Institute list of the 100

best British films of all time and the highest-placed British film of the 1990s.

14 Marlowe, p. 170.

Chapter Ten

1 Biskind, p, 43.

2 Ibid., p, 181.

3 Ibid., p. 231.

4 Ibid., p. 325.

5 Ibid., p. 377.

6 Fleming, p. 122.

7 Phillips, p. 222.

8 Ibid., p. 276.

9 Ibid., p. xix.

10 Sabbag, p. xx.

11 Siegel.

12 Sabbag, p. 72.

13 Biskind, p. 410.

14 Woodward, p. 94.

15 Ibid., pp. 106, 109.

16 Ibid., p. 16.

17 *High Times*, March 1986, p. 42.

18 In all the films depicting heavy cocaine use, there is also heavy drinking. Chronic coke users often say that the powder makes you drink more – and they are right. The combination of the two creates a whole new drug in the body – cocaethylene – which not only contributes to the binge use of both but also to the likelihood of a coke fatality where the actual dose of cocaine was quite small. Breakthrough findings implicating cocaethylene in cocaine overdose deaths were published in the *Journal of Neurochemistry* in 1991.

Chapter Eleven

1 Phillips, p. 10.

2 There is always a debate about the correct way in which to describe this community: people of colour, African-American, black and minority ethnic and so on. However, in the words of Karen Ross in *Black and White Media*, the term 'black' 'still provokes a powerful political reson-

ance and functions as a symbolic signifier of resistance. Therefore, in the context of this chapter I will be using the term 'black' throughout.

3 Null, p. 17.

4 Ibid., p. 19.

5 Starks, p. 183.

6 There was a sequel, *Superfly TNT* (1973), a real dog of a movie written by Alex Haley (later of *Roots* fame). Shot on the cheap in Europe with Ron O'Neal trying to do everything – Priest has got out and, now with all his cash, doesn't know what to do. Neither did Warner Brothers, who passed on the film. Paramount was less choosy.

7 George, p. 103.

8 Ibid., p. 1.

9 Ibid.

10 Ibid.

11 Reeves and Campbell, p. 249.

12 Boyd, p. 18.

13 Ibid.

14 Watkins, p. x.

15 Ibid., p. 183.

16 Ibid., p. 152.

17 How much of this can be put down to the strength of Mafia-controlled union labour on film sets is a matter of conjecture, although it must be said that film directors, especially the likes of Martin Scorsese, have a sympathy with the disadvantaged immigrant growing up in a tough neighbourhood, with the American Dream way off in the distance, and making it any way he can.

18 Desson Howe review in the *Washington Post*, 8 March 1991.

19 Hollings, K., 'Harvey Keitel in *Clockers*', in Hunter, J., ed., *Harvey Keitel: Movie Top Ten*.

20 Less documented on film but equally important to this chapter is the Hispanic community of East Los Angeles – the city's largest and fastest-growing minority group. Mexican-Americans founded the city, but they remain among its poorest inhabitants with all the disadvantages – lack of education and employment opportunities and racism – suffered by the black community. Like their black brothers, hordes of young Chicano males roam the barrios of East LA, getting into gang fights and drug dealing and other crimes. Most of the gangs are deeply territorial, and most of the gang members use drugs.

American Me (1992) was a directorial debut for Edward James Olmos, who took the starring role as Santana in a tale of 30 years of Chicano gang warfare and drugs. Santana founded a street gang but has spent the last 18 years in prison, where he is boss of the 'Mexican Mafia'. Released from Folsom Prison, he goes back to his old neighbourhood and tries to start over but finds that gang ties are stronger than any other allegiances. The title was taken from a sociology book of the same name written in 1948 by Beatrice Griffith about the lives of young Chicanos.

Bound by Honor (aka *Blood In, Blood Out*) was an unusual subject for director Taylor Hackford, more associated with mainstream Hollywood movies like *An Officer and a Gentleman* (1982) and *The Devil's Advocate* (1997). This three-hour epic told the story of three brothers. Miklo is a half-caste who struggles for acceptance in the Chicano community and eventually rises to become leader of the Chicano La Honda gang in San Quentin. Paco chooses the army over prison after being charged with accessory to murder and later joins the drug squad. Cruz is a talented artist who becomes addicted to morphine and heroin after being crippled in an attack by a rival gang.

Chapter Twelve

1 In his review of *Traffic* (28 January 2001), *Observer* critic Philip French compared the film with Dick Powell's *To the Ends of the Earth*, in the grand sweep of its view of international drug trafficking, calling the 1948 movie 'unjustly forgotten'.

2 *The Poppy Is Also a Flower* (1969), based on Ian Fleming's last and unfinished Bond novel, was a bizarre attempt sponsored by Xerox using an all-star cast to drum up support for the United Nations anti-drug effort. Princess Grace of Monaco appeared in a prologue to appeal for international drug control. Terence Young directed Rita Hayworth, Stephen Boyd, Trevor Howard, Omar Sharif, Jack Hawkins, Yul Brynner and Eli Wallach, all acting for $1 each in a limp drama with a narc declaring that cocaine comes from opium.

3 Johnstone, p. 124.

4 Actually they do. In 1998 Carlton TV admitted faking parts of its drug trafficking documentary investigation, *The Connection*.

5 Ted Demme died of a heart attack in January 2002 during a charity basketball game. The coroner said that the cocaine found in Demme's body could have contributed to his death.

Chapter Thirteen

1 Other recent drug films have taken a broader sweep across the contemporary UK drug scene with only limited success in content and style and none at all at the box office. Probably the best of the lot was *Twin Town* (1997) set in Swansea which tells the tale of two young drug-using tearaways Julian and Jeremy. *Trainspotting* director, Danny Boyle, was one of the executive producers, and this film sits well alongside its more famous counterpart. Hanif Kureishi (*My Beautiful Laundrette*) wrote and directed *London Kills Me* (1992), a so-so tale about street drug culture whose characters are sympathetic but ultimately dull. John Strickland's *Greenwich Mean Time* (1999) is an REM, glossy 'style' movie produced by Taylor Hackford which rapidly spirals into Yardie-driven drugs and murder. *Sorted* (2000) employs rave culture as a backdrop to a routine thriller about Matthew Rhys, a northern lad come South to investigate the death of his big-time lawyer brother. The film begins quite well, but the pace sags and unfortunately, instead of being the quintessence of devilish drug baron, Tim Curry hams it up like Dick Dastardly. One reviewer of the adaptation of Martin Amis's *Dead Babies* (2000) thought it was so bad that he took pity on those involved by not naming them. Incredibly, the EU Script Fund and Media Programme forked out money for this *Brideshead Revisited* meets *Trainspotting* mess. One film that tried very hard to capture the south London drug buzz was *South-West Nine* (2002). With its 'gorgeous mosaic of clubbers, scammers, squatters and anarchists', as the *Guardian* put it, the film managed to light on most aspects of modern youth culture, a range of music from reggae to techno and most of the drugs from acid to crack – skipping through its narrative with a certain verve and panache. Given that the UK is now top of Europe's cocaine league, it is probably time for our first major coke film. Perhaps Peter Greenaway could oblige with *A Zed and Two Snorts*?

2 Interview conducted by Far Gone Books.

3 Jessup's trip back into total nothingness is also mirrored in the ketamine experience of the late D. M. Turner, who drowned in his bath with a bottle of ketamine by his side. He wrote in *The Essential Psychedelic Guide* (1994), p. 90: 'I travelled back to the primordial, undifferentiated oneness of being that preceded the Big Bang and the creation of the manifest universe. There was nothing to see or interact with.'

4 Jansen, p. 144.

Chapter Fourteen

1 Hollywood has yet to deal with the controversy over the medical use of marijuana. The only instance I can find is Susan Sarandon in the movie *Stepmom* (1998), where she smokes dope as a cancer patient. Sarandon and her husband Tim Robbins are well-known drug law reform activists.

2 Grady, D. P., from *Reefer Madness to Freddy's Dead: The Portrayal of Marijuana Use in Motion Pictures*, in Loukides, P., and Fuller, L. K., *Beyond the Stars III: The Material World in American Popular Film*, Bowling Green State University, Ohio, 1995.

3 Arnold, J., 'Making Money from Misery? Marketing the Drug Culture', *Drugs in Society*, December 2001, p. 16.

4 In 2000 a group of British comedy writers and actors, including Peter Serafinowicz (the voice of Darth Maul in *Star Wars: Phantom Menace*), wrote a pilot for a sitcom about heroin users called *The Junkies*. The premise was that the predictability of the heroin lifestyle would make it a perfect vehicle for a sitcom, whose appeal is often based on the self-delusion of one character that good times are just around the corner – Harold Steptoe, Del Boy and Alan Partridge would be just three examples. *The Junkies* was inspired by one of the writers overhearing some heroin users talking about the day's plan – which was to buy heroin, use it and then go and buy some more, just like yesterday's plan and the next day's plan. '*Friends* with smack' never made it to the screen, but the producers did scrape enough money together to shoot one episode and launch it on the Net through an indie company called Shooting People. The heroin lifestyle is pretty dull and boring and, sad to say, that's exactly how the pilot comes across.

5 Cooper, M., 'Up in Smoke', *American Film*, March 1987, p. 53.

6 Ibid., p. 56.

7 Groubert, M., 'High Ratings', *High Times*, June 2000, pp. 49-52.

Chapter Fifteen

1 In the final version of the film, directed by Terry Gilliam, Gary Busey has a cameo role as the highway patrolman who stops Duke and suggests he takes a nap somewhere. The scene appears in the book, but not the part where Busey asks Depp for a big kiss.

2 From David Morgan's interview with Gilliam for Morgan's film website, *Wide Angle/Closeup*.

3 Ibid.

4 Christie, p. 260.

5 Ibid., p. 263.

6 Ibid., p. 258.

7 From the introduction to the original screenplay.

8 Owen, p. 101.

9 Terry Gilliam says they wanted to use a lot of Hendrix music in *Fear and Loathing*, but the family wouldn't allow Jimi's music to be used in any film about drugs. A Japanese guitarist, Tomoyasu Hotei, plays 'Star-Spangled Banner' as Nixon images flash by. But these 'keepers of the flame' who deny that Hendrix ever took drugs are the same bunch that brought you the Jimi Hendrix Coffee Table and the Jimi Hendrix Golf Clubs. All in the best possible taste, of course. *Withnail and I* appeared before the Hendrix 'family' laid its dread hand of Stalinist revisionism on Jimi's life, so we are allowed to hear Hendrix's version of 'All Along the Watchtower' as the soundtrack to Withnail's and Marwood's frantic desire to escape the sordidness of their impoverished and hopeless situation.

Bibliography

During the research for this book, I consulted hundreds of articles, reviews, books and several websites – the most notable of these being the Internet Movie Database – www.imdb.com – an incredibly rich source of information in itself but which in turn led to many other valuable online resources. For drug information, one of the finest English-language collections is housed at DrugScope, the leading UK drug charity (www.drugscope.org.uk).

What follows is a selection of some of the most useful articles and books.

Articles

Bell-Metereau, R., '*Altered States* and the Popular Myth of Self-Discovery', *Journal of Popular Film and Television,* winter 1982, pp. 171–79

Block, A.,
 – 'European Drug Traffic and Traffickers Between the Wars: The Policy of Suppression and Its Consequences', *Journal of Social History,* 1989, 23(2), pp. 315–37
 – 'The snowman cometh: Coke in Progressive New York', *Criminology,* 1979, 17(1), pp. 75–99

Bourgois, P., 'In Search of Horatio Alger: Culture and Ideology in the Crack Economy', *Contemporary Drug Problems,* 1989, 16(4), pp. 619–49

Chandler, J. D., 'Frank Sinatra and the Mob', *Crime* magazine, http://crimemagazine.com/sinatra.htm

Chein, I., and Rosenfeld, E., 'Juvenile Narcotics Use', *Law and Contemporary Problems,* 1957, 22(1), pp. 52–68

Delicado, J., 'Hollywood dealer', *High Times,* March 1986, pp. 41–3

Dobkin de Rios, M., and Winkelman, M., 'Shamanism and Altered States of Consciousness: An Introduction', *Journal of Psychedelic Drugs,* 1989, 21(1), pp. 1–7

Gay, G. R., 'An Old Girl: Flyin' Low, Dyin' Slow, Blinded by Snow: Cocaine in Perspective', *International Journal of Addictions,* 1973, 8(6), pp. 1027–42

Giordano, B., 'Exploitation Movies: Bikers, Babes and Slashers', http:// allmovie.com/cg/x.dll?p=avg&sql=MI5

Harding, G., 'Pathologising the Soul: The Construction of a Nineteenth-Century Analysis of Opiate Addiction', in Coomber, R. (ed.), *The Control of Drugs and Drug Users: Reason or Reaction?*, Harwood, 1998

Hopkins, J., 'Cocaine Consciousness: The Gourmet Trip', *Journal of Popular Culture*, 1975, 9(2), pp. 305–14

Inciardi, J., 'The Vilification of Euphoria: Some Perspectives on an Elusive Issue', *Addictive Diseases, [1974]*, 1(3), pp. 241–67

Jones, T. L., 'Operation Underworld: The Springing of Lucky Luciano', http://www.bostonmafia.com/ThomLucky.html

Kane, J., 'Dope in the Cinema', *High Times* (four-part article), 1977–8

Lawrenson, E., and Leigh, D., 'Feeling Needled', *Sight and Sound*, December 2000

Levinthal, C. F. 'Milk of Paradise/Milk of Hell – The History of Ideas about Opium'. *Perspectives in Biology and Medicine*, 28 (4), Summer 1985, pp. 561–577

Long, B., 'Taylorology: The Continuing Exploration of the Life and Death of William Desmond Taylor', *http://www.public.asu.edu/~ialong/Taylor1.txt* and so on for the various issues of the e-zine

Mandel, J., 'The Mythical Roots of Drugs Policy: Soldiers' Disease and Addicts in the Civil War', http://www.druglibrary.org/schaffer/history/soldis.htm

Miller, C., 'The Representation of the Black Male in Film', *http://www.pressroom.com/%7Eafrimale/miller.htm*

Moore, O. J., 'Why Can't the Boyz 'n the Hood Do the Right Thing?', http://gewi.kfunigraz.ac.at/~blimp/full_text/moore/moore.html

Reasons, C., 'Images of Crime and the Criminal: The Dope Fiend Mythology', *Journal of Research in Crime and Delinquency*, 1976, 13(2), pp. 133–44

Reinarman, C., and Levine, H. G., 'Crack in Context: Politics and the Media in the Making of a Drug Scare', *Contemporary Drug Problems*, 1989, 16(4), pp. 535–77

Schlesinger, A., 'The New Mood in Politics', extract from *The Politics of Hope*, Riverside Press, 1962, *http://dept.english.upenn.edu/~afilreis/50s/schles-pol-of-hope.html.*

Sharrett, C., 'Operation Mind Control: *Apocalypse Now* and the search for Clarity', *Journal of Popular Film and Television*, 1982, 8(1), pp. 34–43

Siegel, R. K., 'Cocaine and the Privileged Class: A Review of Historical and Contemporary Images', *Advances in Alcohol and Substance Misuse*, 1984, 4(2), pp. 37–49

Spillane, J., 'Did Drug Prohibition Work?: Reflections on the End of the

First Cocaine Experience in the United States, 1910–1945', *Journal of Drug Issues*, 1998, 28(2), pp. 517–38

Stafford, P., and Eisner, B., 'Who Turned on Whom?', *High Times*, December 1977

Taqi, S., 'The Drug Cinema', *UN Bulletin on Narcotic Drugs*, 1972, 24(4), pp. 19–28

Thompson, A. O., 'Trains, Veins and Heroin Deals', *American Cinematographer*, August 1996

Tuohy, J. W.,
 – 'Extortion 101'
 – 'Johnny Hollywood', Parts One and Two
 – 'Tales from the City of Angels'
 – 'Gone Hollywood: How the Mob Extorted the Hollywood Studio System'
 – 'Bugsy'
 All articles from *http://americanmafia.com*

Whitlock, F., 'Witch Crazes and Drug Crazes: A Contribution to the Social Pathology of Credulity and Scapegoating', *Australian Journal of Social Issues*, 1979, 14(1), pp. 43–54

Winick, C.,
 – 'Tendency Systems and the Effects of a Movie Dealing with a Social Problem', *Journal of Genetics and Psychology*, 1963, 68, pp. 289–305
 – 'A Content Analysis of Drug-Related Films Released During 1971', in US National Commission on Marihuana and Drug Use: Drug Use in America, Appendix Vol.2, 1973, pp. 709–17

Books

Algren, N., *The Man with the Golden Arm*, Rebel Inc, 2000

Anger, K.,
 – *Hollywood Babylon*, Delta, 1975
 – *Hollywood Babylon II*, Arrow, 1986

Ashbrook, J., *Terry Gilliam*, Pocket Essentials, 2000

Bart, P., *Who Killed Hollywood?*, Renaissance Books, 1999

Bernstein, M. (ed.), *Controlling Hollywood: Censorship and Regulation in the Studio Era*, Athlone Press, 2000

Biskind, P. *Easy Riders, Raging Bulls: How the Sex 'n' Drugs 'n' Rock 'n' Roll Generation Saved Hollywood*. Bloomsbury, 1999

Black, G. D.,
 – *The Catholic Crusade against the Movies 1940-1975*, Cambridge University Press, 1997

– *Hollywood Censored: Morality Codes, Catholics and the Movies*, Cambridge University Press, 1994

Block, A. A., *Reader for Drug Wars: Critical Issues in History and Public Policy*, (unpublished) 1991

Bonnie, R. J. and Whitehead, C. H., *The Marihuana Conviction: A History of Marihuana Prohibition in the United States*. University Press of Virginia, 1974.

Boyd, T., *Am I Black Enough for You? Popular Culture from the Hood and Beyond*. Indiana University Press, 1997

Boyer, J., *Bob Rafelson*, Twayne, 1996

Brottman, M. (ed.), *Jack Nicholson: Movie Top Ten*, Creation Books, 1999

Brown, M., *Performance*, Bloomsbury, 1999

Brownlow, K.
– *Behind the Mask of Innocence: Sex, Violence, Prejudice, Crime: Films of Social Conscience in the Silent Era*, Cape, 1990
– *The Parade's Gone By*, Secker and Warburg, 1968

Burroughs, W., *Junkie*, Penguin, 1977

Cameron, I. (ed.), *The Movie Book of Film Noir*, Studio Vista, 1992

Carmen, I. H., *Movies, Censorship and the Law*, University of Michigan Press, 1966

Christie, I. (ed.), *Gilliam on Gilliam*, Faber, 1999

Clarke, D., *All or Nothing at All: A Life of Frank Sinatra*, Macmillan, 1997

Cockburn, A. and St Clair, J., *Whiteout: The CIA, Drugs and the Press*, Verso, 1998

Cohan, S., and Hark, I. R. (eds), *The Road Movie Book*, Routledge, 1997

Cook, J., and Lewington, M., (eds), *Images of Alcoholism*, British Film Institute, 1979

Coppola, E., *Notes on the Making of Apocalypse Now*, Faber, 1995

Corman, R., *How I Made a Hundred Movies in Hollywood and Never Lost a Dime*. DaCapo Press, 1998

Courtwright, D.,
– *Addicts Who Survived: An Oral History of Narcotic Use in America 1923–1965*, University of Tennessee, 1989
– *Dark Paradise: Opiate Addiction in America before 1940*, Harvard University Press, 1982

Cowie, P., *The Apocalypse Now Book*. Faber & Faber, 2000

Crowther, B., *Mitchum – A Film Career of Robert Mitchum*, Robert Hale, 1991

Diawara, M., *Black American Cinema*, Routledge, 1993

DeGrazia, E., *Banned Films: Movies, Censorship and the First Amendment*, Bowker, 1982

Denzin, N., *Hollywood Shot by Shot: Alcoholism in American Cinema*, Aldine de Gruyter, 1991

DiOrio, A., *Little Girl Lost,* Arlington House, 1973

Doherty, T., *Pre-code Hollywood. Sex, Immorality and Insurrection in American Cinema 1930–1934,* Columbia University Press, 1999

Edwards, A., *Judy Garland: A Biography,* Constable, 1974

Eisner, L., *The Haunted Screen: Expressionism in the German Cinema and the Influence of Max Reinhardt,* Thames and Hudson, 1969

Epstein, E. J., *Agency of Fear: Opiates and Political Power in America.* Putnam, 1977

Evans, R., *The Kid Stays in the Picture,* Hyperion, 1994

Feaster, F, and Wood, B., *Forbidden Fruit: The Golden Age of the Exploitation Film,* Midland Marquee Press, 1999

Fleming, C., *High Concept: Don Simpson and the Hollywood Culture of Excess,* Bloomsbury, 1989

French, K., *Apocalypse Now,* Bloomsbury, 1998

Friedrich, O.,
  – *Before the Deluge: A Portrait of Berlin in the 1920s,* Michael Joseph, 1974
  – *City of Nets: A Portrait of Hollywood in the 1940s,* Headline, 1986

Frischauer, W., *Behind the Scenes of Otto Preminger,* William Morrow, 1974

Gabler, N., *An Empire of Their Own: How the Jews Invented Hollywood,* W. H. Allen, 1989

Gaghan, S., *Traffic: The Shooting Script,* Newmarket Press, 2000

Gay, P., *Weimar Culture,* Penguin, 1974

George, N., *Hiphop America,* Penguin, 1998

Gibson, W., *Neuromancer,* Gollancz, 1984

Gollin, R. M., *A Viewer's Guide to Film,* McGraw-Hill, 1992

Goldman, W., *Adventures in the Screen Trade,* Futura, 1985

Graham-Mulhall, S., *Opium, the Demon Flower,* Montrose, 1926

Gray, B., *Roger Corman,* Renaissance Books, 2000

Herr, M., *Dispatches,* Picador, 1979

Higham, C., *Merchant of Dreams: Louis B. Mayer, MGM and the Secret Hollywood,* Sidgwick & Jackson, 1993

Hill, L., *Easy Rider,* BFI, 1996

Hillier, J., *The New Hollywood,* Studio Vista, 1992

Hodge, T., *Trainspotting and Shallow Grave,* Faber, 1996

Hunnings, N. M., *Film Censors and the Law,* Allen & Unwin, 1967

Hunter, J., (ed.),
  – *Dennis Hopper: Movie Top Ten,* Creation Books, 1999
  – *Harvey Keitel: Movie Top Ten,* Creation Books, 1999
  – *Johnny Depp: Movie Top Ten,* Creation Books, 1999

James, D., *That's Blaxploitation!,* St Martin's Griffin, 1995

Jansen, K., *Ketamine: Dreams and Realities,* MAPS, 2001

Johnstone, N., *Abel Ferrara: The King of New York,* Omnibus, 1999

Bibliography

Jonnas, J., *Hep-cats, Narcs and Pipe Dreams: A History of America's Romance with Illegal Drugs*, John Hopkins University Press, 1999

Leab, D., *From Sambo to Superspade*, Secker and Warburg, 1975

Lee, M. A., and Schlain, B., *Acid Dreams: The Complete Social History of LSD*, Pan, 2001

Leff, L. J., and Simmons, J. L., *The Dame in the Kimono: Hollywood, Censorship and the Production Code from the 1920s to the 1960s*, Weidenfeld & Nicholson, 1990

Linson, A., *A Pound of Flesh: Perilous Tales of How to Produce Movies in Hollywood*, Grove Press, 1993

Litwak, M., *Reel Power: The Struggle for Influence and Success in the New Hollywood*, Silman-James, 1986

Lusane, C., *Pipe Dream Blues: Racism and the War on Drugs*, South End Press, 1991

McClelland, D., *Unkindest Cuts: Scissors and the Cinema*, Yoseloff, 1972

McInerney, J., *Bright Lights, Big City*, Penguin, 1984

McWilliams, J., *The Protectors: Harry J. Anslinger and the Federal Bureau of Narcotics 1930–1962*, University of Delaware Press, 1990

Marlowe, A., *How to Stop Time: Heroin from A to Z*, Virago, 1999

Mathews, T. D., *Censored: The Story of Film Censorship in Britain*, Chatto & Windus, 1994

Miles, B., *William Burroughs: El Hombre Invisible*, Virgin, 1992

Monaco, J., *How to Read a Film*, third edition, Oxford University Press, 2000

Moore, J. W., *Homeboys: Gangs, Drugs and Prison in the Barrios of Los Angeles*, Temple University Press, 1978

Morgan, H. W., *Yesterday's Addicts: American Society and Drug Abuse 1865–1920*, University of Oklahoma Press, 1974

Munn, M., *The Hollywood Connection: The Mafia and the Movie Business*, Robson Books, 1993

Musto, D., *The American Disease: Origins of Narcotic Control*, expanded edition, Oxford University Press, 1987

National Council of Public Morals, *The Cinema*, 1917

Nelmes, J. (ed.), *An Introduction to Film Studies*, second edition, Routledge, 1999

Nicholls, P. (ed.), *The Encyclopedia of Science Fiction*, Granada, 1981

Null, G., *Black Hollywood*, Citadel, 1993

Obst, L., *Hello, He Lied & Other Truths from the Hollywood Trenches*, Broadway Books, 1997

O'Neill, E., *Long Day's Journey into Night*, Jonathan Cape, 1992

Owen, A. (ed.) *Smoking in Bed: Conversations with Bruce Robinson*, Bloomsbury, 2000

Parish, J, and Hill, G., *Black Action Films*, McFarland, 1989

Peary, D., *Cult Movies 2*, Vermilion, 1984

Pellerin, C. *Trips: How Hallucinogens Work in the Brain*, Seven Stories Press, 1998

Phelps, G., *Film Censorship*, Victor Gollancz, 1975

Phillips, J., *You'll Never Eat Lunch in this Town Again*, Signet, 1992

Phillips, J. L. and Wynne, R. D., *Cocaine: The Mystique and the Reality*. Avon, 1990

Pickard, R., *Frank Sinatra at the Movies*, Robert Hale, 1994

Pitts, M. R., *Poverty Row Studios 1929–1940*, McFarland, 1997

Prawer, S. S., *Caligari's Children: The Film as Tale of Terror*, DaCapo, 1980

Proctor, B., *William Randolph Hearst: The Early Years, 1863–1910*, Oxford University Press, 1998

Randall, R. S., *Censorship of the Movies*, University of Wisconsin Press, 1968

Reeves, J. L., and Campbell, R, *Cracked Coverage: Television News, the Anti-Cocaine Crusade and the Reagan Legacy*, Duke University Press, 1994

Rhines, J. A., *Black Film/White Money*, Rutgers University Press, 1996

Robb, B. J., *River Phoenix: A Short Life*, Plexus, 1995

Robertson, J., *The Hidden Cinema: British Film Censorship in Action 1913–1972*, Routledge, 1989

Robinson, B., *Withnail and I: Original Screenplay*, Bloomsbury, 1989

Robinson, D., *World Cinema: A Short History*, Eyre Methuen, 1973

Ross, K., *Black and White Media*, Polity Press, 1996

Ross, S. J., *Working-Class Hollywood: Silent Film and the Shaping of Class in America*, Princeton University Press, 1999

Sabbag, R., *Snowblind*, Rebel Inc, 1998

Salewicz, C., *Oliver Stone: The Making of His Movies*, Orion Media, 1997

Sante, L., *Lowlife: Drinking, Drugging, Whoring, Murder, Corruption, Vice and Miscellaneous Mayhem in Older New York*, Granta Books, 1991

Sargeant, J., *Naked Lens: Beat Cinema*. Creation Books, 1997

Schaefer, E., *Bold! Daring! Shocking! True! A History of Exploitation Films, 1919–1959*, Duke University Press, 1999

Schatz, T., *The Genius of the System: Hollywood Filmmaking in the Studio Era*, Henry Holt, 1998

Schumach, M., *The Face on the Cutting Room Floor: The Story of Drugs and Television Censorship*, DaCapo Press, 1975

Sexton, A., *Rap on Rap*, Delta, 1995

Short, M., *Crime Inc: The Story of Organised Crime*, Thames Methuen, 1984

Silver, G. (ed.), *The Dope Chronicles 1850–1950*, Harper & Row, 1979

Silvester, C. (ed.), *The Penguin Book of Hollywood*, Penguin, 1999

Slide, A., *Banned in the USA: British Films in the United States and Their Censorship 1933–1960*, Tauris, 1998

Sloman, L., *Reefer Madness: A History of Marijuana*, St Martin's Griffin, 1998

Smith, K., *Mental Hygiene: Classroom Films 1945–1970*, Blast Books, 1999

Starks, M., *Cocaine Fiends and Reefer Madness: An Illustrated History of Drugs in the Movies*, Cornwall Books, 1982

Stevenson, J, *Addicted: The Myth and Menace of Drugs in Film*, Creation Books, 2000

Stollery, M., *Trainspotting*, York Press, 2001

Streatfeild, D., *Cocaine: An Unauthorised Biography*, Virgin, 2001

Swanberg, W. A., *Citizen Hearst: A Biography of William Randolph Hearst*, Longman, 1962

Thompson, H. S.,
 – *Fear and Loathing in Las Vegas*, Paladin, 1972
 – *Hell's Angels*, Penguin, 1967

Travers, P. (ed.), *The Rolling Stone Film Reader*, Pocket Books, 1996

Trevelyan, J., *What the Censor Saw*, Michael Joseph, 1973

Vachon, C., *Shooting to Kill*, Bloomsbury, 1998

Walker, A., *Stanley Kubrick: Director*, Weidenfeld & Nicholson, 1999

Waters, J., *Shock Value: A Tasteful Book about Bad Taste*, Thunders' Mouth Press, 1995

Watkins, S. C., *Representing: Hip Hop Culture and the Production of Black Cinema*, University of Chicago Press, 1998

Weaver, T., *Poverty Row Horrors: Monogram, PRC and Republic Horror Films of the Forties*, McFarland, 1993

White, A., *Rebel for the Hell of It: The Life of Tupac Shakur*, Quartet, 1997

Woodward, B., *Wired: The Short Life and Fast Times of John Belushi*, Simon & Schuster, 1984

Woronov, M., *Swimming Underground: My Years in the Warhol Factory*, Serpent's Tail, 2000

Yablonsky, L., *Gangsters: Fifty Years of Madness, Drugs and Death on the Streets of America*, New York University Press, 1997

Yacowar, M., *The Films of Paul Morrissey*, Cambridge University Press, 1993

Yule, A., *Al Pacino: A Life on the Wire*, Warner Books, 1991

Zinneman, F., *An Autobiography*, Bloomsbury, 1992

Filmography

All the following were viewed for the writing of this book.

csm = classroom scare movies from the catalogue of somethingweird.com

The Acid Eaters (1968)
Alice in Acidland (1969)
Altered States (1980)
American Beauty (2000)
Another Day in Paradise (1998)
Apocalypse Now (1979)
Apocalypse Now Redux (2001)
Assassin of Youth (1935)
Awakening of the Beast (1969)
Bad Lieutenant (1992)
The Basketball Diaries (1994)
Basquait (1996)
Beyond LSD (csm) (1968)
The Big Chill (1983)
The Big Lebowski (1997)
Black Connection (1974)
Blackout (1997)
Blood and Concrete (1990)
Blood In, Blood Out (1993)
Blow (2001)
Blow Up (1966)
Boogie Nights (1997)
The Boost (1988)
Born to Win (1971)
Boyz N the Hood (1991)
Bright Lights, Big City (1988)
Bringing out the Dead (1999)
Chappaqua (1967)
Christiane F (1981)
Cisco Pike (1971)
Clean and Sober (1988)
Clear and Present Danger (1994)
Clockers (1995)

Cocaine Fiends (1939)
Colors (1988)
The Connection (1962)
Contact (1997)
The Cool and the Crazy (1958)
Dazed and Confused (1993)
Deep Cover (1992)
Devil's Harvest (1948?)
Devil's Sleep (1949)
The Doors (1991)
Drug Addiction (csm) (1966)
Drugstore Cowboy (1989)
Easy Rider (1969)
Ed Wood (1994)
Emerald Forest (1985)
Fast Times at Ridgemount High (1982)
Fear and Loathing in Las Vegas (1998)
Focus on Heroin (csm) (1971)
The French Connection (1971)
The French Connection 2 (1975)
Go (1999)
Gridlocked (1996)
Hatful of Rain (1957)
Highway Patrolman (1991)
Human Traffic (1999)
Hurly Burly (1998)
I'm Dancing As Fast As I Can (1982)
In Too Deep (1999)
Jacob's Ladder (1990)
Jesus' Son (2000)
Juice (1992)
Kids (1995)
Lawnmower Man (1992)
Lenny (1974)
Less than Zero (1987)
Looking for Mr Goodbar (1977)
Lost Weekend (1945)
The Man with the Golden Arm (1955)
The Man with the X-Ray Eyes (1963)
Manchurian Candidate (1962)
Marihuana: Weed with Its Roots in Hell (1936)
Marijuana – the Hidden Danger (csm)
Marijuana: The Great Escape (csm) (1970)
Menace II Society (1993)
Midnight Express (1978)
Mike's Murder (1984)

Monkey on My Back (1957)
More (1969)
Naked Lunch (1991)
The Narcotic Story (csm) (1958)
Narcotics: Pit of Despair (csm) (1967)
New Jack City (1991)
Opium (1919?)
Out of the Blue (1980)
The Pace that Kills (1928)
Panic in Needle Park (1971)
The PCP Story (csm) (197?)
People versus Pot (csm) (1970)
Performance (1970)
Permanent Midnight (1998)
Postcards from the Edge (1990)
Pulp Fiction (1994)
Reefer Madness (1936)
Requiem for a Dream (2001)
Rush (1991)
Saving Grace (2000)
She Shoulda Said No! (aka *Wild Weed*) (1949)
Sid and Nancy (1986)
Slacker (1991)
Smoky Joe's High Ride (csm)
South-West Nine (2001)
Straight out of Brooklyn (1991)
Strange Days (1995)
Superfly (1972)
Sven Klang's Kvintett (1976)
Touch of Evil (1958)
Traffic (2000)
Traffik (1989)
Trainspotting (1995)
Trash (1970)
The Trip (1968)
The Trip Back (csm) (1969)
Up in Smoke (1978)
Valley of the Dolls (1967)
Velvet Goldmine (1998)
Who'll Stop the Rain? (aka *Dog Soldiers*) (1978)
Withnail and I (1987)
Wonder Boys (2000)

Index